PROFESSIONAL JAVA® EE DESIGN PATTERNS

PROFESSIONAL

Java® EE Design Patterns

PROFESSIONAL

Java® EE Design Patterns

Murat Yener
Alex Theedom

wrox™

A Wiley Brand

Professional Java® EE Design Patterns

Published by
John Wiley & Sons, Inc.
10475 Crosspoint Boulevard
Indianapolis, IN 46256
www.wiley.com

Copyright © 2015 by John Wiley & Sons, Inc., Indianapolis, Indiana

Published simultaneously in Canada

ISBN: 978-1-118-84341-3
ISBN: 978-1-118-84358-1 (ebk)
ISBN: 978-1-118-84345-1 (ebk)

Manufactured in the United States of America

10 9 8 7 6 5 4 3 2 1

For general information on our other products and services please contact our Customer Care Department within the United States at (877) 762-2974, outside the United States at (317) 572-3993 or fax (317) 572-4002.

Wiley publishes in a variety of print and electronic formats and by print-on-demand. Some material included with standard print versions of this book may not be included in e-books or in print-on-demand. If this book refers to media such as a CD or DVD that is not included in the version you purchased, you may download this material at http://booksupport.wiley.com. For more information about Wiley products, visit www.wiley.com.

Library of Congress Control Number: 2014946684

To Nilay and all my family (Semra and Musfata Yener), for all your support and time I needed to write this book.

—MURAT

To Mariu, for all your support and encouragement.

—ALEX

ABOUT THE AUTHORS

MURAT YENER is a code geek and open source committer, working at Intel New Devices Group as an Android developer. He has extensive experience with developing Java, web frameworks, JavaEE, and OSGi applications, in addition to teaching courses and mentoring. Murat is an Eclipse committer and one of the initial committers of the Eclipse Libra project, he is currently working on building native and Hybrid mobile apps with HTML5 and mGWT.

Murat has been a user group leader at GDG Istanbul since 2009, organizing, participating, and speaking at events. He is also a regular speaker at JavaOne, EclipseCon, and Devoxx conferences.

Linkedin—www.linkedin.com/in/muratyener

twitter—@yenerm

blog—www.devchronicles.com

ALEX THEEDOM is a Senior Java Developer at Indigo Code Collective indigocodecollective.com (part of the E-scape Group) where he played a pivotal role in the architectural design and development of a microservice based, custom built lottery and instant win game platform.

Prior to that, he developed ATM software for an international Spanish bank and code quality analysis software for a software consultancy.

Alex is experienced with Java web application development in a diverse range of fields including finance, e-learning, lottery and software development. His passion for development has taken him to projects throughout Europe and beyond. He is a blogger at alextheedom.com and can be found helping fellow problem solvers in online forums.

Linkedin—www.linkedin.com/in/alextheedom

Twitter—@alextheedom

Blog—www.alextheedom.com

ABOUT THE TECHNICAL EDITOR

MOHAMED SANAULLA is a Software Developer with over five years of professional experience developing software. He is currently working for India's largest e-Commerce establishment and is also a moderator on the JavaRanch Forums. When he is not working on his PC, he is busy tending to his cute little daughter. He shares his experiments and thoughts on software development at http://blog.sanaulla.info.

CREDITS

ASSOCIATE PUBLISHER
Jim Minatel

PROJECT EDITOR
Adaobi Obi Tulton

TECHNICAL EDITOR
Mohamed Sanaulla

PRODUCTION MANAGER
Kathleen Wisor

COPY EDITOR
Karen A. Gill

**MANAGER OF CONTENT DEVELOPMENT
AND ASSEMBLY**
Mary Beth Wakefield

MARKETING DIRECTOR
David Mayhew

MARKETING MANAGER
Carrie Sherrill

**PROFESSIONAL TECHNOLOGY AND
STRATEGY DIRECTOR**
Barry Pruett

BUSINESS MANAGER
Amy Knies

PROJECT COORDINATOR, COVER
Patrick Redmond

PROOFREADER
Nancy Carrasco

INDEXER
John Sleeva

COVER DESIGNER
Wiley

COVER IMAGE
© iStock.com/pavlen

BACKGROUND
© PhotoAlto Images/Fotosearch

ACKNOWLEDGMENTS

AS MY COAUTHOR Alex always says, we wanted to write a book we would like to own and read for ourselves. To begin with, I want to thank Alex for all his patience, hard work, and great knowledge. Without him, this book wouldn't be nearly as good.

I am grateful to Mary James, our former acquisitions editor, who contacted me about writing a book on Spring but listened to my ideas that formed the basis of this book. Without her support and guidance, this book wouldn't have become a reality. No words would be enough to thank Adaobi Obi Tulton, who patiently worked on all the details while keeping most of the schedule stresses away from us. And thanks, of course, to everyone at Wrox/Wiley who got this book on the shelves. Thanks, also, to Reza Rahman for all his encouragement.

I must thank three important people who had a huge impact on where I am in my professional life in terms of software.

First, thanks to my dad, Mustafa Yener, for buying me my first computer, a C64, at an early age while I was asking for slot cars. That computer is where I wrote my very first codes.

Second, thanks to my thesis advisor, Prof. Mahir Vardar, whom I owe all the early guidance I needed to start my career.

Finally, thanks to my life-time mentor and friend (also my ex-boss) Naci Dai, who taught me almost anything I know about being a professional software developer.

—MURAT

WE ARE VERY PROUD of this, our first book, and hope that you will get as much from reading it as we have writing it. We approached writing this with the perspective that it should be the kind of book we would buy if we hadn't written it. We have achieved that.

However, this book would not have been possible without the dedication, patience, and understanding of the many others who have contributed directly and indirectly to its creation. We would like to acknowledge the contributions made by the dedicated and experienced team at Wiley Publishing. They have stuck with us through thick and thin and believed that it was all possible. We would like to give special thanks to Mary James, our acquisitions editor, whose support made this book a reality. Thanks also to Adaobi Obi Tulton, whose patience and gentle nudges kept us on our toes and whose attention to detail saved us from tripping over ourselves. I would like to thank my coauthor, Murat Yener, for his inspiration and sense of humor that makes this book unique; and finally, but not least, I would like to thank my wife, Maria Eugenia García García, for her total support and understanding while writing this book. Thank you.

—ALEX

CONTENTS

FOREWORD

Ignorant men raise questions that wise men answered a thousand years ago

—JOHANN WOLFGANG VON GOETHE

Design patterns are our link to the past and the future. They make up a foundational language that represents well understood solutions to common problems that talented engineers before us have added to our collective knowledge base. Design patterns or blueprints exist in every engineering field in one way or another. Software development is no different. Indeed, design patterns are probably our most tangible link to engineering rather than the more organic and less regimented world of the artisan or craftsman. The art and science of design patterns was brought to the world of software engineering—and more specifically to enterprise Java—by the seminal Gang of Four (GoF) book. They have been with us ever since through our adventures in J2EE, Spring, and now modern lightweight Java EE. This is for very good reasons. Server-side Java developers tend to write the type of mission critical applications that need to stand the test of time and hence benefit the most from the discipline that design patterns represent.

It really takes a special kind of person to write a book on design patterns, let alone a book on how to utilize design patterns in Java EE applications. You require not only basic knowledge of APIs and the patterns themselves, but deep insight that can only come with hard-earned experience, as well as an innate ability to explain complex concepts elegantly. I am glad Java EE now has Murat and Alex to accomplish the mighty feat.

This book fulfills a much needed gap and fills it well. It is also very good that the book is on the cutting edge and covers Java EE 7 and not just Java EE 6 or Java EE 5. In fact many of the design patterns covered, like Singleton, Factory, Model-View-Controller (MVC), Decorator, and Observer, are now incorporated right into the Java EE platform. Others like Facade, Data Access Object (DAO), and Data Transfer Object (DTO) fit elegantly on top. Murat and Alex tackle each pattern, explain its pragmatic motivation, and discuss how it fits into Java EE.

It is an honor and a privilege to write a small opening part of this very important book that I hope will become a very useful part of every good Java EE developer's bookshelf. I hope you enjoy the book, and that it helps you write better, more satisfying enterprise Java applications.

M. REZA RAHMAN
Java EE/GlassFish Evangelist
Oracle Corporation

INTRODUCTION

THIS BOOK DISCUSSES THE CLASSIC DESIGN PATTERNS that were first mentioned in the famous book by the GoF[1] and updates them specifically for Java EE 6 and 7.

In every chapter we describe the traditional implementation of each pattern and then show how to implement it using Java EE-specific semantics.

We use full code examples to demonstrate both the traditional and Java EE implementations and color each chapter with real-life stories that show the use (or misuse) of the pattern.

We investigate the pros and cons of each pattern and examine their usages. Each chapter finishes with some exercises that challenge your understanding of the pattern in Java EE.

WHO THIS BOOK IS FOR

This book is for everyone with any level of experience. It covers almost everything about a pattern, from how it is referred to in other books, to code on basic Java implementation, to Java EE implementation, and finally real life examples of how and when to use a specific pattern. It also has real life war stories that talk about good and bad practices.

Having some basic knowledge of design patterns and Java EE will aid you as you read this book.

If you are already experienced with patterns and basic Java implementations, you may prefer to jump into Java EE implementations. Refreshing your memory and knowledge of design patterns could prove helpful.

WHAT THIS BOOK COVERS

This book covers all classical design patterns that Java EE offers as part of standard implementation, besides some new patterns. The coverage goes back to Java EE5 and is up to date for the latest version available, which is Java EE 7.

We hope this book will be a reference you will keep on your shelf for a long time.

HOW THIS BOOK IS STRUCTURED

Each chapter focuses on a design pattern. If the pattern is classical, a simple Java implementation is given after the explanation of the pattern. Each chapter offers war stories telling a good or bad real life example about the pattern focused on/in the chapter. The war story is followed by a Java EE implementation, example, and explanation. Each code sample given can be run by itself. Finally, each chapter ends with when and how to use the pattern effectively.

WHAT YOU NEED TO USE THIS BOOK

Any modern computer with an operating system that has a Java Virtual Machine (JVM) implementation is sufficient to run the samples given in this book. For ease of coding, you need an integrated development environment (IDE) of your own choice. The sample can run on any popular modern IDEs including Eclipse, NetBeans, and IntelliJ.

You need the Java Development Kit (JDK) for Java EE7 to be able to compile and run the code samples, but some of the code samples would also work on previous Java EE JDKs.

You can use any Java EE7–compliant application server to run the samples. We ran all the code samples on Glassfish, which is the reference implementation server, and TomEE, which is the Java EE version of the popular Java web server Tomcat. You can use any server, but because Glassfish is the reference implementation, you might want to try it for the samples.

To run the samples in this book, you need the following:

➤ An operating system that has a JDK for Java EE7, such as Linux, Mac OS X, or Windows

➤ Java EE 7 JDK

➤ An IDE of your choice, such as Eclipse for Java EE Developers, NetBeans, or IntelliJ

➤ Java EE 7–compliant application server such as GlassFish or TomEE

The source code for the samples is available for download from the Wrox website at:

www.wrox.com/go/projavaeedesignpatterns

MOTIVATION FOR WRITING

In November 2011, after having a debate on Java EE versus Spring for a project, I went back to my desk and wrote a blog post titled "Java EE 6 and the Ewoks,"[2] which became popular pretty quickly. The story was based on the TV show *How I Met Your Mother*. In this show, Barney, who is the playboy character, introduced a theory that was focused on Ewoks, the teddy bear–like creatures introduced in Episode VI of *Star Wars*. Fans have mixed feelings on Ewoks.

According to Barney, those born before May 25, 1973, when *Return of the Jedi* was released, think Ewoks are childish and simply hate them. However, those born after that date find Ewoks cute because they remind them of teddy bears.

Now back to my story. Engaging in a debate with a customer about Java EE versus Spring made me realize that it's similar to the Ewok theory. Those who are old enough to have used J2EE 1.4 (EJB 1.0/2.0/2.1) in corporate projects had a slow, unproductive development environment with RAM-eating and buggy IDEs and servers taking several minutes to boot. The architecture was over engineered and probably failed, resulting in a migration to Spring. Those users tended to hate Java EE with a passion, no matter what version they used. The release of Java EE 5 was underrated and did not really impress anyone.

Java EE will never be J2EE again. It is now open, has a large community and reshapes itself by assimilating good ideas from frameworks such as Spring and Hibernate. The first great change was the architecture and style of coding. Enterprise JavaBeans (EJB) followed the lightweight Plain Old Java Object (POJO) model, almost unusable entity beans were replaced with Java Persistence API (JPA), REST and Web Services became standard and integral parts of the run time, and annotations replaced XML configuration. Still, some might argue that Java EE 5 was not ready for the huge shift because it was not as mature as Spring, and the development environment was still not responsive enough. Using Spring on Tomcat instead of EJBs and Java EE 5 on an application server greatly increased the development productivity, but Java EE 5 was still a big step forward towards designing, leveraging, and architecting the Enterprise Java platform from scratch.

This shift was followed by Java EE 6 and 7, which used the same principles and ideas as Java EE 5. Java EE is a great choice for development, but the debate was not over, thanks to the Ewok theory.

It was a hot August day when I first got a call from Wrox/Wiley about whether I would be interested in writing a Spring book. I was experienced and confident with implementing and developing in Spring, but there were already tons of books written about it, which made it hard to see the value in writing a new one.

Besides, I was using Java EE more than ever since version 6 had been released. Considering the Spring versus Java EE debates, my blog posts, and the Ewoks, I felt like writing about Java EE. However, just like Spring, there were many great Java EE books that I admired. I always had the feeling that some properties of Java EE were underrated. Java EE has great built-in implementations of design patterns with simple use of annotations.

The classic patterns listed in the GoF book were used extensively in almost all languages, frameworks, and platforms. J2EE was no exception and neither was Java EE. Actually Java EE took a bold step in providing default implementations for many of those patterns, but still even most of the experienced developers underestimated the value of those out of the box implementations.

I had been blogging about those patterns for almost a year, so I decided to present a counteroffer to write a book on the "classic" design patterns in Java EE. As you are reading this book now, you may guess the feedback was positive.

This book fills the gap between the Java EE platform with the classic design patterns from the GoF book as well as talking about new patterns. This way we did not write just another Java EE book but a catalogue for design patterns in Java EE.

I started blogging, writing and giving talks on design patterns in Java EE to extend my knowledge and experience on a platform I really believed in, so the best thing about writing this book for me was that I had the chance to write about something I was really passionate about. Although my blog had simpler examples, I was already using it as a reference when I needed, so writing a book, which is more formally and properly formatted while still following the same idea was a great opportunity.

Every chapter that my coauthor Alex and I wrote had the same goal: Write content that we would like to read ourselves. The result is a book that we both want to keep as a reference.

We hope that you enjoy reading this book as much as we enjoyed writing it.

CONVENTIONS

To help you get the most from the text and keep track of what's happening, we've used a number of conventions throughout the book.

> **NOTE** *Notes indicates notes, tips, hints, tricks, or asides to the current discussion.*

As for styles in the text:

➤   We *highlight* new terms and important words when we introduce them.

➤   We show keyboard strokes like this: Ctrl+A.

➤   We show file names, URLs, and code within the text like so: `persistence.properties`.

➤   We present code in two different ways:

```
We use a monofont type with no highlighting for most code examples.
We use bold to emphasize code that is particularly important in the present
context or to show changes from a previous code snippet.
```

SOURCE CODE

As you work through the examples in this book, you may choose either to type in all the code manually or to use the source code files that accompany the book. All the source code used in this book is available for download at `www.wrox.com`. Specifically for this book, the code download is on the Download Code tab at:

`www.wrox.com/go/projavaeedesignpatterns`

You can also search for the book at www.wrox.com by ISBN (978-1-118-84341-3) to find the code. A complete list of code downloads for all current Wrox books is available at `www.wrox.com/dynamic/books/download.aspx`.

Each chapter starts with introducing a basic Java implementation of the pattern, if there is any. Next, the chapter lists a Java EE implementation of the pattern that can only compile and run on the Java EE JDK and a Java EE–compliant application server.

Most of the code on `www.wrox.com` is compressed in .ZIP, .RAR, or a similar archive format appropriate to the platform. Once you download the code, just decompress it with an appropriate compression tool.

ERRATA

We make every effort to ensure that there are no errors in the text or in the code. However, no one is perfect, and mistakes do occur. If you find an error in one of our books, like a spelling mistake or a faulty piece of code, we would be very grateful for your feedback. By sending in errata, you may save another reader hours of frustration. At the same time, you will be helping us provide even higher quality information.

To find the errata page for this book, go to:

`www.wrox.com/go/projavaeedesignpatterns`

Then click the Errata link. On this page, you can view all errata that has been submitted for this book and posted by Wrox editors.

If you don't spot "your" error on the Book Errata page, go to `www.wrox.com/contact/techsupport .shtml` and complete the form there to send us the error you have found. We'll check the information and, if appropriate, post a message to the book's errata page and fix the problem in subsequent editions of the book.

P2P.WROX.COM

For author and peer discussion, join the P2P forums at `http://p2p.wrox.com`. The forums are a web-based system for you to post messages relating to Wrox books and related technologies and interact with other readers and technology users. The forums offer a subscription feature to e-mail you topics of interest of your choosing when new posts are made. Wrox authors, editors, other industry experts, and your fellow readers are present on these forums.

At `http://p2p.wrox.com`, you will find a number of different forums that will help you, not only as you read this book, but also as you develop your own applications. To join the forums, just follow these steps:

1. Go to `http://p2p.wrox.com` and click the Register link.

2. Read the terms of use and click Agree.

3. Complete the required information to join, as well as any optional information you wish to provide, and click Submit.

4. You will receive an e-mail with information describing how to verify your account and complete the joining process.

> **NOTE** *You can read messages in the forums without joining P2P, but in order to post your own messages, you must join.*

Once you join, you can post new messages and respond to messages that other users post. You can read messages at any time on the web. If you would like to have new messages from a particular forum e-mailed to you, click the Subscribe to This Forum icon by the forum name in the forum listing.

For more information about how to use the Wrox P2P, be sure to read the P2P FAQs for answers to questions about how the forum software works, as well as many common questions specific to P2P and Wrox books. To read the FAQs, click the FAQ link on any P2P page.

CONTACT THE AUTHORS

If you have any questions regarding the contents of this book, the code, or any other related matter you can contact the authors directly on their blogs and via Twitter.

Murat Yener:

➤ **Blog**—devchronicles.com

➤ **Twitter**—@yenerm

Alex Theedom:

➤ **Blog**—alextheedom.com

➤ **Twitter**—@alextheedom

NOTES

1. *Design Patterns: Elements of Reusable Object-Oriented Software* (Addison-Wesley, 1994): Erich Gamma, Richard Helm, Ralph Johnson, John Vlissides.
2. *Java EE 6 and the Ewoks:* http://www.devchronicles.com/2011/11/javaee6-and-ewoks.html.

PROFESSIONAL

Java® EE Design Patterns

PART I
Introduction to Java EE Design Patterns

1

A Brief Overview of Design Patterns

WHAT'S IN THIS CHAPTER?

➤ An overview of design patterns

➤ A short history about design patterns and why they are important

➤ The use of design patterns in the real world

➤ The history and evolution of Java Enterprise Edition

➤ The emergence of enterprise patterns

➤ How these design patterns have evolved in the enterprise environment

➤ Why and how patterns become anti-patterns

This book is aimed at bridging the gap between the traditional implementation of design patterns in the Java SE environment and their implementation in Java EE.

If you are new to design patterns, this book will help you get up to speed quickly as each chapter introduces the design pattern in a simple-to-understand way with plenty of working code examples.

If you are already familiar with design patterns and their implementation but are not familiar with their implementation in the Java EE environment, this book is perfect for you. Each chapter bridges the gap between the traditional implementation and the new, often easier, implementation in Java EE.

If you are an expert in Java, this book will act as a solid reference to Java EE and Java SE implementations of the most common design patterns.

This book focuses on the most common Java EE design patterns and demonstrates how they are implemented in the Java EE universe. Each chapter introduces a different pattern by explaining its purpose and discussing its use. Then it demonstrates how the pattern is implemented in Java SE and gives a detailed description of how it works. From there, the book demonstrates how the pattern is now implemented in Java EE and discusses its most common usage, its benefits, and its pitfalls. All explanations are accompanied by detailed code examples, all of which can be downloaded from the website accompanying this book. At the end of each chapter, you'll find a final discussion and summary that rounds up all you have read in the chapter. There are even some interesting and sometimes challenging exercises for you to do that will test your understanding of the patterns covered in the chapter.

WHAT IS A DESIGN PATTERN?

> *Design patterns are "descriptions of communicating objects and classes that are customized to solve a general design problem in a particular context."*
>
> —GANG OF FOUR

Design patterns offer solutions to common application design problems. In object-oriented programming, design patterns are normally targeted at solving the problems associated with object creation and interaction, rather than the large-scale problems faced by the overall software architecture. They provide generalized solutions in the form of boilerplates that can be applied to real-life problems.

Usually design patterns are visualized using a class diagram, showing the behaviors and relations between classes. A typical class diagram looks like Figure 1-1.

Figure 1-1 shows the inheritance relationship between three classes. The subclasses `CheckingAccount` and `SavingsAccount` inherit from their abstract parent class `BankAccount`.

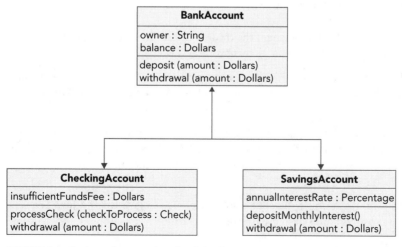

FIGURE 1-1: A class diagram showing inheritance

Such a diagram is followed by an implementation in Java showing the simplest implementation. An example of the singleton pattern, which will be described in later chapters, is shown in Figure 1-2.

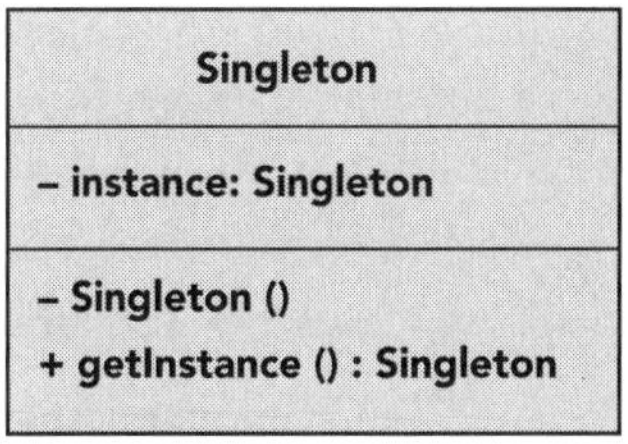

And here is an example of its simplest implementation.

```java
public enum MySingletonEnum {
    INSTANCE;
    public void doSomethingInteresting(){}
}
```

Singleton
– instance: Singleton
– Singleton () **+ getInstance () : Singleton**

FIGURE 1-2: The singleton pattern class diagram

How Patterns Were Discovered and Why We Need Them

Design patterns have been a hot topic since the famous Gang of Four (GoF, made up of Erich Gamma, Richard Helm, Ralph Johnson, and John Vlissides) wrote the book *Design Patterns: Elements of Reusable Object-Oriented Software*,[1] finally giving developers around the world tried and tested solutions to the commonest software engineering problems. This important book describes various development techniques and their pitfalls and provides 23 object-oriented programming design patterns. These patterns are divided into three categories: creational, structural, and behavioral.

But why? Why did we suddenly realize we needed design patterns so much?

The decision was not that sudden. Object-oriented programming emerged in the 1980s, and several languages that built on this new idea shortly followed. Smalltalk, C++, and Objective C are some of the few languages that are still prevalent today. They have brought their own problems, though, and unlike the development of procedural programming, this time the shift was too fast to see what was working and what was not.

Although design patterns have solved many issues (such as spaghetti code) that software engineers have with procedural programming languages like C and COBOL, object-oriented languages have introduced their own set of issues. C++ has advanced quickly, and because of its complexity, it has driven many developers into fields of bugs such as memory leaks, poor object design, unsafe use of memory, and unmaintainable legacy code.

However, most of the problems developers have experienced have followed the same patterns, and it's not beyond reason to suggest that someone somewhere has already solved the issues. Back when object-oriented programming emerged, it was still a pre-Internet world, and it was hard to share experiences with the masses. That's why it took a while until the GoF formed a collection of patterns to well-known recurring problems.

Patterns in the Real World

Design patterns are infinitely useful and proven solutions to problems you will inevitably face. Not only do they impart years of collective knowledge and experience, design patterns offer a good vocabulary between developers and shine a light on many problems.

However, design patterns are not a magic wand; they do not offer an out-of-the-box implementation like a framework or a tool set. Unnecessary use of design patterns, just because they sound cool or you want to impress your boss, can result in a sophisticated and overly engineered system that doesn't solve any problems but instead introduces bugs, inefficient design, low performance, and maintenance issues. Most patterns can solve problems in design, provide reliable solutions to known problems, and allow developers to communicate in a common idiom across languages. Patterns really should only be used when problems are likely to occur.

Design patterns were originally classified into three groups:

➤ **Creational patterns**—Patterns that control object creation, initialization, and class selection. Singleton (Chapter 4, "Singleton Pattern") and factory (Chapter 6, "Factory Pattern") are examples from this group.

➤ **Behavioral patterns**—Patterns that control communication, messaging, and interaction between objects. The observer (Chapter 11, "Observer Pattern") is an example from this group.

➤ **Structural patterns**—Patterns that organize relationships between classes and objects, providing guidelines for combining and using related objects together to achieve desired behaviors. The decorator pattern (Chapter 7, "Decorator Pattern") is a good example of a pattern from this group.

Design patterns offer a common dictionary between developers. Developers can use them to communicate in a much simpler way without having to reinvent the wheel for every problem. Want to show your buddy how you are planning to add dynamic behavior at run time? No more step-by-step drawings or misunderstandings. It's plain and simple; you just utter a few words: "Let's use a decorator pattern to address this problem!" Your friend will know what you are talking about immediately, no further explanation needed. If you already know what a pattern is and use it in a right context, you are well on your way to developing a durable and maintainable application.

> ### SUGGESTED READING
>
> It's strongly suggested that you read *Design Patterns: Elements of Reusable Object-Oriented Software* by Erich Gamma, Richard Helm, Ralph Johnson, and John Vlissides (Addison-Wesley, 1995) or *Head First Design Patterns* by Eric Freeman, Elisabeth Robson, Bert Bates, and Kathy Sierra (O'Reilly, 2004). Both are great companions to this book and are invaluable guides for learning design patterns.

DESIGN PATTERN BASICS

One key point regarding design patterns is that overuse or unnecessary use can be troublesome. As soon as some developers learn new patterns, they show a great desire to use them whenever they can. However, doing so often results in their project being bloated with singletons or overwrapping via façades or unnecessarily complex decorators. Design patterns are answers to problems, so unless there is a problem or a chance for a problem to appear, there is no point implementing a pattern. To give an example, using the decorator pattern just because there is a slim chance that an object's behavior might change in the feature introduces development complexity today and a maintenance nightmare in the future.

ENTERPRISE PATTERNS

Java 1.0 quickly became popular after it was released in early 1996. The timing was perfect for the introduction of a new language that would remove the complexity of memory management, pointers, and the syntax of C/C++. Java offered a gradual learning curve that allowed many developers to adopt it quickly and to start programming in Java. However, there was something else that accelerated the shift: applets. An applet is a small application that runs in a website in a separate process from the web browser and adds functionality to the website that would not be possible with HTML and CSS alone. An example would be an interactive graph or streaming video feed.

With the rapid growth of the Internet, static web pages soon became archaic and uninteresting. The web user wanted a better, faster, and more beautiful surfing experience. Along came applets, which offered unbelievable interactivity, effects, and action to the then-static World Wide Web. Soon, dancing Duke (the symbol of Java) became the trend among modern websites. However, nothing remains still for long on the Internet. Users wanted even more, yet applets failed miserably at adapting to those wants, so they did not maintain their popularity.

Nevertheless, applets were the driving force behind the Java platform's fast adaptation and popularity. Today (as this book is written) Java is still among the two most popular programming languages in the world.[2]

Java to Enterprise Java

Following the release of the Standard Edition of Java, IBM introduced Enterprise JavaBeans (EJB) in 1997, which was adopted by Sun in 1999 and formed part of the Enterprise Java Platform (J2EE) 1.2. In 1998 and prior to the release of J2EE,[3] Sun released a professional version of Java labeled JPE. However, it wasn't until after EJB was released that vendors and developers became interested in adopting enterprise Java. With the release of J2EE 1.3 in 2001, Java became a key player in the enterprise world, and its position was sealed with the release of J2EE 1.4 in 2003.

Version 1.4 was one of the greatest milestones in Java's history. It was widely adopted and maintained its popularity for many years even though new versions were released. Vendors and corporations were slow to adopt the newer versions, even though many had reasons to complain about J2EE1.4. Using it was like driving a monster truck to the shops instead of a family sedan. It was definitely powerful, but it was simply too complicated and bloated with XML files, and neither the frameworks nor the containers were lightweight.

Yet J2EE became the most popular enterprise development platform. It had a set of features that made it a great choice for enterprise development.

➤ **Portability**—The JVM let Java code run on any operating system. Developers could develop on Windows, test on Linux, but go into production on a UNIX system.

➤ **Security**—J2EE offered its own role-based security model.

➤ **Transactions**—J2EE offered built-in transactions.

➤ **Language features from J2SE**—J2SE offered easy syntax, garbage collection, and great object-oriented programming features.

However, J2EE was not perfect. Soon enough, the complex structure of the platform with its heavy use of XML configurations created the perfect problem-ridden environment.

The Emergence of Enterprise Java Patterns

The complex programming models of J2EE soon led many projects into deep waters. Applications developed with J2EE technologies tended to contain excessive amounts of "plumbing" code such as JNDI lookup code, XML configuration files, and try/catch blocks that acquired and released JDBC resources. Writing and maintaining such code proved a major drain on resources and was the source of many bugs and performance issues. The EJB component model aimed to reduce complexity when implementing business logic, but it did not succeed in this aim. The model was simply too complex and often overused.

After just a few years from the first release at the JavaOne conference in 2000, Deepak Alur, John Crupi, and Dan Malks gave a talk titled "Prototyping Patterns for the J2EE Platform," which introduced several patterns targeted at common problems experienced in the design of J2EE applications. This talk would become a book. The following year, they published a book called *Core J2EE Patterns: Best Practices and Design Strategies*.[4] In addition to the 15 already well-known patterns, the authors introduced 6 new J2EE design patterns. The new patterns included Context Object and Application Controller for the Presentation tier, Application Service and Business Object for the Business tier, and Domain Store and Web Service Broker for the Integration tier.

Some of those patterns evolved from the "classic" GoF patterns, whereas others were new and addressed the flaws of J2EE. In the following years, several projects and frameworks such as Apache Camel were released that made the life of enterprise developers easier. Even some, led by Rod Johnson,[5] made a bold step by moving away from J2EE and releasing the Spring Framework. Spring soon became popular, and its popularity influenced great changes in the new programming model behind Java EE. Today most of those patterns are still valid and in use. However, some are obsolete and no longer required thanks to the simplified programming model of Java EE.

Design Patterns Versus Enterprise Patterns

Enterprise patterns differ from design patterns in that enterprise patterns target enterprise software and its problems, which greatly differ from the problems of desktop applications. A new approach, Service Oriented Architecture (SOA), introduced several principals to follow when building well-organized, reusable enterprise software. Don Box's[6] four tenets of SOA formed the basis of these fundamental principles. That set of principles addressed common needs of enterprise projects.

> **DON BOX'S FOUR TENETS OF SOA**
>
> 1. Boundaries are explicit. 2. Services are autonomous. 3. Services share schema and contract, not class. 4. Service compatibility is determined based on policy.

However, "classical" patterns still have something to offer. With the release of Java EE 5, Enterprise Java was back in the spotlight, something that third-party frameworks such as Spring and Struts had hogged for too long. The release of Java EE 6 was an even greater step forward and made the platform more competitive.

Today in Java EE 7, most "classic" design patterns described in the GoF book are embedded in the platform ready to be used "out of the box." Unlike the J2EE era, most of these patterns can be implemented via annotations and without the need for convoluted XML configuration. This is a huge leap forward and offers the developer a simplified programming model.

Although there are several great books on design patterns and the new features of Java EE, there seems to be a missing link on how those patterns are implemented in Java EE.

Plain Old Design Patterns Meet Java EE

Even from day zero, Java has been friendly toward design patterns. Some of the patterns have a built-in implementation that is ready to use, such as the observer pattern in Java SE. Java itself also uses many design patterns; for example, the singleton pattern is used in the system and runtime classes, and comparators are a great example of the implementation of the strategy pattern.

The tradition has continued with Enterprise Java, but especially Java EE, which has built-in implementations of many of the patterns described in the GoF book. Most of these patterns can be enabled and used with simple and easy-to-use annotations. So instead of looking at class diagrams and writing boiler plate code, any developer with experience can enable a pattern with just a few lines of code. Magical? Well, not quite. Because the Java EE run time has a more sophisticated design, it can offer many capabilities, relying on the power of the underlying platform. Most of the functionality that those patterns need would not be available without Java EE's superset of features such as EJB and Context and Dependency Injection (CDI). The Java EE container does most of the work for you as it adds many embedded services and functionality to the server. The drawback is that it has resulted in a heavyweight server runtime environment, especially compared to basic web servers such as Apache Tomcat. However, this has improved, and the latest runtime builds on Java EE 7 are more lightweight.

Still, why do people continue to need design patterns in enterprise applications? Well, patterns are needed now more than ever before. Most of the enterprise applications are built for corporations by different teams of developers, and different parts need to be reused often. Unlike solving a common problem pattern on your own or in a small team, your solutions are now exposed to the whole corporation and beyond to potentially the whole world (if your project is open source). It is easy to introduce a poorly designed application and let it become a corporate tradition or development strategy. Because libraries, utility classes, and application programming interfaces (APIs) are exposed to more developers, it has become even harder to break compatibility and make radical changes. Changing one return type or even adding a new method to an interface may break all projects relying on that piece of code.

It is clear that enterprise software development requires a higher level of discipline and coordination between developer teams. Design patterns are a good way to approach this problem. However, most enterprise developers still do not make good use of classical design patterns even though they have been in Java EE since version 5.0. Although enterprise patterns can solve many issues, the original design patterns continue to have much to offer. They are well worn and proven solutions, they have stood the test of time, and they have been implemented in almost all object-oriented languages.

Finally, because most of those patterns are already integrated in the Java EE platform, there is no need to write the full implementation code. Some may require a little XML configuration, but most of the patterns can be implemented by applying an annotation to the class, method, or member variable. Want to create a singleton? Just add the `@Singleton` annotation to the top of your class file. Need to implement the factory pattern? Just add the `@Produces` annotation, and the method will become the factory of the given return type.

Java EE also sets the standards. The `@Inject` annotation serves as a default implementation and can be mixed and matched with almost any other framework (the Spring Framework) because they use the same annotation.

When Patterns Become Anti-Patterns

Design patterns represent collected wisdom, but this doesn't mean you have to use them all the time. Just like the famous American psychologist Abraham Maslow[7] so aptly stated, "If the only tool you have is a hammer, you tend to see every problem as a nail." If you try to address all problems with only the patterns you know, they simply won't fit, or worse, they'll fit badly and cause more problems. Even more, unnecessary use of patterns tends to overcomplicate the system and result in poor performance. Just because you like the decorator pattern does not mean you need to implement the pattern on every object. Patterns work best when the conditions and the problems require their use.

SUMMARY

Java and design patterns have had a long journey to arrive at where they are now. Once they were separate, with no knowledge of each other, but now they are together, to be forever integrated in the Java Enterprise Edition. To understand this intimate paring, you must know their history. Already you have discovered the roots of your favorite couple and how they found each other. You've read about J2EE's rocky beginnings and how the GoF gave light to 23 design patterns. You've seen how frameworks like Spring came up behind Java and took over and how the reinvented Java EE is now fighting back and gaining ground. The knowledge contained in this book will prepare you to tackle with confidence the majority of the design issue that you will face during your development career. You can rest easy knowing that the years of struggle the Java Enterprise Edition has endured combined with the inherent wisdom of design patterns have resulted in an endurably strong and flexible programming language and environment.

Enjoy this invaluable guide to design patterns in Java EE, and use the wisdom gained here in every project you're involved in.

NOTES

1. *Design Patterns: Elements of Reusable Object-Oriented Software* (Addison-Wesley, 1994): Erich Gamma, Richard Helm, Ralph Johnson, John Vlissides.
2. According to the TIOBE index, Java appears at number two after C: http://www.tiobe.com/index.php/content/paperinfo/tpci/index.html.
3. Before version 5, Java EE used to be called J2EE. From this point J2EE will be used to refer to pre-Java EE 5.

4. *Core J2EE Patterns: Best Practices and Design Strategies* (Prentice Hall 2003, 2nd Edition): Deepak Alur, Dan Malks, John Crupi.
5. Rod Johnson (@springrod) is an Australian computer specialist who created the Spring Framework and cofounded SpringSource. http://en.wikipedia.org/wiki/Rod_Johnson_(programmer).
6. Don Box (@donbox) is a distinguished engineer: http://en.wikipedia.org/wiki/Don_Box.
7. Abraham Maslow (1908–1970) American Psychologist.

The Basics of Java EE

WHAT'S IN THIS CHAPTER?

➤ Introduction to the core concepts of Java EE

➤ Discussion of the multitier structure of an enterprise application

➤ Explanation of Java EE–compliant servers and the web profile

➤ Convention over configuration overview

➤ Content Dependency Injection overview

➤ Interceptor overview

WROX.COM CODE DOWNLOADS FOR THIS CHAPTER

The wrox.com code download for this chapter is found at www.wrox.com/go/projavaeedesignpatterns on the Download Code tab. The code is in the Chapter 02 download and individually named according to the names throughout the chapter.

The Java EE programming model has been simplified substantially since J2EE. Annotations have replaced the XML descriptors files, convention over configuration have replaced the tedious manual configuration, and dependency injection hides the creation and lookup of resources. Developers need to reconsider their approach to design and coding.

The development of Java EE enterprise applications has gotten easier. All that you need is a POJO (Plain Old Java Object) annotated with some metadata and, depending on the annotation used, the POJO becomes an Enterprise JavaBeans (EJB, stateful or stateless), a servlet, a JSF backing bean, a persistence entity, a singleton, or a REST web service. You can optionally declare many of these services using XML in a deployment descriptor.

Listing 2-1 shows how to make a POJO into a singleton bean that is instantiated and initialized at start-up and then managed by the container simply by adding the

@Singleton and @Startup annotations to the class and @PostConstruct to the initialization method. See Chapter 4, "Singleton Pattern," for a detailed explanation of the use of these annotations.

LISTING 2-1: POJO becomes a container-managed singleton bean with the addition of some annotations

```
package com.devchronicles.singleton;

import java.util.HashMap;
import java.util.Map;
import javax.annotation.PostConstruct;
import javax.ejb.Singleton;
import javax.ejb.Startup;

@Startup
@Singleton
public class CacheSingletonBean {

    private Map<Integer, String> myCache;

    @PostConstruct
    public void start(){
        myCache = new HashMap<Integer, String>();
    }

    public void addUser(Integer id, String name){
        myCache.put(id, name);
    }

    public String getName(Integer id){
        return myCache.get(id);
    }
}
```

The aim of Java EE has not changed; it continues to recognize the requirement that developers and enterprises have for distributed and transactional applications that harness speed, security, and reliability. The Java EE platform is designed to make the production of large-scale, multitiered applications easier, more reliable, and more secure.

MULTITIER ARCHITECTURE

The architecture of a Java EE application is separated into tiers: the Client tier, the Middle tier (which consists of the Web layer and the Business layer), and the Enterprise Information Systems (EIS) tier. Each tier has unique responsibilities and utilizes different Java EE technologies. The segregation of an application into distinct tiers brings greater flexibility and adaptability. You have the choice of adding or modifying just a specific layer rather than refactoring the entire application. Each tier is physically separate and located on different machines. And in the case of a web application, the Client tier is distributed globally.

Java EE works within the realm of the Middle tier, although it touches both the Client and the EIS tiers. The Middle tier receives requests from the Client tier application. The Middle tier's Web layer processes the request and prepares a response, which it sends back to the Client tier, whereas the Business layer applies the business logic before persisting it in the EIS tier. Within the Middle tier, there is fluid communication between the layers and the EIS tier, while preparing the response to the Client tier. A multitier architecture can be represented visually, as in Figure 2-1.

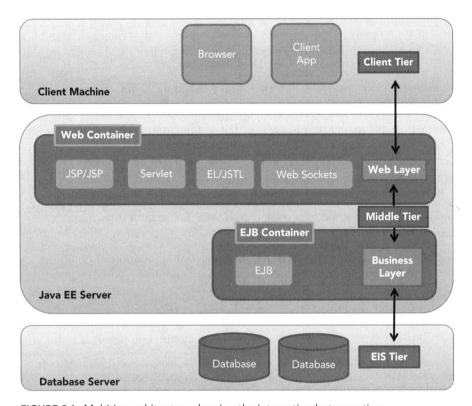

FIGURE 2-1: Multitier architecture showing the interaction between tiers

THE CLIENT TIER

The Client tier is usually a browser that connects to the Java EE server via Hypertext Transfer Protocol (HTTP), although it can be any application on any machine as long as it behaves as a client in a server-client relationship. The client application sends a request to the server for a resource; the server then processes the request and returns a response. This is usually the extent of the relationship between the client and the server.

> **NOTE** *The Client tier is often referred to as the Presentation tier.*

THE MIDDLE TIER

The Java EE server sits on the Middle tier and provides two logical containers: the web container and the EJB container. These containers roughly correspond to the Web layer and the Business layer, respectively. Each layer has distinct but sometimes overlapping responsibilities.

The MVC pattern is commonly used to clearly separate the view generation responsibilities of the Web layer from the data modeling responsibilities of the Business layer. Chapter 14, "Model Viewer Controller Pattern," discusses in detail how to implement this separation of concerns.

Web Layer

The Web layer manages the interactions between the Client tier and the Business layer.

The Web layer receives a request for a resource from the Client tier. The request may include data that the user inputted, such as a username and password or sign-up information. The request is processed and, if necessary, an interaction between the Web layer and the Business layer takes place. The response is dynamically prepared in one of several forms (usually in the form of a HyperText Markup Language [HTML] web page for a response originating from a browser) and sent to the client.

The Web layer maintains the user's states in a session and may even perform some business logic and temporarily persist data in memory.

The technologies that are typically used in the Web layer relate to the management of the interactions between the Client tier and the Middle tier and the construction of the response. Servlets control the web flow and manage interactions while JavaServer Pages (JSP), Expression Language (EL), and JavaServer Pages Standard Tag Library (JSTL) prepare the response to the client. This is just a snapshot of the technologies that you can use in the Web layer. For a complete list, see Figure 2-2.

In Java EE 7, four new technologies were added to the EE universe: WebSockets, Concurrency Utilities, Batch, and JSON-P. You can use all but WebSockets in both layers.

Business Layer

The Business layer executes business logic that resolves business problems or satisfies a particular business need within the business domain.

Normally, this would involve data that has been retrieved from the database in the EIS tier or collected from the client. In a banking domain, a transaction fee might be applied to a transaction amount and sent to the client via the Web layer for the client to confirm the transaction. In an e-commerce domain, a different tax rate might be applied to a product depending on the physical location of the client before being passed to the Web layer, and the web page would be rendered according to this info.

The Business layer is where the core logic of the business application resides. Business logic is wrapped up in the EJB, and the data used by the business logic is retrieved from the EIS tier via Java Persistence API (JPA), Java Transaction API (JTA), and Java Database Connectivity (JDBC).

It is common to request and modify data via web services that use JAX-RS and JAX-WS. (See Chapter 13, "REST," for more on this topic.) This is just a snapshot of the technologies that you can use in the web layer. For a complete list, see Figure 2-2.

Full Product Requirements [2]	JSR Reference	Optional	Web Profile[3]	New in Java EE7	Web Container	EJB Container
Java API for WebSocket	JSR 356					
Java API for JSON Processing	JSR 353					
Java Servlet 3.1	JSR 340					
JavaServer Faces 2.2	JSR 344					
Expression Language 3.0	JSR 341					
JavaServer Pages 2.3	JSR 245					
Standard Tag Library for JavaServer Pages (JSTL) 1.2	JSR 52					
Batch Applications for the Java Platform	JSR 352					
Concurrency Utilities for Java EE 1.0	JSR 236					
Contexts and Dependency Injection for Java 1.1	JSR 346					
Dependency Injection for Java 1.0	JSR 330					
Bean Validation 1.1	JSR 349					
Enterprise JavaBeans 3.2 (except for EJB entity beans and associated EJB QL, which have been made optional)	JSR 345		1			1
Managed Beans 1.0	JSR-316					
Interceptors 1.2	JSR 318					
Java EE Connector Architecture 1.7	JSR 322					
Java Persistence 2.1	JSR 338					
Common Annotations for the Java Platform 1.2	JSR 250					
Java Message Service API 2.0	JSR 343					
Java Transaction API (JTA) 1.2	JSR 907					
JavaMail 1.5	JSR 919					
Java API for RESTful Web Services (JAX-RS) 2.0	JSR 339					
Implementing Enterprise Web Services 1.4	JSR 109					
Java API for XML-Based Web Services (JAX-WS) 2.2	JSR 224					
Web Services Metadata for the Java Platform	JSR 181					
Java API for XML-Based RPC (JAX-RPC) 1.1	JSR 101					
Java API for XML Registries (JAXR) 1.0	JSR 93					
Java Authentication Service Provider Interface for Containers 1.1	JSR 196					
Java Authorization Contract for Containers 1.5	JSR 115					
Java EE Application Deployment 1.2	JSR 88					
J2EE Management 1.1	JSR 77					
Debugging Support for Other Languages 1.0	JSR 45					
Java Architecture for XML Binding (JAXB) 2.2	JSR 222					

1. ENTERPRISE JAVABEANS (EJB) 3.2 LITE
2. SOURCE: JAVA PLATFORM, ENTERPRISE EDITION 7 (JAVA EE 7), JSR 342, EE.9.7 FULL JAVA EE PRODUCT REQUIREMENTS
3. SOURCE: JAVA PLATFORM, ENTERPRISE EDITION 7 (JAVA EE 7), WEB PROFILE SPECIFICATION, JSR 342, WP.2.1 REQUIRED COMPONENTS

FIGURE 2-2: Technology used in the Web and Business layers

NOTE *The Middle tier is often referred to as the Logic tier, Data Access tier, and Application tier.*

THE EIS TIER

The EIS tier consists of data storage units, often in the form of databases, but they can be any resource that provides data. It may be an antiquated legacy system or a file system.

> **NOTE** *The EIS tier is often referred to as the Data tier, Persistence tier, and Integration tier.*

JAVA EE SERVERS

As you have seen, the Middle tier hosts the Java EE server, which provides the Java EE functionality needed for an enterprise application.

Java EE is based on 30 standards, called Java Specification Requests (JSRs) (http://www.oracle .com/technetwork/java/javaee/tech/index.html). These requests go through the Java Community Process (JCP) before they can become accepted as part of the Java EE universe. The JCP is an open process in which anyone can participate and give feedback on JSRs or even submit their own JSR (https://www.jcp.org/en/home/index).

These specifications are bundled together and represent the technologies that a server application must implement to be able to claim that it is Java EE compliant.

Additionally, Oracle requires that the server application passes the Technology Compatibility Kit (TCK). This is a nontrivial test suite that checks that the application server behaves as the specification requires. This ensures that if you develop your application following the Java EE specifications, you will be able to deploy and execute it on any Java EE application.

At the time of writing, three application servers have been certified fully compatible with Java EE 7. They are GlassFish Server Open Source Edition 4.0 (http://glassfish.java.net), Wildfly 8.0.0 (http://wildfly.org), and TMAX JEUS 8 (http://tmaxsoft.com/product/jeus/ certification/). Eleven application servers are Java EE 6 compatible (http://en.wikipedia .org/wiki/Java_Platform,_Enterprise_Edition#Java_EE_6_certified).

THE JAVA EE WEB PROFILE

The Java EE web profile is a subset of technologies that comprise the most appropriate technologies required for the development of web-based enterprise applications. The profile reduces the size and complexity of the platform to just the technologies required for the development of a modern web application. The web profile is a complete stack comprising technologies related to workflow and core functionality (Servlet), presentation (JSF and JSP), business logic (EJB lite), transactions (JTA), persistence (JPA), the new WebSocket, and much more. It omits a lot of enterprise-related technologies such as the Concurrency Utilities, Java

Message Services, JAX-RPC, JAXR, and JAX-WS. See Figure 2-2 for a complete rundown of the technologies included in the web profile.

CORE PRINCIPLES OF JAVA EE

The core principles of Java EE include a number of design paradigms and patterns that are essential to the way you develop enterprise applications. At the center of Java EE is the design paradigm of convention over configuration: a way to simplify the development of enterprise applications without losing flexibility and obscuring its code's purpose. It is not a new idea and has been a part of other frameworks including Grails, Ruby on Rails, and Spring Boot for some time—in some cases for nearly a decade. Thankfully, it has made its way into the heart of Java EE, where it helps others write beautiful code.

Java EE makes good use of its component model, which includes the components Entities, JavaBeans, EJBs, Managed Beans, Servlets, SOAP, and RESTful web services. All these components can be "injectable" dependencies; the container manages, in some way, their life cycle (from instantiation to destruction)—whether they are bound to a context or not—and their decoupling from dependent components via dependency injection.

A loosely coupled application allows for extensibility: Old classes can be swapped with new ones with no requirement to change the dependent class. Dependency injection decouples an object from its dependencies, whereas interceptors decouple business concerns from technical and cross-cutting concerns. Such technological concerns would be performance and logging, and a cross-cutting concern would be security.

CONVENTION OVER CONFIGURATION

All class names should start with a capital letter as part of convention. It's not obligatory; the class will still compile if it starts with a lowercase letter, but starting with a capital letter makes the code easier to read and maintain. When setting up a project in an IDE, you only need to specify the type of the project and its name for the most appropriate directory structure to be created; the most common application programming interfaces (APIs) to be imported; and the default files such as web.xml, index.jsp, etc. to be created with appropriate default settings for ease of development. You do all of this based on agreed convention.

The amount of work you have to do and the decisions you have to make as a developer are substantially reduced when you rely on convention. You don't specify any configuration that is considered conventional; you are required to specify only the unconventional. This has a significant effect. With just a few annotations on a POJO, you can do away with a lot of your ugly XML deployment descriptors and application configuration files. As you have seen in Listing 2-1, you need to apply just three annotations to make a POJO into a singleton bean that will be instantiated and initialized at start-up and then managed by the container.

> **NOTE** *Convention over configuration is also known as coding by convention.*

CONTEXT AND DEPENDENCY INJECTION

Dependency injection is a design pattern (see Chapter 5, "Dependency Injection and CDI") that decouples the relationship between a component and its dependencies. It does this by injecting the dependency into an object rather than the object creating the dependency by using the new keyword. By removing the creation of the dependency from the object and delegating that responsibility to the container, you can swap out the dependency for another compatible object at compile time and run time.

Beans that the container manages are called Context and Dependency Injection (CDI)-managed beans and are instantiated when the container starts up. All POJOs that have a default constructor and are not created using the new keyword are CDI beans that are injected into an object based on type matching. To be injected, the receiving object must declare a field, constructor, or method using the @Inject annotation. Then the type of the declared object is used to determine which dependency to inject.

In Listing 2-2, you have a POJO that has a default constructor and therefore will be managed as a CDI bean, and in Listing 2-3, you inject the managed bean. The container knows to inject the Message bean based on its type. The container manages only one CDI bean of type Message, so this is the bean it injects.

LISTING 2-2: Dependency injection example—Dependency

```java
package com.devchronicles.basicsofjavaee;

public class Message {

    public String getMessage(){
        return "Hello World!!";
    }

}
```

LISTING 2-3: Dependency injection example—Receiver

```java
package com.devchronicles.basicsofjavaee;

import javax.inject.Inject;

public class Service {

    @Inject
    private Message message;

    public void showMessage(){
        System.out.println(message.getMessage());
    }
}
```

An inquiring mind might ask: What happens if the container is managing more than one bean of type Message? For this to be true, Message would have to be an interface that has more than one concrete implementation. This is where it becomes more interesting . There are several strategies that you can employ to resolve these types of ambiguities. You will encounter several of these during the course of this book. If curiosity has gotten the better of you, skip to Chapter 5.

Context is the distinguishing feature between EJBs and CDI-managed beans. CDI beans exist within a defined context; EJBs do not. CDI beans are created within the context of a scope; they exist for the life of the scope and are destroyed when the scope finishes. There are four scopes that are annotated as follows: `@ApplicationScope`, `@ConversationScope`, `@SessionScope`, and `@RequestScope`. The CDI container controls the life of a bean based on the bean's defined scope. For example, a bean annotated with `@SessionScope` exists for as long as the HTTP session is alive; at the end the scope, the bean is destroyed and marked for garbage collection. This behavior is in contrast to that of EJBs, which are not bound to a scope. This means that you must explicitly remove the bean by calling a method annotated by the `@Remove` annotation.

INTERCEPTORS

Most applications have concerns that don't comfortably fit into the core concern of the application logic but cannot be cleanly separated from the application's design or implementation. These concerns are cross-cutting and affect different parts of the application. They are often responsible for duplicate code and interdependencies that make the system less extensible. The implementation of these noncore concerns as interceptors allows them to be decoupled from the core concern. You do this by logically separating their implementation and intercepting method calls to the core and invoking the appropriate method.

You implement interceptors using the annotation `@Interceptors` followed by the class name of the crossing-cutting concern. In Listing 2-4, the `setValue` method is intercepted upon its invocation by the `LoggerInterceptor.class`.

LISTING 2-4: Core method intercepted by logger interceptor

```
@Interceptors(LoggerInterceptor.class)
public void setValues(Integer value, String name) {
    this.value = value;
    this.name = name;

}
```

The logger interceptor can access the intercepted method's parameters and perform the cross-cutting logic before returning to fully execute the intercepted method.

In Listing 2-5, the logger interceptor accesses the parameters of the `setValues` method and logs them to the system logger.

LISTING 2-5: The logger interceptor

```
@AroundInvoke
public logger(InvocationContext ic) throws Exception {
    Object[] params = ic.getParameters();
    logger.warning("Parameters passed: " + params);
}
```

You can define interceptors in the business code and in the deployment descriptor files. This aspect of interceptors and much more is discussed in Chapter 8, "Aspect-Oriented Programming (Interceptors)."

SUMMARY

In this chapter, you have seen a brief summary of Java EE and the history of the current principles of it.

You have discovered how the architecture should be layered properly in a Java EE project. We also provide a long JSR compatibility list to help you determine which container best suits your project. Finally the chapter focused on Core Principles of Java EE by presenting convention over configuration and giving a brief summary of CDI.

Next, we will be ready to move on to each pattern, focusing on their implementations and providing specific examples.

EXERCISES

1. Think about a banking application where you need to integrate into the mainframe back end and provide services for web, mobile, and native desktop clients.

2. Think about implementing the web application for the project you designed in the first step. Which layer should host the web application?

3. After a long debate, the bank you are working for decided to move away from the mainframe, asking you to design a substitute system. What parts of the current project will be impacted?

PART II
Implementing Design Patterns in Java EE

3

Façade Pattern

WHAT'S IN THIS CHAPTER?

➤ An introduction to the intent of the façade pattern

➤ A brief discussion of the benefits that the pattern brings

➤ Three ways that the pattern can be implemented: POJO, stateless, and stateful session bean façade

➤ The important differences between the stateful and the stateless session bean façade

➤ When and where to use this pattern

➤ Warnings about its use and potential pitfalls

WROX.COM CODE DOWNLOADS FOR THIS CHAPTER

The wrox.com code downloads for this chapter are found at www.wrox.com/go/projavaeedesignpatterns on the Download Code tab. The code is in the Chapter 03 download and individually named according to the names throughout the chapter.

The façade pattern is one of the structural design patterns described in the GoF[1] book. The intent behind it is to encapsulate complicated business logic in a higher-level interface that makes access to a subsystem easier to use. This is often done by grouping related method calls and invoking them sequentially from one method.

From a higher-level view, every API can be considered an implementation of the façade pattern since they provide a simple interface which hides its complexity. Any call to an API's method results in the invocation of many other methods from a subsystem hidden behind it. An example of a façade would be the javax.servlet.http.HttpSession interface. This hides the complicated logic associated with maintaining the session while exposing its functionality via a handful of simple-to-use methods.

WHAT IS A FAÇADE?

The GoF[1] book describes this pattern as "providing a unified interface to a set of interfaces in a subsystem." *Head First Design Patterns*[2] gives the same explanation and points out that, while hiding the complexity of the subsystem, the façade pattern offers the full power of the subsystem via an easier-to-use interface.

To give a basic real-world example of how the façade pattern works, imagine a washing machine with only two wash modes: heavily soiled and lightly soiled. For each mode, the washing machine must execute a predefined set of operations: set water temperature, heat water, set duration of wash cycle, set duration of spin cycle, add detergent, add bleach, add fabric softener, and so on. Each mode requires a different set of washing instructions (different amounts of detergent, higher or lower temperature, longer or shorter spin durations, and so on).

The simple interface provides two wash modes that hide the complicated logic of selecting the appropriate water temperature, the duration of the spin and wash cycle, and the different methods for adding detergent, bleach, or fabric softener. The user of the washing machine does not have to think about the complicated logic of how to wash the clothes (decide the temperature, cycle duration, and so on). The only decision the user must make is whether the clothes are heavily soiled or lightly soiled. This is in essence the façade pattern applied to a washing machine design. Later on in this chapter, you will see an implementation of this use case.

The façade pattern is commonly implemented for the following purposes and situations:

- ➤ Provide a simple and unified access to a legacy back-end system.

- ➤ Create a public API to classes, such as a driver.

- ➤ Offer coarse-grained access to available services. Services are combined, such as in the washing machine example.

- ➤ Reduce network calls. The façade makes many calls to the subsystem, while the remote client makes only one call to the façade.

- ➤ To encapsulate flow and inner details of an app for security and simplicity.

> **NOTE** *Façades are sometimes implemented as singleton abstract factories.*

WAR STORY

In the early dark days of J2EE, I was working as a junior developer for a huge banking application where we implemented almost all the J2EE design patterns. All Enterprise JavaBeans (EJB) were wrapped by a façade, and every service EJB using that façade was wrapped with another façade. We also had interfaces for the façades to ensure we didn't break the API. In J2EE, EJB needs a local and remote interface, so writing one EJB meant writing four interfaces and two classes. We didn't have spaghetti code, but we had more layers than a meat lasagna. We were quite happy in our little world—that was, until other teams started to use our core services. Very soon, both the performance of the system and our ability to handle change requests started to suffer.

We contracted a famous and expensive consultant from one of our server vendors to analyze our system. He had a few meetings, spent some time browsing our code base, and concluded that some refactoring was in order, so he deleted all façades and related interfaces. The result was that we had less code to maintain and much better performance, so everyone was happy. The moral of this story is to use patterns—even the simple ones—sparingly and only when you need them, and definitely don't show off your knowledge of patterns.

Façade Class Diagram

As can be seen in the class diagram in Figure 3-1, the façade pattern provides a simple interface to an underlying system. It encapsulates the complicated granular logic.

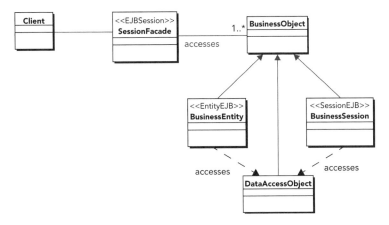

FIGURE 3-1 Class diagram of the façade pattern

IMPLEMENTING THE FAÇADE PATTERN IN PLAIN CODE

Implementing the façade pattern isn't complicated. It doesn't enforce a strict structure or rule set. Any method that provides easy access to a complicated flow could be considered an implementation of the façade pattern.

Now you'll implement the washing machine example given in the introduction as shown in Listing 3-1. You need two methods—`heavilySoiled` and `lightlySoiled`—that represent the two washing modes. All complicated work (the selection of water temperature, spin cycle duration, decision to add bleach or not) is performed in methods invoked from within the façade.

LISTING 3-1: Implementation of the washing machine analogy

```java
public class WashingMachine {

    public void heavilySoiled() {
        setWaterTemperature(100);
        setWashCycleDuration(90);
        setSpinCycleDuration(10);
        addDetergent();
        addBleach();
        addFabricSoftener();
        heatWater();
        startWash();
    }

    public void lightlySoiled() {
        setWaterTemperature(40);
        setWashCycleDuration(20);
        setSpinCycleDuration(10);
        addDetergent();
        heatWater();
        startWash();
    }
}


// to use the façade
new WashingMachine().lightlySoiled();
```

If you want to use this functionality, just invoke the façade's `lightlySoilded` or `heavilySoilded` method and let it do the complicated logic of washing the clothes. All complicated logic is kept hidden by the façade and exposed via its two methods.

The implementation of the methods is decoupled from the client. This decoupling allows the implementation to change without affecting any change in the way the client accesses the washing services. The client knows nothing about the implementation of these methods, and it doesn't care. All that it is interested in is obtaining the service it requires.

This example demonstrates one of many of the benefits of the façade pattern. This book does not go into detail about the benefits of the façade pattern, so what follows is a brief summary of the most important ones:

➤ A reduction in coupling because the client knows nothing about the subsystem

➤ Increased maintainability and manageability when changes are required

➤ Reuse of functionality because it encourages the reuse of controls and fine-grained logic

➤ Consistency of service execution by invoking the same method consistently from one invocation to the next

➤ Reduction in business logic complexity by grouping related methods and invoking them from one method invocation

➤ Centralization of security and transaction control management

➤ Testable and mockable pattern implementations

> **NOTE** *You may see this implementation referred to as the POJO façade to distinguish it from the stateful and stateless implementations that you will see later in this chapter.*

IMPLEMENTING THE FAÇADE PATTERN IN JAVA EE

Unlike many other patterns described in this book, Java EE does not offer a built-in implementation of this method. Nevertheless, it is straightforward to implement using stateful or stateless EJB. Using EJB offers the advantage of easy access to other EJB that the façade might require.

Façade with Stateless Beans

To demonstrate this implementation, assume that you have three EJBs as shown in Listing 3-2 with distinct but related functionality: CustomerService, LoanService, and AccountService.

LISTING 3-2: Code for three EJBs that form the subsystem to the façade

```java
package com.devchronicles.facade;

import javax.ejb.Stateless;

@Stateless
public class CustomerService {

    public long getCustomer(int sessionID) {
        // get logged in customer id
        return 100005L;
    }

    public boolean checkId(long x) {
        // check if customer id is valid
        return true;
    }
}

package com.devchronicles.facade;

import javax.ejb.Stateless;

@Stateless
public class LoanService {
    public boolean checkCreditRating(long id, double amount) {
        // check if customer is eligible for the amount
        return true;
    }
```

continues

LISTING 3-2 *(continued)*

```
    }

package com.devchronicles.facade;

import javax.ejb.Stateless;

@Stateless
public class AccountService {

    public boolean getLoan(double amount) {
        // check if bank vault has enough
        return true;
    }

    public boolean setCustomerBalance(long id, double amount) {
        // set new customer balance
        return true;
    }

}
```

You can group these service EJB in a logical collection of related functionality to form an implementation of the façade pattern, such as in Listing 3-3.

LISTING 3-3: Implementation of the stateless façade

```
package com.devchronicles.facade;

import javax.ejb.Stateless;
import javax.inject.Inject;

@Stateless
public class BankServiceFacade {

    @Inject
    CustomerService customerService;

    @Inject
    LoanService loanService;

    @Inject
    AccountService accountService;

    public boolean getLoan(int sessionId, double amount) {
        boolean result = false;
        long id = customerService.getCustomer(sessionId);

        if(customerService.checkId(id)){
            if(loanService.checkCreditRating(id, amount)){
                if(accountService.getLoan(amount)){
                    result = accountService.setCustomerBalance(id, amount);
                }
            }
        }
        return result;
    }
}
```

A façade can invoke other façades in other subsystems, which in turn encapsulate their own logic and flow. This shows one of the benefits of using façades: a simplified hierarchy of method calls. There's one façade for each subsystem, and these subsystems communicate with each other via the façades.

Façade with Stateful Bean

The same bean can be implemented as a stateful session bean or even as a singleton bean as long as it hides some complicated logic and exposes an easy-to-use interface to the client. The only change is the addition of the `@Stateful` annotation, which marks the bean a stateful EJB.

In J2EE (pre 5.0), the use of the façade pattern was encouraged in the implementation of the session façade pattern. However, even in the simplified approach of Java EE, façades still have their place when control and encapsulation of the workflow are required.

WHERE AND WHEN TO USE THE FAÇADE PATTERN

The façade pattern should be used to encapsulate complicated (business) logic at a high level and provide a cleaner single point of access via an API.

Whenever you are in the position to provide an interface or an API to someone, think first about the complexity of the logic and the changes that might occur. The façade pattern does a good job of providing a clean API while hiding the parts subject to change.

However, unnecessarily wrapping methods in a façade is bad practice and adds unnecessary layers. Premature encapsulation could result in too many invocations and layers that don't add value.

When implementing the session façade, you must determine if the use case requires state to be maintained. A use case that invokes only one method of the façade to receive the service that it needs is considered nonconversational, so there is no need to save the conversational state between one method invocation and the next. You should implement this façade as a stateless session bean.

On the other hand, if the conversational state must be maintained between method invocations, the most appropriate way to implement the façade is as a stateful session bean.

You must be careful in the use of the stateful session façade because it ties up server resources until the client that provoked the conversation releases them or times out. This could mean that, for the majority of the time the stateful session bean façade is bound to the client, it is doing nothing; it's just maintaining state and using resources. And, unlike stateless session bean façades, it cannot be reused and shared between other clients because each request creates a new instance of the stateless façade, maintaining the state for that client's session.

So take care when using this pattern. Analyze the use case and make appropriate decisions.

SUMMARY

You can implement the façade pattern as a POJO, a stateless session bean, or a stateful session bean. The various ways to implement the façade pattern solve different problems for different use case scenarios. But the variety of implementations does not distract from its principle intent: providing a high-level simple interface to a more complicated subsystem.

Take care when deciding to implement the façade as a stateful session bean to ensure that it will not cause resource consumption issues.

A well-designed application makes good use of the façade pattern to encapsulate complicated logic and decouple subsystems from clients; however, the premature and overuse of the façade pattern can lead to a more complicated system with multiple layers.

The session façade pattern is akin to the boundary in the entity-control-boundary architectural pattern, and it is related to the adapter and wrapper patterns.

EXERCISES

1. List some public API implementations of the façade pattern and explain how they hide the complicated logic of the subsystem.

2. Develop a façade that hides the complicated logic of an order and payment system.

3. Encapsulate method invocations to the two subsystems—payment and order—in just two methods.

4. Develop the façade as a singleton.

NOTES

1. *Design Patterns: Elements of Reusable Object-Oriented Software* (Addison-Wesley, 1994): Erich Gamma, Richard Helm, Ralph Johnson, John Vlissides.
2. *Head First Design Patterns* (O'Reilly, 2004): Eric Freeman, Elisabeth Robson, Bert Bates, Kathy Sierra.

Singleton Pattern

WHAT'S IN THIS CHAPTER?

➤ The different ways that a developer can implement the singleton design pattern, besides its common usage and pitfalls

➤ The problems that using static members and methods causes in multithreaded environments

➤ The advances that were made in Java 5 SE with the introduction of the enum type and how it can be used to create thread-safe singletons

➤ The use of the @Singleton annotation in Java EE and how this has radically changed the way the singleton pattern is implemented in session beans

➤ The use of BEAN- and CONTAINER-managed concurrency and how the @LockType annotation controls access to business methods

➤ The main issues that have dogged the singleton pattern and why it is considered an anti-pattern that has fallen out of favor

WROX.COM CODE DOWNLOADS FOR THIS CHAPTER

The wrox.com code download for this chapter is found at www.wrox.com/go/ projavaeedesignpatterns on the Download Code tab. The code is in the Chapter 04 download and individually named according to the names throughout the chapter.

The singleton pattern is one of the easiest, most well-known design patterns, but it has fallen out of fashion. Some even consider it as an anti-pattern, which will be discussed later in this chapter. However, enterprise frameworks such as Spring make heavy use of it, and Java EE offers an elegant and easy-to-use implementation. In this chapter, you will see why singletons are needed, why they fell out of fashion, how they can be useful in Java EE applications, and how you can implement them.

The singleton pattern is one of the creational patterns described in the GoF[1] book. A singleton class guarantees the production of only one instance of its own type. Having only one instance can be useful in several cases, such as with global access and when caching expensive resources; however, it may introduce some problems of race conditions if the singleton is used in a multithread environment. Because most programming languages do not provide a built-in mechanism to create singletons, developers must code their own implementations.

However, Java EE has a built-in mechanism that gives the developer a simple way to create a singleton via the addition of an annotation to the class.

WHAT IS A SINGLETON?

According to GoF, the singleton pattern is used to "ensure a class only has one instance, and provide a global point of access to it." *Head First Design Patterns*[2] offers the same explanation and points. Singletons are often used in combination with factory patterns (discussed in Chapter 6, "Factory Pattern").

Singletons are commonly used for the following purposes and situations:

➤ To access shared data across the whole application domain, such as configuration data

➤ To load and cache expensive resources only once, allowing global shared access and improve performance

➤ To create an application logger instance, because normally only one is required

➤ To manage objects within a class implementing the factory pattern

➤ To create a façade object, because normally only one is necessary

➤ To lazily create static classes, since singletons can be lazily instantiated

Spring uses singletons when creating beans (by default, Spring beans are singletons), and Java EE uses singletons internally, such as in the service locator. Java SE also uses the singleton pattern in the implementation of the `runtime` class. So singletons are definitely helpful if you use them in the right context.

Nevertheless, the aggressive use of the singleton pattern may mean unnecessarily caching resources and not letting the garbage collector reclaim objects and free valuable memory resources. It also may mean you do not really use the advantages of object creation and inheritance. An unusually high usage of singletons is considered a sign of poor object-oriented design, which may cause memory and performance issues. Another problem is that singletons are not great when it comes to unit testing. Later, this chapter discusses in more detail the issues surrounding the use of the singleton pattern.

Singleton Class Diagram

As you can see from the class diagram in Figure 4-1, the singleton pattern is based on a single class that holds a reference to the only instance of itself while controlling its creation and its access via the single getter method.

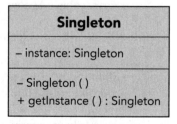

FIGURE 4-1 The singleton pattern class diagram

Implementing the Singleton Pattern in Plain Code

Because you need to guarantee that singletons serve only one instance, the first thing to do is control the object's creation. You can do this easily by making the constructor invisible to the outer world.

```
package com.devchronicles.singleton;

public class MySingleton {

    private MySingleton() {
        // Implemetation code here.
    }
}
```

Next, you need a method that creates the instance or returns it if the instance was already created. Because an instance of MySingleton does not yet exist, you must mark the creation method as static to allow access via the class name; for example: MySingleton.getInstance().

At comment 1 in Listing 4-1, you test the creation of the singleton and create it if it does not exist; otherwise, you return the instance that was created in a previous call to the getInstance() method. Each subsequent calls returns the previously created MySingleton object instance. The code might appear to be functioning, but it is actually buggy and not complete. Because the object creation method is not atomic, it is prone to error in race conditions. It allows more than one instance of the singleton to be created in a multithreaded environment.

LISTING 4-1: Simple implementation of the singleton pattern

```
package com.devchronicles.singleton;

public class MySingleton {
    private static MySingleton instance;

    private MySingleton() {}

    public static MySingleton getInstance() {
        if (instance==null){ // 1
            instance=new MySingleton();
        }
        return instance;
    }
}
```

To fix the race condition problem, you need to acquire a lock and not release it until the instance is returned. In Java, you can implement the locking mechanism via the synchronized keyword, as shown in Listing 4-2.

LISTING 4-2: Synchronizing the singleton for thread safety

```
package com.devchronicles.singleton;

public class MySingleton {

    private static MySingleton instance;

    private MySingleton() {}

    public static synchronized MySingleton getInstance() {
        if (instance==null){
            instance=new MySingleton();
        }
        return instance;
    }
}
```

Another approach is to create the singleton instance at the same time you load the class, as shown in Listing 4-3. This prevents needing to synchronize the creation of the singleton instance and creates the singleton object once the JVM has loaded all the classes (and therefore before a class can call the getInstance() method). This occurs because static members and blocks are executed when the class is loaded.

LISTING 4-3: Creating the singleton object at the time of class loading

```
package com.devchronicles.singleton;

public class MySingleton {

    private final static MySingleton instance=new MySingleton();

    private MySingleton() {}

    public static MySingleton getInstance() {
        return instance;
    }
}
```

Another approach is to use a static block, as shown in Listing 4-4. However, this leads to lazy initialization because the static block is invoked before the constructor is called.

LISTING 4-4: Creating the singleton object in a static block

```
package com.devchronicles.singleton;

public class MySingleton {

    private static MySingleton instance=null;

    static {
        instance=new MySingleton();
    }
```

```
        private MySingleton() {}

        public static MySingleton getInstance() {
            return instance;
        }
    }
```

Double-checked locking is another highly popular mechanism to create singletons. It is considered more secure than other methods because it checks the instance of the singleton once before locking on the singleton class and again before the creation of the object. Listing 4-5 shows this method.

LISTING 4-5: Implementing the double-checked locking

```
package com.devchronicles.singleton;

public class MySingleton {

    private volatile MySingleton instance;

    private MySingleton() {}

    public MySingleton getInstance() {
            if (instance == null) { // 1
                synchronized (MySingleton.class) {
                    if (instance == null) { // 2
                        instance = new MySingleton();
                    }
                }
            }
            return instance;
    }
}
```

The getInstance() method checks the private MySingleton instance member twice (once at comment 1 and then again at comment 2) for being null before creating and assigning a MySingleton instance.

However, none of those approaches is 100 percent safe. For example, the Java Reflection API allows developers to change the access modifier of the constructor to Public, thus exposing the singleton to the possibility of re-creation.

The best way to create singletons in Java is by using the enum type, which was introduced in Java 5 and is shown in Listing 4-6. This approach is also heavily advocated by Joshua Bloch in his book *Effective Java*.[3] Enum types are singletons by nature, so JVM handles most of the work required to create a singleton. Thus, by using an enum type, you free yourself from the task of synchronizing object creation and provision and avoid problems associated with initialization.

LISTING 4-6: Enum type implementation of the singleton pattern

```
package com.devchronicles.singleton;

public enum MySingletonEnum {
    INSTANCE;
    public void doSomethingInteresting(){}
}
```

In this example, a reference to the instance of the singleton object is obtained by the following:

```
MySingletonEnum mse = MySingletonEnum.INSTANCE;
```

Once you have the singleton's reference, you can call any of its methods like so:
`mse.doSomethingInteresting();`.

WAR STORY

Several years ago, a close friend of mine who owned a small software company asked my help to interview a candidate. Because I always find software job interviews great engineer-to-engineer experience, I didn't hesitate to jump at the opportunity. The candidate had only a few years of job experience but graduated from a good university and was definitely sharp. We had a long chat about Java, JPA, Spring, and other well-known Java frameworks. He was eager to learn and try new stuff and handled all questions calmly.

After about an hour, the interview was finished, but we continued to talk casually. I asked him about the books he had recently read, and his reply was *Head First Design Patterns*. I inquired about which pattern he found most interesting or simply wanted to talk about. Not surprisingly, it was the singleton pattern. This made my spider senses tingle. The candidate thought the singleton pattern was simple and easy to implement, so it would be a safe topic. The truth was, it wasn't. If he had chosen another pattern such as the decorator, I would not have had the opportunity to dive into the more advanced topics of this seemingly simple pattern.

I then asked the candidate how he would implement a singleton. He responded with the classic private constructor method, which clearly showed he hadn't read *Effective Java* and had no clue about the enum type singleton. Later I asked, "What if I used reflection to change the access level of the constructor back to public?" He was surprised, but I could clearly see from his eyes that he was more interested in going back home and trying this out. He couldn't come up with a solution, but he also didn't make up a nonsense response. He was busier digesting and thinking about the reflection idea.

This job candidate may have missed the right answer, but he showed he was passionate and eager to learn. He was hired and became one of the best developers I have ever worked with.

IMPLEMENTING THE SINGLETON PATTERN IN JAVA EE

All the code examples so far have demonstrated the use of singletons within the context of Java SE. Although you can use them in Java EE, there is a more elegant and easy-to-use approach: singleton beans.

Singleton Beans

In Chapter 2, "The Basics of Java EE," you saw the use of stateless and stateful session beans via a simple annotation configuration. Luckily, singletons offer a similar approach. Just by adding the @Singleton annotation to a class, you can turn it into a singleton bean as shown in Listing 4-7.

LISTING 4-7: The implementations of the singleton pattern using @singleton

```
package com.devchronicles.singleton;

import java.util.HashMap;
import java.util.Map;
import javax.annotation.PostConstruct;
import javax.ejb.Singleton;
import java.util.logging.Logger;

@Singleton
public class CacheSingletonBean {

    private Map<Integer, String> myCache;

    @PostConstruct
    public void start(){
        Logger.getLogger("MyGlobalLogger").info("Started!");
        myCache = new HashMap<Integer, String>();
    }

    public void addUser(Integer id, String name){
        myCache.put(id, name);
    }

    public String getName(Integer id){
        return myCache.get(id);
    }
}
```

With the simple use of annotations, Java EE does not need a configuration XML file. You may see a beans.xml file in the project, but most of the time it remains empty. You only need it for starting the Context and Dependency Injection (CDI) container. The @Singleton annotation marks the class as a singleton EJB, and the container handles creation and usage of the single instance.

If you execute this bean code on your server, you will not see logger output from the singleton because the method annotated with @PostConstruct has not been invoked. Why is that?

Using Singletons at Startup

Singletons in Java EE are initialized lazily by default. This might suit most situations: allowing the instance to be created only when it is needed and accessed for the first time. However, you may want to create the instance at startup to allow access to the singleton without delay, especially if it's expensive to create the instance or it's guaranteed that you will need the bean from the start of the application. To ensure that the instance is created at startup, use the @Startup annotation on the class as shown in Listing 4-8.

LISTING 4-8: Invoking the singleton at startup

```
package com.devchronicles.singleton;

import java.util.HashMap;
import java.util.Map;
import javax.annotation.PostConstruct;
import javax.ejb.Singleton;
import javax.ejb.Startup;
import java.util.logging.Logger;

@Startup
@Singleton
public class CacheSingletonBean {

    private Map<Integer, String> myCache;

    @PostConstruct
    public void start(){
        Logger.getLogger("MyGlobalLogger").info("Started!");
        myCache = new HashMap<Integer, String>();
    }

    public void addUser(Integer id, String name){
        myCache.put(id, name);
    }

    public String getName(Integer id){
        return myCache.get(id);
    }
}
```

If you relaunch your server, the post construct method is invoked because the singleton is now created at server startup. The logger should now receive the message Started!.

Determining Startup Order

This may bring up another question. What if the singleton you have just created depends on another resource? How do you wait for the other resource to be ready? Although this may look like a corner case, it definitely is not. Think about a singleton, which loads and caches some messages from the database. This may look trivial, but even basic read-only database access may be dependent on other services. What if the connection pool is created by another singleton or, better yet, what if the logging depends on another singleton? Java EE offers a simple annotation to fix this situation. You can use the @DependsOn annotation and pass it the name of the bean on which the class depends (see Listing 4-9). Now you can easily determine the starting order of the singletons.

LISTING 4-9: Specifying startup order using @depends annotation

```java
package com.devchronicles.singleton;

import java.util.HashMap;
import java.util.Map;
import javax.annotation.PostConstruct;
import javax.ejb.Singleton;
import javax.ejb.Startup;
import javax.ejb.DependsOn;
import javax.ejb.EJB;

@Startup
@DependsOn("MyLoggingBean")
@Singleton
public class CacheSingletonBean {

    private Map<Integer, String> myCache;

    @EJB
    MyLoggingBean loggingBean;

    @PostConstruct
    public void start(){
        loggingBean.logInfo("Started!");
        myCache = new HashMap<Integer, String>();
    }

    public void addUser(Integer id, String name){
        myCache.put(id, name);
    }

    public String getName(Integer id){
        return myCache.get(id);
    }
}
```

Next let's create another singleton bean (Listing 4-10), which the previous bean already referenced.

LISTING 4-10: Specifying startup order

```java
package com.devchronicles.singleton;

import javax.annotation.PostConstruct;
import javax.ejb.Singleton;
import javax.ejb.Startup;
import java.util.logging.Logger;


@Startup
@Singleton
```

continues

LISTING 4-10: *(continued)*

```
public class MyLoggingBean {

    private Logger logger;

    @PostConstruct
    public void start(){
        logger = Logger.getLogger("MyGlobalLogger");
        logger.info("Well, I started first!!!");
    }

    public void logInfo(String msg){
        logger.info(msg);
    }
}
```

Here you can also use the `@PostConstruct` annotation to test that your bean has been created and its life cycle has begun. Methods annotated with `@PostConstruct` are invoked on newly constructed beans after all dependency injection has been done and before the first business method is invoked. Of course, in real life, you need to use singleton beans inside other beans. Later chapters will focus more on integration and access of EJB and whether they should be singletons.

The preceding example beans run when the server is started. `CacheSingletonBean` waits to run because it depends on `MyLoggingBean` initialization. The logger output is similar to the following:

```
> Well, I started first!!!
> Started!
```

Your singleton bean might depend on the initialization of a sequence of other beans. In this case, you can specify multiple beans in the `@DependsOn`. The following singleton bean depends on `MyLoggingBean` and `MyInitializationBean`:

```
@Startup
@DependsOn({"MyLoggingBean","MyInitializationBean"})
@Singleton
public class CacheSingletonBean {
    // Implementation code here.
}
```

The order in which `MyLoggingBean` and `MyInitializationBean` are initialized is determined by their own `@DependsOn` annotations. If neither bean explicitly depends on the other, the beans are initialized by the container in an unspecified order.

Managing Concurrency

The most important problem you'll face is concurrency. With the Java EE implementation, you no longer need to worry about the creation of the bean, but you may still need to be careful about method access because your singleton will be exposed in a concurrent environment. Java EE, again, solves this issue with annotations.

Java EE offers two types of concurrency management: *container-managed concurrency* and *bean-managed concurrency*. In container-managed concurrency, the container is responsible for handling anything related to read and write access, whereas bean-managed concurrency expects the developer to handle concurrency using traditional Java methods such as synchronization. You can enable bean-managed concurrency via the ConcurrencyManagementType.BEAN annotation.

Java EE uses container-managed concurrency by default, but you can explicitly declare it with the ConcurrencyManagementType.CONTAINER annotation:

```
@Startup
@DependsOn("MyLoggingBean")
@ConcurrencyManagement(ConcurrencyManagementType.CONTAINER)
@Singleton
public class CacheSingletonBean {
    // Implementation code here.
}
```

Now you'll get back to the example and use the @Lock annotations to control the access. See Listing 4-11.

LISTING 4-11: Managing concurrency using @locktype

```
package com.devchronicles.singleton;

import java.util.HashMap;
import java.util.Map;
import javax.annotation.PostConstruct;
import javax.ejb.ConcurrencyManagement;
import javax.ejb.ConcurrencyManagementType;
import javax.ejb.DependsOn;
import javax.ejb.EJB;
import javax.ejb.Lock;
import javax.ejb.LockType;
import javax.ejb.Singleton;
import javax.ejb.Startup;

@Startup
@DependsOn("MyLoggingBean")
@ConcurrencyManagement(ConcurrencyManagementType.CONTAINER)
@Singleton
public class CacheSingletonBean {

    private Map<Integer, String> myCache;

    @EJB
    MyLoggingBean loggingBean;

    @PostConstruct
    public void start(){
        loggingBean.logInfo("Started!");
        myCache = new HashMap<Integer, String>();
    }
```

continues

LISTING 4-11: *(continued)*

```
@Lock(LockType.WRITE)
public void addUser(Integer id, String name){
    myCache.put(id, name);
}

@Lock(LockType.READ)
public String getName(Integer id){
    return myCache.get(id);
}
}
```

Two lock types control access to the bean's business methods: `@Lock(LockType.WRITE)`, which locks the bean to other clients while the method is being invoked, and `@Lock(LockType.READ)`, which allows concurrent access to the method and does not lock the bean to other clients. Methods that affect change to data are usually annotated with `WRITE` access to prevent access to the data as it updates. In this example, the `addUser()` method is annotated with the `WRITE` lock type so that if any client calls the `getName()` method, it has to wait until the `addUser()` method returns before it can complete its call. This may result in the container throwing a `ConcurrentAccessTimeoutException` if the `addUser()` method does not complete in the specified timeout period. You can configure the timeout period via an annotation, which you will see an example of in Listing 4-12.

You can set the `LockType` annotation at the class level. It applies to all business methods that don't explicitly configure their own `LockType`. Because the default `LockType` is `WRITE`, it is normally sufficient to configure just the methods that require concurrent access.

LISTING 4-12: Defining the singleton's concurrent timeout access

```
import java.util.logging.Logger;
import javax.annotation.PostConstruct;
import javax.ejb.Singleton;
import javax.ejb.Startup;
import javax.ejb.DependsOn;
import javax.ejb.ConcurrencyManagement;
import javax.ejb.ConcurrencyManagementType;
import javax.ejb.AccessTimeout;
import java.util.Map;
import javax.ejb.EJB;
import java.util.HashMap;
import javax.ejb.Lock;
import javax.ejb.LockType;
import java.util.concurrent.TimeUnit;

@Startup
@DependsOn("MyLoggingBean")
@ConcurrencyManagement(ConcurrencyManagementType.CONTAINER)
@Singleton
@AccessTimeout(value=120000) // default in milliseconds
```

```java
public class CacheSingletonBean {

    private Map<Integer, String> myCache;

    @EJB
    MyLoggingBean loggingBean;

    @PostConstruct
    public void start(){
        loggingBean.logInfo("Started!");
        myCache = new HashMap<Integer, String>();
    }

    @AccessTimeout(value=30, unit=TimeUnit.SECONDS)
    @Lock(LockType.WRITE)
    public void addUser(Integer id, String name){
        myCache.put(id, name);
    }

    @Lock(LockType.READ)
    public String getName(Integer id){
        return myCache.get(id);
    }
}
}
```

The `@AccessTimeout` annotation can have different `TimeUnit` constants, such as `NANOSECONDS`, `MICROSECONDS`, `MILLISECONDS`, and `SECONDS`. If no `TimeUnit` value is given, the value is interpreted as milliseconds by default. You can also place this annotation at the class level and apply it to all methods that don't explicitly define an access timeout annotation.

WHERE AND WHEN TO USE THE SINGLETON PATTERN

As a rule of thumb, heavy use of singletons may be a sign of misuse. You should use singletons where it makes sense, such as caching frequently accessed but expensive-to-load data, sharing data for global access, or using single point of contact purposes (such as logging).

Creating and caching unnecessary resources has a negative impact on memory, CPU resources, and initial startup, so handle singletons with care when using them for caching data. However, singletons can be quite handy and can be configured easily in a Java EE container. For serious caching solutions, consider a framework such as the widely used Ehcache (`http://www.ehcache.org/`) or Apache's distributed caching system Java Caching System (`http://commons.apache.org/proper/commons-jcs/`).

You can use a singleton to control access to back-end systems that are not thread safe or have licensing issues. Using the `LockType.WRITE` annotation on methods allows sequential access to such systems in which multiple concurrent access would cause problems with performance or licensing.

SUMMARY

It has been briefly mentioned that the singleton pattern has fallen out of favor to the point in which many developers and architects now consider it an anti-pattern. The singleton pattern's unpopularity extends from problems caused by its overuse and abuse and its evident shortcomings in multithreaded applications.

Programmers have overused and abused the singleton pattern because it is a simple pattern to implement. So every class becomes a singleton. This has presented a nightmare for developers who must maintain the code, and it has become an even greater challenge for those who have to refactor the singletons into object-oriented code when it is discovered that more than one instance of a singleton class is required.

The use of singleton classes has made testability more complicated because global states need to be instantiated to run a simple unit test. Furthermore, singletons have made tests less deterministic because these states might change, affecting the outcome of the tests.

You have seen in the code examples the numerous difficulties that singletons pose in multithread environments. It was difficult to create a singleton that was guaranteed thread safe before Java SE 5 and the introduction of the enum type.

However, with the advances made in Java EE, the problem of thread-safe singletons has largely been resolved with the @Singleton annotation and container control concurrency.

The container controls the creation of the singleton and ensures that no business method is called before the @PostContrust completes. The container also controls the concurrency of access to the bean via the @ConcurrencyManagement annotation, and its associated @LockType annotation allows fine-grain access control over each method.

By no means has every problem of the singleton been resolved. There could still be problems in multinode environments if the bean is used to access back-end non-thread-safe resources. Bottlenecks and tight coupling of classes could be additional problems.

Even though the singleton pattern has suffered from abuse and overuse by developers, leading to its eventual relegation to an anti-pattern, it has nevertheless matured substantially since it was introduced by GoF and should be reconsidered as a valuable and viable design pattern.

EXERCISES

1. Design a web page hit counter with two methods: one method that increments the count, and one method that gets the latest count. Ensure that it is thread safe by defining the appropriate lock types.

2. Design a simple cache that stores a list of books for a library management application. The data should be loaded into the cache on application startup. Add methods to retrieve books based on different criteria, such as ISBN, author, and genre.

3. Design a complex cache that reads data from a database at startup. The data retrieval methods should query the cache first, and if the requested data is not found, the bean should query the database. If the data requested is found in the database, it should be stored in the cache.

4. Add to exercise 3 a mechanism that deletes infrequently accessed data from the cache and updates out-of-date data. Ensure that the entire life cycle of the cache is appropriately managed.

NOTES

1. *Design Patterns: Elements of Reusable Object-Oriented Software* (Addison-Wesley, 1994): Erich Gamma, Richard Helm, Ralph Johnson, John Vlissides.
2. *Head First Design Patterns* (O'Reilly, 2004): Eric Freeman, Elisabeth Robson, Bert Bates, Kathy Sierra.
3. *Effective Java* (Addison-Wesley, 2008): Joshua Bloch.

Dependency Injection and CDI

WROX.COM CODE DOWNLOADS FOR THIS CHAPTER

The wrox.com code download for this chapter is found at www.wrox.com/go/
projavaeedesignpatterns on the Download Code tab. The code is in the Chapter 05
download and individually named according to the names throughout the chapter.

Dependency injection (DI) is one of the few well-known and accepted design patterns that
was *not* listed in the book by the Gang of Four.[1] Today, it has been used widely in modern
programming languages both internally and as a best practice to promote loose coupling.

J2EE was designed to handle the most complex systems but failed miserably by
overcomplicating the development of even the simpler systems. The original design of
J2EE relied on heavyweight complexity and tight coupling, which led to the popularity of
frameworks such as Spring and Pico container. In 2004, Martin Fowler published an article
on the inversion of control containers and the dependency of the injection pattern.[2] Most
vendors did not support and encourage developers to use the J2EE container. However,
soon the lightweight containers took over, they became officially supported and, even more,
Spring became the unofficial de facto standard and led to the redesign of Enterprise Java from
scratch.

WHAT IS DEPENDENCY INJECTION?

The dependency injection pattern is based on the idea of inverting the control. Instead of creating hard dependencies and creating new objects either with the new keyword or lookups, you inject the needed resource into the destination object. This approach has many benefits:

➤ The client does need not to be aware of the different implementations of the injected resources, making design changes easier.

➤ Unit testing using mock objects is much easier to implement.

➤ Configuration can be externalized, reducing the impact of changes.

➤ A loosely coupled architecture allows pluggable structures.

The basic idea behind DI is to change the place where objects are created and to use an injector to inject the specific implementations to the destination objects at the right moment. This may sound like an implementation of the factory pattern (see Chapter 6, "Factory Pattern"), but the whole concept is much more than simple object creation. Inversion of Control (IoC) changes the whole wiring between objects and lets the injector do the work (most of the time magically). Instead of calling a factory to provide an implementation to the caller, the injector works proactively to determine when a destination object needs the target object and performs the injection in the appropriate way.

IMPLEMENTING DI IN PLAIN CODE

Java did not offer a standard DI implementation out of the Enterprise JavaBeans (EJB) container until the introduction of Context and Dependency Injection (CDI). Although there are various DI frameworks, such as Spring and Guice, it is not difficult to code a basic implementation.

The simplest implementation of DI is a factory that creates the dependency on request via a getInstance() method. Now you'll implement an example that shows how to do this in plain code.

The simple DI implementation should separate the resolution of dependencies from the behavior of the class. This means a class should have specific functionality without defining how it obtains a reference to the classes it depends on. This decouples object creation from where the object is used: the essence of DI.

You will start by looking at an example in Listings 5-1, 5-2, 5-3 and 5-4 that is highly coupled, and refactor it to use your home-grown DI.

LISTING 5-1: UserService class that creates a new dependency in the constructor

```
package com.devchronicale.di;

class UserService {

    private UserDataRepository udr;

    UserService() {
        this.udr = new UserDataRepositoryImpl();
```

```
    }
    public void persistUser(User user) {
        udr.save(user);
    }
}
```

LISTING 5-2: UserDataRepository interface

```
package com.devchronicale.di;

public interface UserDataRepository {
    public void save(User user);
}
```

LISTING 5-3: Concrete implementation of the UserDataRepository

```
package com.devchronicale.di;

public class UserDataRepositoryImpl implements UserDataRepository {
    @Override
    public void save(User user) {
        // Persistence code here
    }
}
```

LISTING 5-4: User class

```
package com.devchronicale.di;

public class User {
    // User Specific Code Here
}
```

In Listing 5-1, the UserService class provides business logic services for user management, such as persisting the user to the database. In this example, the object creation is done in the constructor. This couples the business logic (the class's behavior) to the object creation.

You'll refactor this example by taking the object creation out of your class and putting it in a factory.

In Listing 5-5, an implementation of the UserDataRepository is created and passed to the constructor of the UserService class. You change the constructor of the UserService class to accept this new parameter.

LISTING 5-5: UserServiceFactory that creates UserService objects

```
package com.devchronicale.di;

public class UserServiceFactory {
    public UserService getInstance(){
        return new UserService(new UserDataRepositoryImpl());
    }
}
```

In Listing 5-6, the UserService constructor asks for an instance of the UserDataRepository to be "injected" into the constructor. The UserService class is decoupled from the UserDataReposityImpl class. The factory is now responsible for the creation of the object and "injects" the implementation into the constructor of the UserService. You have successfully separated the business logic from object creation.

LISTING 5-6: The refactored UserService class

```
package com.devchronicale.di;

class UserService {

    private UserDataRepository udr;

    UserService(UserDataRepository udr) {
        this.udr = udr;
    }

    public void persistUser(User user) {
        udr.save(user);
    }
}
```

WAR STORY

When I was given the task of writing an Android application, I decided to research Dependency Injection Frameworks for mobiles. As a software developer with Enterprise Development experience, this seemed like the right route to take. The Android user interface (UI) system was already reliant on a DI-like structure that bound XML-based UI components to Java code, so it seemed wise to implement a fully functioning DI framework to achieve blown functionality.

I worked on a beautiful architecture in which all objects and resources were wired together. The injection worked like a charm; however, the application did not. The app start-up took much longer than similar apps, and the navigation was not so smooth either. We all believed DI was a must-have to achieve loose coupling and well-organized code, so we looked for problems in other areas. We mastered sleek, lightweight UI and asynchronous background tasks so we wouldn't lock the app and to minimize the work done on start-up, but nothing really worked.

It soon dawned on us that the root of the problem was the DI framework. It was searching for all injection resources and references, while the app was starting and trying to perform all the wiring at the beginning of the app's life cycle. This might be a good idea on a server start-up, which has many users, few restarts, and huge amounts of memory. But it wasn't a good idea on a mobile device, where we had a single user, many restarts, and limited memory.

> Our solution was to hard-wire the resources. Even though this gave us an "uglier" app, the app started up in lightning speed, solving our performance issue.
>
> The moral of this story is not that DI is a bad pattern to implement on mobile devices but that a poor implementation of DI (whether on a mobile device or not) in the wrong context can cause huge problems.

IMPLEMENTING DI IN JAVA EE

J2EE did not offer DI out of the box until Java EE 5. Instead, in J2EE, beans and resources were accessed using Java Naming and Directory Interface (JNDI) context lookups. This approach caused hard-wiring and relied on a heavyweight server-based container, which made testing almost harder than writing the actual code.

With the release of Java EE 5 and EJB 3, DI became an integral part of the Enterprise Java platform. To get rid of XML-based configuration, several annotations were introduced to perform injection:

➤ `@Resource` (JSR250) is for injecting data sources, Java Message Service (JMS), URL, mail, and environment variables.

➤ `@EJB` (JSR220) is for injecting EJB.

➤ `@WebServiceRef` is for injecting web services.

With the release of Java EE 6, CDI, and EJB 3.1, DI became a much more capable, and thus more interesting, topic in Java EE.

In EJB 3.1, an interface was no longer mandatory for EJBs. Also, a new EJB web profile was introduced that offers a simplified lighter EJB container. A new and improved injection annotation `@Inject` was introduced (JSR229 and JSR330), which also provided a common interface for injection between other DI frameworks in the Java realm.

The `@Inject` annotation DI is type safe because it injects a dependency based on the type of the object reference. If you were to refactor the code in Listing 5-1, you would remove the constructor and add an `@Inject` annotation to the `UserDataRepository` field. The code would look something like Listing 5-7.

LISTING 5-7: The refactored UserService class using @Inject

```
package com.devchronicale.di;

import javax.inject.Inject;

class UserService {

    @Inject
```

continues

LISTING 5-7: *(continued)*

```
    private UserDataRepository udr;

    public void persistUser(User user) {
        udr.save(user);
    }
}
```

The CDI container constructs a single `UserDataRepositoryImpl` instance as a container managed bean and injects it anywhere it finds `@Inject` annotating a field of type `UserDataRepository`.

You can inject a container-managed bean into constructors, methods, and fields, regardless of the access modifier, although fields must not be final, and the method must not be abstract.

Some important questions arise. What happens if there is more than one implementation of the `UserDataRepository` interface? How does the CDI container identify the correct implementation to inject? To disambiguate the concrete implementations of the `UserDataRepository` interface, you can annotate the concrete class using a developer-defined qualifier.

Imagine having two implementations of the `UserDataRepository` interface: one for a Mongo DB collection (a document based database) and another for a MySQL database (relational database). You would have to create two qualifiers (one for the Mongo implementation and another for the MySQL implementation), the concrete class would be annotated at the class level with the relevant qualifier, and in the class in which the `UserDataRepository` is to be injected, a field would be annotated with the same qualifier.

If you refactor the `UserService` class in Listing 5-7 to use the Mongo implementation of the `UserDataRepository`, you would add `@Mongo` to the `udr` field as follows:

```
@Inject @Mongo
private UserDataRepository udr;
```

The use of qualifiers is discussed in more depth below and in Chapter 6.

The @Named Annotation

Another great achievement was the introduction of the `@Named` annotation instead of String qualifiers. Ambiguities in EJB dependencies were resolved by using a String in the `beanName` attribute of the `@EJB` annotation that specified the implementation to be injected: `@EJB(beanName="UserDataRepository")`. The `@Name` annotation also supports disambiguation with the use of a `String` attribute. In Listing 5-8, the Mongo implementation of the `UserDataRepository` is injected into the `udr` field.

LISTING 5-8: The @Named annotation used to disambiguate

```
package com.devchronicale.di;

import javax.inject.Inject;
```

```
import javax.inject.Named;

class UserService {

    @Inject
    @Named("UserDataRepositoryMongo")
    private UserDataRepository udr;

    public void persistUser(User user) {
        udr.save(user);
    }
}
```

An explicit annotation of the Mongo implementation is required by a corresponding @Named annotation appropriately named. In Listing 5-9, the Mongo implementation of the UserDataRepository interface is annotated with the same String name as that used to disambiguate the injected implementation in Listing 5-8.

LISTING 5-9: The concrete implementation requires an @Named annotation

```
package com.devchronicale.di;

import javax.inject.Named;

@Named("UserDataRepositoryMongo")
public class UserDataRepositoryMongo implements UserDataRepository {

    @Override
    public void save(User user) {
        // Persistence code here
    }
}
```

The use of Strings to identify dependencies is legacy because it is not type safe and is discouraged in the CDI specification JSR-299. However, there is a use of the @Named annotation that avoids the need to use String identifiers at the point of injection.

```
@Inject @Named
private UserDataRepository UserDataRepositoryMongo;
```

In Listing 5-9, the name of the implementation to inject is inferred from the name of the field UserDataRepositoryMongo. What is effectively happening is that @Named is being replaced by @Named("UserDataRepositoryMongo").

Context and Dependency Injection (CDI)

Context and Dependency Injection (CDI) brought full-fledged dependency injection and context support to the Java EE platform, which used to be EJB specific and far more limited. After EJB 3 was introduced, JBoss introduced Seam (a web application framework), which had become quite popular, by supporting direct interaction between JavaServer Faces (JSF) and JavaBeans as well as EJB. The success of Seam led to the design of JSR299, WebBeans. Just as Hibernate, a famous Java Persistence Framework, inspired Java Persistence API (JPA) standardization, Seam inspired and formed the core implementation of CDI.

CDI can work with any Plain Old Java Object (POJO) by instantiating and injecting objects into each other. The following types of objects are injectable:

➤ POJOs

➤ Enterprise resources such as data source and queues

➤ Remote EJB references

➤ Session beans

➤ EntityManager objects

➤ Web services references

➤ Producer fields and objects returned by producer methods

CDI Versus EJB

Although CDI and EJB seem to be rivals, they work in harmony. CDI can work alone without an EJB container. Actually, CDI can power a desktop application or any web application that doesn't rely on the EJB container. CDI provides the factory and injection to any JavaBean.

However, EJBs still require the EJB container. Even the simplified architecture of EJBs is more complex than POJOs, so EJBs still need the EJB container. The EJB container provides additional services such as security, transactions, and concurrency that EJBs need.

Simply put, the CDI container is a lighter, powerful, but less functional container for POJOs. Still, both containers are so well integrated that CDI annotations can act as a gateway and standard interface to interact with the EJB container. For example, the `@Inject` annotation can work with either POJOs or EJBs and can inject any combination of each by invoking the right container to handle the job.

CDI Beans

A container managed bean is little more than a POJO that conforms to some simple rules:

➤ It must have a no-argument constructor, or the constructor must declare an `@Inject` annotation.

➤ The class must be a top-level concrete class or must be annotated with `@Decorate`; it cannot be a nonstatic inner class.

➤ It cannot be defined as an EJB.

➤ If the bean is defined as a managed bean by another Java EE technology, such as the JSF technology, it will also be managed by the container.

Any class conforming to these requirements will be instantiated and managed by the container and is injectable. No special annotation is required to define the class as a managed bean.

The container looks for bean-inside-bean archives. There are two types of bean archives: explicit and implicit. An explicit archive contains a `bean.xml` deployment descriptor, which is normally empty. The CDI scans the classes in the archive looking for any class that conforms to the bean requirements detailed earlier and manages and injects any such class that is not annotated with `@Vetoed`. This annotation excludes that class from being managed by the container.

In some cases, it may not be desirable to allow the container to manage any conformant bean it finds. If you want to restrict what the CDI container considers to be a managed bean, you can define the *bean-discovery-mode* property in the `bean.xml` deployment descriptor. Listing 5-10 shows a snippet of the `bean.xml` file that defines the `bean-discovery-mode` property as `ALL`.

LISTING 5-10: The bean discovery mode is set in the bean.xml

```
<?xml version="1.0" encoding="UTF-8"?>
<beans xmlns="http://xmlns.jcp.org/xml/ns/javaee"
       xmlns:xsi="http://www.w3.org/2001/XMLSchema-instance"
       xsi:schemaLocation="http://xmlns.jcp.org/xml/ns/javaee
                          http://xmlns.jcp.org/xml/ns/javaee/beans_1_1.xsd"
       version="1.1" bean-discovery-mode="all">
  ...
</beans>
```

The `bean-discovery-mode` property can take one of three values: `ALL`, `NONE`, or `ANNOTATED`. The `ALL` property instructs the CDI container to manage all beans that it finds in the archive. This is the default. The `NONE` property means that the CDI container will manage no beans, and the `ANNOTATED` property makes the archive behave like an implicit archive. In this case, the container scans for beans with annotated scope types.

An implicit bean archive does not contain a `bean.xml` deployment descriptor. This signals to the CDI container that the container should only manage beans with a scope. Further details about scoped beans are discussed later in the section, "Contexts and Scope."

The @Inject Annotation

The `@Inject` annotation and its capabilities have already been covered. Before CDI in Java EE was introduced, each DI framework offered its own way of injecting resources. When the Java EE CDI container was released to work alongside the EJB container, `@Inject` annotation became a unique and abstract interface for almost all inject operations. The `@Inject` annotation lets you use any appropriate container or DI framework referenced for the case.

Contexts and Scope

Context is the difference between EJBs and CDI containers. Each CDI bean's life cycle is bound to a context scope. The CDI offers four different scopes:

➤ **@RequestScoped**—Duration is a user's HTTP request.

➤ **@SessionScoped**—Duration is a user's HTTP session.

➤ **@ApplicationScoped**—State is shared across all users for the duration of the application.

➤ **@ConversationScoped**—Scope duration is controlled by the developer.

A bean annotated with a scope holds state for the duration of the scope and shares that state with any client that runs in the same scope. For example, a bean in the request scope holds state for the lifetime of the HTTP request, and a bean with session scope holds state for the lifetime of the HTTP session. The scoped bean is automatically created when it is needed and destroyed when the context in which it takes part finishes.

The scope annotations are often used to give scope to beans that are used via Expression Language (EL) in Facelet pages.

Naming and EL

A bean annotated with @Named is accessible through EL. By default, the name used in the expression is the name of the class with the first letter in lowercase. To refer to getter methods that start with get or is, omit the get or is part of the method name. Listing 5-11 shows an example.

LISTING 5-11: The @Named annotation makes a bean visible to EL

```
package com.devchronicale.di;

import javax.enterprise.context.RequestScoped;
import javax.inject.Named;

@Named // Defining that this is a managed bean
@RequestScoped // Defines the scope
public class User {

    private String fullName;

    public String getFullName(){
        return this.fullName;
    }

// some methods not included for brevity
}
```

This is a simple implementation of a named bean that returns a String when the getFullName() method is called. In a Facelets page, you would refer to this method as user.fullname.

```
<h:form id="user">
    <p><h:outputText value="#{user.fullname}"/></p>
</h:form>
```

CDI Beans for Backing JSF

As in the previous example, CDI Beans can serve as backing beans for JSF pages. You can access named beans via the name of the bean with a lowercased first letter. You can access Getter/Setter fields and methods within JSF pages using Java conventions. Details of JSF go beyond the scope of this book, but Listing 5-11 demonstrates a basic usage of CDI Beans with JSF.

Qualifiers

This section looks at how you would construct the qualifier classes.

In Listing 5-12, you create a qualifier named Mongo that you can use to annotate fields. If you want to use this annotation on a *METHOD*, a *PARAMETER*, or a class/interface (*TYPE*), you can add it to the @Target annotation.

LISTING 5-12: Create a custom qualifier named @Mongo

```
package com.devchronicale.di;

import static java.lang.annotation.ElementType.FIELD;
import static java.lang.annotation.RetentionPolicy.RUNTIME;

import java.lang.annotation.Retention;
import java.lang.annotation.Target;

import javax.inject.Qualifier;

@Qualifier
@Retention(RUNTIME)
@Target({FIELD})
public @interface Mongo {}
```

The discussion regarding the varied use of annotations continues in more depth in Chapter 6.

Alternatives

In the examples so far, you learned how you can disambiguate between two distinct implementations of the UserDataRepository interface by using qualifiers. You normally make this choice of implementation at development time by changing the source code. However, you can also make this choice at deployment time by using the @Alternative annotation and some configuration in the bean.xml deployment descriptor.

Adapting the examples so far, you annotate the two implementations of the UserDataRepository interface with @Alternative and add some configuration XML to the bean.xml file. This is where you decide which implementation to inject.

```
@Alternative
public class UserDataRepositoryMongo implements UserDataRepository {...}

@Alternative
public class UserDataRepositoryMySQL implements UserDataRepository {...}
```

The implementation that you use in the application is declared in the bean.xml file:

```
<beans ...>
    <alternatives>
        <class>com.devchronicale.di.UserDataRepositoryMongo</class>
    </alternatives>
</beans>
```

Alternatives are often used during the testing phase of development to create mock objects.

Stereotypes

You can think of stereotypes as templates that define the characteristics of a specific functionality of a bean type. For example, a bean that is used at the model layer of an Model View Controller (MVC) application requires certain annotations to perform its function. These would include the following:

```
@Named
@RequestScoped
@Stereotype
@Target({TYPE, METHOD, FIELD})
@Retention(RUNTIME)
```

Only `@Named` and `@RequestScoped` are enough to define a Model bean. Others are required to create an annotation called `@Model`.

You could apply these annotations on every bean that requires them, or you could define a stereotype called `@Model` and apply only that to the beans. The latter makes your code much easier to read and maintain.

To create a stereotype, you define a new annotation and apply the required annotations as in Listing 5-13.

LISTING 5-13: Stereotype annotation

```
@Named
@RequestScoped
@Stereotype
@Target({TYPE, METHOD, FIELD})
@Retention(RUNTIME)
public @interface Model {}
```

Any bean annotated with `@Model` has a request scope (`@RequestScoped`) and is visible to EL (`@Named`). Luckily, the CDI container that comes with this stereotype has already been defined.

A typical use of the stereotype annotation is to combine with alternative annotation so you have a way to annotate mock objects.

Other Patterns via CDI

CDI unleashed a great power to Java EE developers. CDI goes beyond being just a simple DI framework by making the implementation of all those patterns possible with minimal code.

The chapters that follow dive deep into details of these patterns; however, to whet your appetite, here's a brief introduction to these CDI-powered patterns.

Chapter 7, "Decorator Pattern," covers the decorator pattern. Decorators wrap a target object to dynamically add new responsibilities at run time. Each decorator can be wrapped by another, which allows for a theoretically unlimited number of decorated target objects at run time. The decorator pattern uses the `@Decorator` and the `@Delegate` annotations. You must specify the decoration order in `beans.xml`.

The factory pattern is covered in Chapter 6. Factories minimize the usage of the `new` keyword and can encapsulate the initialization process and different concrete implementations. The factory pattern uses the `@Produces` annotation to mark producer methods. Target object can inject or observe the produced objects.

The observer pattern and events are addressed in Chapter 11, "Observer Pattern." The observer pattern changes the direction of a message, thus the order of caller and the callee. With the help of the observer pattern, instead of aggressively checking a resource, an object can subscribe to the changes on the resource. The observer pattern in Java EE uses the `@Observes` annotation and events. The target observer(s) can observe any fired event.

Aspects and interceptors are the focus of Chapter 8, "Aspect-Oriented Programming (Interceptors)." They let you change execution flow at run time. Any aspect or interceptor can be marked to cut the execution and kick in at the given point. This approach enables dynamic changes even on a large code base.

SUMMARY

In this chapter, you have seen the concept of dependency injection in Java EE. The dependency injection concept lets us build loosely coupled systems easier than one can ever imagine. We have seen how dependency injection allows us to eliminate the use of a new keyword, thus, manual object creation.

We also focused on CDI, which unleashes a huge potential by leveraging a whole new container. With the help of CDI, dependency injection can be applied to any object and many patterns that are discussed in this book are easy to implement.

EXERCISES

1. Design a service class which will return some string to the client.

2. Implement a file reader and inject it to the service you developed before.

3. This time implement an object which reads the html content as a string from a fixed URL.

4. Think about what you need to refactor in the service class to be able to inject both data providers with the same reference.

5. Is there a way to dynamically inject each implementation depending on different circumstances? For example can you make sure the file reader is injected during development but the http reader is used during production?

NOTES

1. *Design Patterns: Elements of Reusable Object-Oriented Software* (Addison-Wesley, 1994): Erich Gamma, Richard Helm, Ralph Johnson, John Vlissides.
2. Inversion of Control Containers and the Dependency Injection Pattern (Martin Fowler, 2004): `http://martinfowler.com/articles/injection.html`.

Factory Pattern

WHAT'S IN THIS CHAPTER?

➤ What the factory pattern is and why you need it

➤ How to implement the various flavors of the factory pattern: the factory method and the abstract factory

➤ How to implement the factory pattern in Java EE using the @Producers and @Inject annotations

➤ How to create custom annotations and the @Qualifier to disambiguate concrete implementations

WROX.COM CODE DOWNLOADS FOR THIS CHAPTER

The wrox.com code download for this chapter is found at www.wrox.com/go/ projavaeedesignpatterns on the Download Code tab. The code is in the Chapter 06 download and individually named according to the names throughout the chapter.

The factory design pattern is one of the widely used core design patterns in modern programming languages. It is used not only by web and application developers, but by the developers of run times and frameworks such as Java and Spring.

The factory pattern has two variations: the factory method and the abstract factory. The intent of these patterns is the same: to provide an interface for creating families of related or dependent objects without specifying their concrete classes. This chapter introduces you to both of these variations and shows you examples of how to implement them.

You will see how the factory pattern has been implemented in Java SE, how that differs from its implementation in Java EE, and how it takes advantage of context dependency injection.

WHAT IS A FACTORY?

As one of the creational patterns, the factory's purpose is to create objects. The creational logic is encapsulated within the factory and either provides a method that returns a newly created object (factory method pattern) or delegates the creation of the object to a subclass (abstract factory pattern). In both cases, the creation of the object is abstracted away from where it will be used.

The client need not be aware of the different implementations of the interface or class. The client only needs to know the factory (factory method or abstract factory) to use to get an instance of one of the implementations of the interface. Clients are decoupled from the creation of the objects.

The decoupling occurs as the result of applying the dependency inversion principle and brings many practical advantages, of which the most important is the decoupling of higher-level classes from lower-level classes. This decoupling allows the implementation of the concrete classes to be changed without affecting the client, thus reducing coupling between classes and increasing flexibility.

The factory pattern gives us the opportunity to decouple object creation from the underlying system by encapsulating the code responsible for creating the objects. This approach simplifies our life when it comes to refactoring as we now have a single point where the refactoring changes happen.

Often the factory itself is implemented as a singleton or as a static class because normally only one instance of the factory is required. This centralizes factory object creation, allowing for greater organization and maintainability of source code and the reduction of errors when changes and updates are made.

> **NOTE** *Dependency Inversion Principle:*
>
> 1. *High-level modules should not depend on low-level modules. Both should depend on abstractions.*
> 2. *Abstractions should not depend on details. Details should depend on abstractions.*[1]

In Java EE, dependency injection is employed to deliver the decoupling of higher-level classes from lower-level classes when implementing the factory pattern. The combined use of the `@Producers` and `@Inject` annotations makes their implementation relatively simple.

FACTORY METHOD

The GoF[2] book describes the factory method pattern as such: "Defines an interface for creating an object, but lets subclasses decide which class to instantiate." *Head First Design Patterns*[3] adds that the "factory method lets a class defer instantiation to subclasses."

Factories minimize the usage of the `new` keyword and can encapsulate the initialization process and the different concrete implementations. The ability to centralize those needs minimizes the effect of adding or removing concrete classes to the system and the effects of concrete class dependencies.

The factory method class diagram is shown in Figure 6-1.

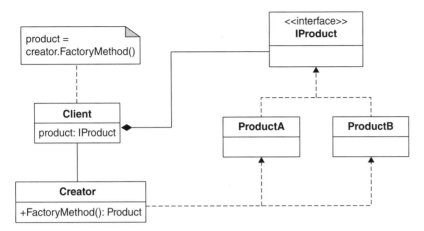

FIGURE 6-1: The class diagram shows the structure of the factory method pattern. You can see how the object creation is encapsulated in the subclasses.

WAR STORY

At one time, I was developing a desktop application with a friend. At the beginning, we were not sure if we needed a full-blown database or not. This was long before no-SQL and document-based data stores, so our only option was to use XML. Nevertheless, we were not sure if XML files would be sufficient to store the data. Meanwhile, we had already started developing the application and needed a concrete persistence implementation to save data. Because we wanted the flexibility to change the system from using XML to using SQL, we decided to create all the data access objects (DAOs) via the implementation of the factory pattern. This way we could easily switch from XML to SQL or vice versa. Within a few weeks, we realized that we really underestimated the data needs of the system. XML was definitely an adequate solution and was now out of question, so we were stuck with an SQL-based database for the rest of the project. In the end, we didn't really use our DAO factory.

However, as we were completing the application, our clients asked for a demo platform. It was not enough to demonstrate the capabilities of the application and let them play for a day or two. They wanted more time to evaluate the application. This meant we needed to install a functioning application on the network to allow the clients time to properly evaluate the application and see that it rocked. We didn't want to install the full application because there was no way to ensure that the client wouldn't make a copy, and we definitely didn't want to build a demo application from scratch. Suddenly, I came up with a brilliant idea. The demo application needed to persist the data in order to function sufficiently, so that the client could evaluate it, but not enough that the client could make a pirate copy of the application. The idea was to temporarily store the data in memory. If we could

continues

continued

easily change our DAOs to an in-memory data store instead of persisting the data in a database, we could leave the clients to try the demo version for as long as they wanted. (Without a persistent data store, the application would make no sense at all!) Because we already had the DAO factory, we only needed to implement the in-memory DAO classes and tweak the factory code to return them when our database was not present.

The result was so successful that I implemented another factory to control print jobs to print to a nonformatted text file instead of the real printer for the demo version. These changes that took advantage of the factory pattern meant that we could easily leave clients to evaluate our application for as long as they wanted and, because the clients could not print formatted copies and persist financial data, the application was useless in production.

Designing the system using factories was not a huge win at first but was a life saver in the end. Design patterns tend to address future problems if they are used in the right context.

Implementing the Factory Method in Plain Code

The factory method does not have boilerplate code for its implementation. Listings 6-1 to 6-6 show implementations of the factory pattern using a `DrinksMachine` that dispenses different types of drinks depending on the implementation of its subclasses.

LISTING 6-1: DrinksMachine abstract class extended by concrete implementations

```
public abstract class DrinksMachine {

    public abstract Drink dispenseDrink();

    public String displayMessage(){
        return "Thank for your custom.";
    }
}
```

LISTING 6-2: CoffeeMachine implementation of the DrinksMachine abstract class

```
public class CoffeeMachine extends DrinksMachine {

    public Drink dispenseDrink() {
        return new Coffee();
    }
}
```

LISTING 6-3: SoftDrinksMachine implementation of the DrinksMachine abstract class

```java
public class SoftDrinksMachine extends DrinksMachine {

    public Drink dispenseDrink() {
        return new SoftDrink();
    }
}
```

LISTING 6-4: The Drink interface

```java
public interface Drink {}
```

LISTING 6-5: SoftDrink implementation of the Drink interface

```java
public class SoftDrink implements Drink {
    SoftDrink() {
        System.out.println("Soft drink");
    }
}
```

LISTING 6-6: Coffee implementation of the Drink interface

```java
public class Coffee implements Drink {

    Coffee() {
        System.out.println("Coffee");
    }
}
```

This implementation shows how the subclasses of the DrinksMachine abstract class determine the drink that is dispensed. This allows any implementation of the DrinksMachine class to dispense any object of the Drink type. Each subclass of the DrinksMachine's abstract class determines which drinks are dispensed.

This is a simple implementation in which the dispenseDrink method dispenses only one type of drink. A more illustrative example would show the dispenseDrink method receiving the name of a drink and then constructing and returning the requested drink object. Listing 6-7 shows how to achieve this.

LISTING 6-7: CoffeeType enum

```java
public enum CoffeeType {EXPRESSO, LATTE}


public Drink dispenseDrink(CoffeeType type) {

    Drink coffee = null;

    switch (type) {
```

continues

LISTING 6-7: *(continued)*

```
        case EXPRESSO: coffee = new Expresso();
        case LATTE:    coffee = new Latte();
    }

    return coffee;
}
```

For brevity, this chapter shows only a code snippet of the enum type `CoffeeType` that defines the type of coffee and the `dispenseDrink` method of the concrete `Coffee` class.

ABSTRACT FACTORY

The factory method pattern is straightforward and useful to implement, but in more complex systems, you need to organize it. This problem leads you to a new pattern called the abstract factory pattern.

The abstract factory pattern is described in both the GoF book and *Head First Design Patterns* as "provides an interface for creating families of related or dependent objects without specifying their concrete classes."

What abstract factories offer is the encapsulation of a group of factories and control over how the client accesses them. This chapter does not go into all the details of how to implement abstract factories but instead offers a brief introduction for basic understanding.

The abstract factory class diagram is shown in Figure 6-2.

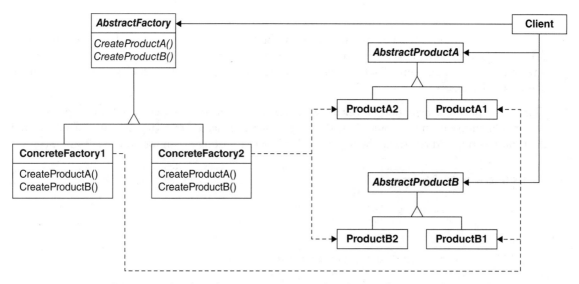

FIGURE 6-2: As can be seen in the class diagram, you can use the abstract factory pattern to group existing factories and encapsulate how you access them.

Implementing the Abstract Factory in Plain Code

To demonstrate the abstract factory design pattern, this chapter extends the drinks machine example by adding a factory that produces two different types of drinks machine: basic and gourmet.

The "families of related or dependent objects" that the abstract factory creates are the coffee machine and the soft drinks machine. You must create an interface for the factories to implement. In Listing 6-8, you create the `AbstractDrinksMachineFactory` interface.

LISTING 6-8: Interface for the abstract factory

```
public interface AbstractDrinksMachineFactory {
    public DrinksMachine createCoffeeMachine();
    public DrinksMachine createSoftDrinksMachine();
}
```

The concrete implementations of this interface are the `GourmetDrinksMachineFactory` and the `BasicDrinksMachineFactory` classes. For brevity, only the `GourmetDrinksMachineFactory` is shown in Listing 6-9.

LISTING 6-9: Implementation of the AbstractDrinksMachineFactory

```
public class GourmetDrinksMachineFactory implements AbstractDrinksMachineFactory{

    public DrinksMachine createCoffeeMachine() {
        return new GourmetCoffeeMachine();
    }

    public DrinksMachine createSoftDrinksMachine() {
        return new GourmetSoftDrinksMachine();
    }

}
```

Each factory implements the abstract factory's `create` method in a different way and, depending on which factory is instantiated, a different implementation of a coffee and soft drinks machine is created.

```
AbstractDrinksMachineFactory factory = new GourmetDrinksMachineFactory();
DrinksMachine CoffeeMachine = factory.createCoffeeMachine();
CoffeeMachine.dispenseDrink(CoffeeType.EXPRESSO);
```

This shows a `GourmetDrinksMachineFactory` being instantiated. Its coffee machine's creation method is invoked to create the coffee machine object that this implementation requires.

The full code for this implementation is in the Chapter 06 download.

IMPLEMENTING THE FACTORY PATTERN IN JAVA EE

The factory pattern is not tricky to implement, as you have seen in the preceding examples. Java EE offers a simple and elegant way to implement the factory pattern via annotations and dependency injection. In the Java EE world, you use the `@Produces` annotation to create an object, and you use `@Inject` to inject the created object (or resource) where it's required. The simplest implementation in Java EE of the factory method follows in Listing 6-10.

LISTING 6-10: Simple implementation of the factory method using producer methods

```java
package com.devchronicles.producer;
import javax.enterprise.inject.Produces;

public class EventProducer {

    @Produces
    public String getMessage(){
        return "Hello World";
    }

}
```

The `getMessage` method is annotated with `@Produces` and results in String objects containing the text `Hello World`. Although the type produced in this example is a string, you can produce anything you need, including interfaces, classes, primitive data types, Java array types, and core Java types.

To use the produced object, you need to inject the same type into the class where you are going to use it, as demonstrated in Listing 6-11.

LISTING 6-11: Injecting a string created by the factory

```java
package com.devchronicles.factory;

import javax.ejb.Stateless;
import javax.ejb.TransactionAttribute;
import javax.ejb.TransactionAttributeType;
import javax.inject.Inject;

@Stateless
@TransactionAttribute(TransactionAttributeType.REQUIRED)
public class EventService {

    @Inject
    private String message;

    public void startService(){
        System.out.println("Start service call " + message);
    }
}
```

When you run and invoke the `startService` method, the string value in the producer method is injected into the *message* member of `EventService` and printed to the console. This is the simplest possible implementation of the factory pattern in Java EE. However, it raises one important question: How does the Context Dependency Injection (CDI) container know that it must inject the string produced by the `getMessage` method into the *message* member of `EventService`?

The answer: The CDI container relies on types to determine where to inject the produced type. In this example, the produced type is a string, as is the injected type. So it matches the produced type with the inject type and injects it.

You might argue that in a real system, you need to produce and inject different instances of the same object type. How does the CDI container know where to inject each produced type? It does this by using an annotation configuration called a *qualifier.*

In real-world projects, you probably want to return different object types instead of a simple string so that you can create different objects by type.

LISTING 6-12: MessageA bean

```java
package com.devchronicles.factory;

@Alternative
public class MessageA {

    private String message;

    public String getMessage(){
        return message;
    }

    public void setMessage(String message){
        this.message = message;
    }

}
```

LISTING 6-13: MessageB bean

```java
package com.devchronicles.factory;

@Alternative
public class MessageB {
    private String message;

    public String getMessage(){
        return message;
    }

    public void setMessage(String message){
        this.message = message;
    }
}
```

LISTING 6-14: Factory implementation that creates message beans

```
package com.devchronicles.factory;

import javax.enterprise.inject.Produces;

public class EventProducer {

    @Produces
    public MessageA messageAFactory(){
        return new MessageA();
    }

    @Produces
    public MessageB messageBFactory(){
        return new MessageB();
    }

}
```

In this example, you have created two beans: MessageA in Listing 6-12 and MessageB in Listing 6-13. You have annotated them with @Alternative, which disables them so that the container does not attempt to inject their instances when it finds a matching injection point. You annotate them so the factory in Listing 6-14 will produce the instances. If you didn't annotate, the container would throw an exception while loading the application. It would read something like this:
CDI deployment failure:WELD-001409 Ambiguous dependencies for type [MessageA]. The ambiguity is caused by the two instances of MessageA that are created: one by the container and the other by the @Produces method. The container doesn't know which instance to inject into the *message* member of the EventService. You will see a way to resolve this ambiguity later in the chapter.

LISTING 6-15: Injecting the beans created by the factory using the @Inject annotation

```
package com.devchronicles.factory;

import javax.ejb.Stateless;
import javax.ejb.TransactionAttribute;
import javax.ejb.TransactionAttributeType;
import javax.enterprise.event.Event;
import javax.inject.Inject;

@Stateless
@TransactionAttribute(TransactionAttributeType.REQUIRED)
public class EventService {

    @Inject
    private MessageA messageA;

    @Inject
    private MessageB messageB;

    public void startService(){

        messageA.setMessage("This is message A");
```

```
        messageB.setMessage("This is message B");

        System.out.println("Start service call " + messageA.getMessage());
        System.out.println("Start service call " + messageB.getMessage());

    }
}
```

In the EventService class shown in Listing 6-15, the containers inject the two beans produced by the factory into the *messageA* and *messageB* member variables of the EventService class. You can use these objects as you would normally.

An alternative implementation is to use the @Qualifier and @interface annotations to mark the type you want to inject. The example that follows uses custom annotations to create two qualifiers: @LongMessage in Listing 6-16 and @ShortMessage in Listing 6-17.

LISTING 6-16: ShortMessage qualifier

```
@Qualifier
@Retention(RetentionPolicy.RUNTIME)
@Target({ElementType.METHOD, ElementType.FIELD})
public @interface ShortMessage {}
```

LISTING 6-17: LongMessage qualifier

```
@Qualifier
@Retention(RetentionPolicy.RUNTIME)
@Target({ElementType.METHOD, ElementType.FIELD})
public @interface LongMessage {}
```

You use these qualifiers to annotate the producer methods as shown in Listing 6-18 and their matching injection points as shown in Listing 6-19.

LISTING 6-18: Using the qualifiers to disambiguate the beans

```
public class EventProducer {

    @Produces @ShortMessage
    private MessageA messageAFactory(){
        return new MessageA();
    }

    @Produces @LongMessage
    private MessageB messageBFactory(){
        return new MessageB();
    }

}
```

LISTING 6-19: Injecting the created beans using qualifiers to disambiguate

```
@TransactionAttribute(TransactionAttributeType.REQUIRED)
public class ClientMessage {

    @Inject @ShortMessage
    private MessageA messageA;

    @Inject @LongMessage
    private MessageB messageB;

    public void doEvent(){
        messageA.setMessage("This is a long email message.");
        messageB.setMessage("This is a short SMS message.");
        System.out.println(messageA.getMessage());
        System.out.println(messageB.getMessage());
    }
}
```

The @Target annotation specified on the qualifier interface determines where you can use the qualifier. The values can be one or all of the following—*TYPE*, *METHOD*, *FIELD*, and *PARAMETER*—and their meanings are self-explanatory.

Alternatively, you can achieve the same implementation via the use of an enum type defined in the @interface class, Listing 6-20 shows this implementation.

LISTING 6-20: Custom annotation type

```
@Qualifier
@Retention(RetentionPolicy.RUNTIME)
@Target({ElementType.METHOD})
public @interface MyEvent {
    Type value();
    enum Type{ LOGGING, MESSAGE }
}
```

With the help of this custom annotation, you can use different methods to create string objects marked with your annotation. In Listing 6-21 strings are produced by the messageAFactory and the messageBFactory methods.

LISTING 6-21: Using the custom annotations to disambiguate the beans

```
public class EventProducer {

    @Produces
    @MyEvent(MyEvent.Type.LOGGING)
    public String messageAFactory(){
        return "A message";
    }

    @Produces
```

```
    @MyEvent(MyEvent.Type.MESSAGE)
    public String messageBFactory(){
        return "Another message";
    }

}
```

You use these annotations to annotate the producer methods and their matching injection points as shown in Listing 6-22.

LISTING 6-22: Injecting the created beans using custom annotations to disambiguate

```
package com.devchronicles.observer;

import javax.ejb.Stateless;
import javax.ejb.TransactionAttribute;
import javax.ejb.TransactionAttributeType;
import javax.enterprise.event.Event;
import javax.inject.Inject;

@Stateless
@TransactionAttribute(TransactionAttributeType.REQUIRED)
public class EventService {

    @Inject
    @MyEvent(MyEvent.Type.LOGGING)
    private String messageA;

    @Inject
    @MyEvent(MyEvent.Type.MESSAGE)
    private String messageB;

    public void startService(){
        System.out.println("Start service call " + messageA);
        System.out.println("Start service call " + messageB);
    }

}
```

A simpler approach would be to use the @Named annotation rather than creating your own annotation type. This is implemented as in Listing 6-23.

LISTING 6-23: Using @Named annotations to disambiguate

```
package com.devchronicles.factory;
import javax.enterprise.inject.Produces;

public class EventProducer {

    @Produces
    @Named("Logging")
    public String messageAFactory(){
```

continues

LISTING 6-23: *(continued)*

```java
            return "A message";
    }

    @Produces
    @Named("Message")
    public String messageBFactory(){
        return "Another message";
    }

}
```

You use @Name to annotate the producer methods and their matching injection points, as shown in Listing 6-24.

LISTING 6-24: Injecting using @Named annotations

```java
@Stateless
@TransactionAttribute(TransactionAttributeType.REQUIRED)
public class EventServiceName {

    @Inject
    @Named("Logging")
    private String messageA;

    @Inject
    @Named("Message")
    private String messageB;

    public void startService(){
        System.out.println("Start service call " + messageA);
        System.out.println("Start service call " + messageB);
    }

}
```

Although this appears simpler than creating your own annotation type, in complicated systems, it may not be a wise or a type-safe choice. The named annotation works with the String provided in quotes and is far from being type safe. The compiler can't warn you of potential bugs.

Harness the Power of CDI

If your application has multiple implementations of an interface and you want to implement a factory pattern to produce the required instances of these objects, you are going to have a factory class with multiple methods annotated with the @Produces annotation. This will become verbose and difficult to maintain. Fortunately, Java EE provides a solution in the form of the @Any annotation and the imaginative use of enum types, annotation literals, and the Instance class.

What would take many tens if not hundreds of lines of code to produce each instance, you can accomplish in just four lines of code. You can achieve this by collecting all instances of a particular interface implementation and selecting the one you want to use by using the `@Any` annotation.

The `@Any` annotation instructs the container that all beans implementing the given interface should be injected at that injection point. In the listing below the code `private Instance<MessageType>`, `messages` injects instances of all dependencies that implement the `MessageType` interface into the member variable *messages*.

Once all dependencies have been injected, you need a way to distinguish between them and select the one you want to use. This is where the use of annotation literals and enum types comes into play. In the listings that follow, you define an `@Message` qualifier and the enum literals `SHORT` and `LONG`. These distinguish between the implementations of the `MessageType` interface.

To select the dependency, compare it with the enum type of the qualifier of each implementation by creating an `AnnotationLiteral` of the type you are searching for, retrieve it, and return it to the client.

Now you'll see how this is implemented in code. You will use the example of a factory that produces `ShortMessage` and `LongMessage` objects, each implementing the `Message` interface annotated as either `SHORT` or `LONG`.

LISTING 6-25: MessageType interface

```
public interface MessageType {
    public String getMessage();
    public void setMessage(String message);
}
```

LISTING 6-26: ShortMessage implementation of message interface

```
@Message(Message.Type.SHORT)
@Dependent
public class ShortMessage implements MessageType{

    private String message;

    @Override
    public String getMessage() {
        return message;
    }

    @Override
    public void setMessage(String message) {
        this.message = message;
    }
}
```

LISTING 6-27: LongMessage implementation of message interface

```java
@Message(Message.Type.LONG)
@Dependent
public class LongMessage implements MessageType {

    private String message;

    @Override
    public String getMessage() {
        return message;
    }

    @Override
    public void setMessage(String message) {
        this.message = message;
    }
}
```

Each concrete implementation of the `MessageType` interface, as shown in Listing 6-25, is annotated with an `@Message` qualifier denoting the message type as either `Message.Type.SHORT` or `Message .Type.LONG` as implemented in Listing 6-26 and Listing 6-27 respectively. The `@Message` qualifier is implemented in the same manner, as can be seen is Listing 6-28, as the qualifier used in the Custom Annotation Type example shown earlier.

LISTING 6-28: Custom message annotation

```java
@Qualifier
@Retention(RetentionPolicy.RUNTIME)
@Target({ElementType.FIELD, ElementType.TYPE})
public @interface Message {
    Type value();
    enum Type{ SHORT, LONG }
}
```

To create the annotation literal that you use to make the comparison between the type you want and the type of the dependency, you extend the abstract class `AnnotationLiteral` and implement `Message` as the custom message qualifier. Listing 6-29 shows how this is done.

LISTING 6-29: Annotation literal used to retrieve required message type

```java
public class MessageLiteral extends AnnotationLiteral<Message> implements Message {

    private static final long serialVersionUID = 1L;
    private Type type;

    public MessageLiteral(Type type) {
        this.type = type;
```

```
        }

        public Type value() {
            return type;
        }

    }
```

Now that you have all the parts of the puzzle, you can put it together in the `MessageFactory` class shown in Listing 6-30.

LISTING 6-30: The Factory implementation

```
@Dependent
public class MessageFactory {

    @Inject
    @Any
    private Instance<MessageType> messages;

    public MessageType getMessage(Message.Type type) {
        MessageLiteral literal = new MessageLiteral(type);
        Instance<MessageType> typeMessages = messages.select(literal);
        return typeMessages.get();
    }

}
```

In the factory class, all dependencies that implement the `MessageType` interface are injected into the member variable *messages*. Then, from the method `getMessage`, you use the `Message.Type` parameter to create a new `MessageLiteral` that you use to select the `MessageType` implementation that you want from *messages*, which in turn is returned to the client.

The client injects the factory and calls the `getMessage` method passing in the `Message.Type` that it requires, as can be seen in Listing 6-31.

LISTING 6-31: Client using the Factory implementation

```
@TransactionAttribute(TransactionAttributeType.REQUIRED)
@ApplicationScoped
public class Client {

    @Inject
    MessageFactory mf;

    public void doMessage(){
        MessageType m = mf.getMessage(Message.Type.SHORT);
        m.setMessage("This is a short message");
```

continues

LISTING 6-31: *(continued)*

```
            System.out.println(m.getMessage());

            m = mf.getMessage(Message.Type.LONG);
            m.setMessage("This is a long message");
            System.out.println(m.getMessage());
        }
    }
```

This chapter has deviated quite substantially from the original GoF implementation of the factory pattern. In fact, you could argue that this is not really a true factory pattern implementation but rather a select and inject pattern. Nevertheless, the new and dynamic functionality of CDI allows you to be creative in the way you implement traditional patterns and improve on classic design.

WHERE AND WHEN TO USE THE FACTORY PATTERNS

The traditional implementation of the factory pattern has changed substantially since the GoF first espoused its usage.

Abstract factories are considered an effective way to hide object creation, especially if the creation is complex. And the more complex the object creation, the more justifiable is the use of a factory to create the object. If it is important that objects are created in a consistent manner and their creation is strictly controlled, you should consider an implementation of the factory pattern.

However, in the brave new world of the CDI environment, where the container instantiates managed objects, the use of an abstract factory is arguably moot. Your best attempt to implement the factory pattern uses the @Produce annotation that still allows you to hide complicated creational logic in the producer method and inject the resulting object into the client.

Alternatively, you can harness the power of the CDI environment and let the container create the objects and then select the instantiation you want to use from a pool of similar objects. However, you are limited to simple objects that can be instantiated satisfactorily by calling the default constructor.

SUMMARY

In this chapter, you have seen how to implement the various flavors of the factory pattern in a non-CDI environment. And in a CDI environment, you have seen how producer methods and the @Inject annotation have radically changed the way you implement and use the factory pattern in Java EE.

You have discovered how to harness the power of the container's automatic instantiation of bean objects and how to select and use them in your code.

Hopefully, you have no doubt that the implementation of the factory pattern in a Java EE is substantially more elegant and by far the simpler and cleaner way to generate objects.

EXERCISES

1. Create a vehicle factory that produces different types of cars and vans by using the abstract factory pattern.

2. Implement that same vehicle factory as in the previous exercise but use `@Produce`, qualifiers, and enum types.

3. By harnessing the power of the CDI container, implement a way to have multiple objects of the same type and to select the type you require based on type-safe logic.

NOTES

1. Wikipedia.org: `http://en.wikipedia.org/wiki/Dependency_inversion_principle`.
2. *Design Patterns: Elements of Reusable Object-Oriented Software* (Addison-Wesley, 1994): Erich Gamma, Richard Helm, Ralph Johnson, John Vlissides.
3. *Head First Design Patterns* (O'Reilly, 2004): Eric Freeman, Elisabeth Robson, Bert Bates, Kathy Sierra.

Decorator Pattern

WROX.COM CODE DOWNLOAD FOR THIS CHAPTER

The wrox.com code download for this chapter is found at www.wrox.com/go/
projavaeedesignpatterns on the Download Code tab. The code is in the Chapter 07
download and individually named according to the names throughout the chapter.

The GoF[1] book describes the decorator pattern as "Attach additional responsibilities to an
object dynamically" and gives a Graphical User Interface Toolkit as an example. This is an
excellent real-world example because adding new styles or behaviors to a user interface (UI)
toolkit is the perfect job for the decorator pattern.

The *Head First Design Patterns*[2] book gives a coffee shop as an example of different options
such as whip cream being added to the product. The addition of each new condiment wraps
the beverage object and adds new behavior to the description and price. This example has been
the best-fit solution since the authors had a similar real-life experience. See the next War Story.

The decorator pattern relies on component and decorator objects, which implement the same
interface. The decorator has an instance variable that implements the same interface so it can

wrap either a component object or another decorator. Sharing the same interface allows decorators to decorate the base component or another decorator. With a proper implementation, it is simple to call all relevant function implementations in order from the last decorator to the inner target component object. In most cases, it should not be difficult to adapt an existing system to use the decorator pattern.

WHAT IS A DECORATOR?

The decorator pattern is one of the structural patterns described in the book of GoF. Its purpose is to wrap a target object so that you can dynamically add new responsibilities at run time. Each decorator can wrap another one, which allows for a theoretically unlimited number of decorating of target objects.

Although this runtime behavior is much more flexible than inheritance via subclassing, it introduces a level of complexity to concrete subclassing as it makes it more difficult to determine the types and behaviors of objects prior to executing the application.

Decorators are used in almost all languages and all platforms, from the UI to the back end. Most frameworks and run times use the decorator pattern to add flexibility and runtime–specific behavior.

In Java EE, you implement the decorator pattern without boilerplate code. However, unlike the majority of the patterns in this book, you often add XML configuration to the `bean.xml`.

WAR STORY

Several years ago, we won a contract to complete a food and drinks ordering and payment system for a company that then provided it as a point of sale (POS) service to its clients.[3] These clients were restaurants, cafés, and bars. We had no knowledge of the domain, so we made some reasonable assumptions based on the limited knowledge and information we had at the time. Luckily, most assumptions worked out well.

One of our design rules was that if an add-on option changes the price of a product, it should be added as a new product. So if the restaurant serves extra portions for an additional price, a new item should be added to the menu. However, if an option like extra cheese was free, that information could be added as a side note to the order.

This rule had worked well for every client until one day we met with a café owner whose business operated slightly differently. The café was focused on selling deserts, but it also offered pizza as a savory option. Pizza was the only meal item on the whole menu. Because the café didn't specialize in pizza, it did not offer set pizzas but instead let its customers create their own pizzas from a long list of toppings, and it charged for each topping. This was quite a sensible way for the café to offer its customers pizza because only a few of its customers would want to eat pizza. However, it was catastrophic for our system because of our design rule: If an add-on option changes the price of a product, it should be added as a new product. Because each topping had a different price, we needed to calculate all the combinations of toppings and enter a new pizza to the menu for each combination.

As you know, $n!$ algorithms grow large quickly, which in this case would have resulted in a long list of pizzas after only a few combinations. Because this was not acceptable, we suggested to the client that he enter several pizzas with a fixed number of toppings (1 topping, 2 topping, 3 topping), and he could add a note to the order to record the customer's choice of topping. With this solution, we could shorten the list from $n!$ to n.

Still, this solution was not really reasonable. Because the system was already up and running, we needed to find a way to fix it without breaking other parts. We needed a way to add functionality at run time. We needed to "decorate" the existing pizza object with toppings. Clearly, the answer was to implement the decorator pattern. And that is what we did. Each topping the customer chose wrapped the pizza object in a similar way to the example used in the *Head First Design Patterns* book.

Decorator Class Diagram

As is seen in the class diagram in Figure 7-1, the decorator pattern introduces some boilerplate code to an existing class hierarchy. The pattern introduces a shared interface between the target class and the decorator. The decorator must have a reference to an instance of this interface.

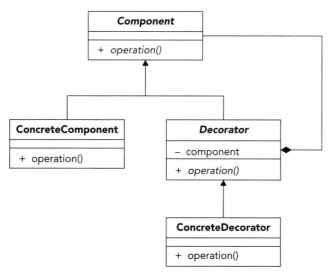

FIGURE 7-1: Class diagram of the decorator pattern

IMPLEMENTING THE DECORATOR PATTERN IN PLAIN CODE

If the classes are in the design stage, the addition of decorators shouldn't be too much of an issue. However, if the decorator is to be implemented in an existing system, you might need to refactor some classes. For example, the target class should implement the same interface that the decorator implements.

This chapter demonstrates the use of the decorator pattern using a simplified POS system for a pizza restaurant. Each pizza can be "decorated" with extra toppings, such as double cheese and free chili.

First, you will create the `Order` interface, which is implemented by the `Pizza` class and by the decorator's `Extra` abstract class. The `Extra` class is extended by the extra toppings classes: `DoubleExtra`, `NoCostExtra`, and `RegularExtra`.

You'll start by creating the `Order` interface in Listing 7-1.

LISTING: 7-1: The Order interface

```
public interface Order {
    public double getPrice();
    public String getLabel();
}
```

In Listing 7-2, you'll create the class that represents a pizza (Four Seasons, Margarita, Hawaiian, and so on) on the menu. This is the target object to be decorated.

LISTING: 7-2: The class to be decorated implements the Order interface

```
public class Pizza implements Order {

    private String label;
    private double price;

    public Pizza(String label, double price){
        this.label=label;
        this.price=price;
    }

    public double getPrice(){
        return this.price;
    }

    public String getLabel(){
        return this.label;
    }
}
```

The following code creates a Four Seasons pizza.

```
Order fourSeasonsPizza = new Pizza("Four Seasons Pizza", 10);
```

Next, you need to create the decorators that will decorate the pizza with extra toppings. Use an abstract class so that the concrete classes do not have to implement all the business methods of an interface. An abstract decorator will create a blueprint that other decorators can extend.

Perhaps you have different topping types (cheese, chili, pineapple, and so on). Imagine that the customer wants to order the meal a little spicier, and the restaurant will not charge for that extra topping. So you need a decorator that does not add to the price of the pizza but provides proper labeling (that extra chili has been requested). Also, the customer may ask for two extra portions of cheese, and if the system prints "cheese" twice, the chef may think it is a bug and add only one portion of cheese. So you need another concrete decorator to allow for proper labeling of double toppings. Listing 7-3 accomplishes your goals.

LISTING 7-3: The abstract decorator that adds extra toppings

```
public abstract class Extra implements Order {

    protected Order order;
    protected String label;
    protected double price;

    public Extra(String label, double price, Order order) {
        this.label=label;
        this.price=price;
        this.order=order;
    }

    // Price can be a big issue, so delegate this to concrete implementation
    public abstract double getPrice();

    // Should be okay to provide standard labeling
    public String getLabel() {
        return order.getLabel()+", "+this.label;
    }
}
```

Now that you have the abstract decorator, you can add specific behaviors and create concrete decorators. You'll start with the RegularExtra decorator, which adds a charge and a label to the target object (the pizza). Because the labeling function is already provided by the abstract decorator and inherited by all subclasses that extend it, you only need to implement the pricing functionality. Listing 7-4 takes care of that.

LISTING 7-4: The decorator that adds extra toppings

```
public class RegularExtra extends Extra {

    public RegularExtra(String label, double price, Order order) {
        super(label, price, order);
    }

    public Double getPrice() {
        return this.price+order.getPrice();
    }
}
```

Next, you need to create the NoCostDecorator, which modifies the label string but does not add to the cost of the pizza. See Listing 7-5.

LISTING 7-5: The decorator that adds extra toppings at no cost

```
public class NoCostExtra extends Extra {

    public NoCostExtra(String label, double price, Order order) {
        super(label, price, order);
    }

    public Double getPrice() {
        return order.getPrice();
    }
}
```

Finally, in Listing 7-6, you implement the DoubleExtra decorator to avoid printing the topping twice on the label. The decorator doubles the price and adds the keyword double in front of the target label.

LISTING 7-6: The decorator that adds double toppings

```
public class DoubleExtra extends Extra {

    public DoubleExtra(String label, double price, Order order) {
        super(label, price, order);
    }

    public Double getPrice() {
        return (this.price*2)+order.getPrice();
    }

public String getLabel() {
        return order.getLabel()+ ", Double " + this.label;
    }
}
```

Now that the decorator pattern has been implemented to add extra toppings to your pizza, you can test your implementation.

```
Order fourSeasonsPizza = new Pizza("Four Seasons Pizza", 10);
fourSeasonsPizza = new RegularExtra("Pepperoni", 4, fourSeasonsPizza );
fourSeasonsPizza = new DoubleExtra("Mozzarella", 2, fourSeasonsPizza );
fourSeasonsPizza = new NoCostExtra("Chili", 2, fourSeasonsPizza );

System.out.println(fourSeasonsPizza.getPrice());
System.out.println(fourSeasonsPizza.getLabel());
```

The output in the console will be as follows:

```
18.0
Pizza, Pepperoni, Double Mozzarella, Chili
```

But wait! There is a potential bug! Chili is not free if you order it as a side dish, but the chef is happy to offer it free on a pizza. You need to make sure the system accounts for those differences. Just imagine that these values and labels come from a database. What would you do to create different behaviors for chili? One option might be to create two chili objects: one labeled as "with pizza." Clearly, this would be a hack, leaving a backdoor open for any waiter to order free chili for his friends. Another option would be to create an additional constructor method in the abstract class that does not take a price parameter. Any decorator that does not charge for extras could implement this.

IMPLEMENTING THE DECORATOR PATTERN IN JAVA EE

Unlike most other patterns described in this book, you implement the decorator pattern by declaring the decorator classes in the `bean.xml` deployment descriptor (except when annotated with `@Priority`; see the following section "Decorators Without XML Configuration"). Luckily, this configuration is simple and gives you the advantage of pluggability and control over the order in which the decorators are invoked.

The decorator implementation in Java EE introduces two new annotations: `@Decorator` and `@Delegate`. `@Decorator` annotates the decorator class, and `@Delegate` annotates the delegate injection point where the class to be decorated is injected.

You will use the example of a shop that wants to discount some of its products. It will use a decorator to apply this discount to the regular retail price. In Listing 7-7, you start by creating the interface that you will use to connect the decorator with the object you want to decorate.

LISTING 7-7: The Product interface

```
public interface Product {
    public void setLabel(String label);
    public void setPrice(double price);
    public String getLabel();
    public double getPrice();
    public String generateLabel();
}
```

The interface introduces the `generateLabel` method, which the decorator implements to add its discounting behavior. In Listing 7-8, you create the `Table` class. It is the product that you want to be decorated; therefore, it implements the `Product` interface.

LISTING 7-8: The class to be decorated implements the Product interface

```
public class Table implements Product {

    private String label = "Dining Table";
    private double price = 100.00;

    public void setLabel(String label) {
        this.label = label;
```

continues

LISTING 7-8 *(continued)*

```
    }

    public void setPrice(double price) {
        this.price = price;
    }

    public String getLabel() {
        return label;
    }

    public double getPrice() {
        return price;
    }

    public String generateLabel() {
        return  price + ", " + label;
    }

}
```

You create the PriceDiscountDecorator decorator by implementing the Product interface. This class implements the generateLabel method and adds its discounting behavior. The decorator reduces the price of a product by 50 percent and adds the text "(Discounted)" to the product's label.

To enable the container to identify this class as a decorator, you must annotate it with @Decorator. The delegate injection point (the instance that will be decorated) is annotated with @Delegate and must be an injected field, an initializer method parameter, or a bean constructor method parameter. The delegate type must be the interface implemented by the classes that you want to be decorated—in this case, Product. The CDI container injects any available instance of the Product interface into the *product* member variable as shown in Listing 7-9.

LISTING 7-9: The PriceDiscountDecorator decorator

```
@Decorator
public class PriceDiscountDecorator implements Product {

    @Any
    @Inject
    @Delegate
    private Product product;

    public String generateLabel() {
        product.setPrice(product.getPrice() * 0.5);
        product.setLabel(product.getLabel() + " (Discounted)");
        return product.generateLabel();
    }

    // Not all methods shown
}
```

Finally, you must declare the decorator in bean.xml. Although most of the configuration has already been done via annotations, you still need to add some XML configuration to make the decorator work. The configuration might seem disappointing because you have already annotated your decorator; nevertheless, the configuration is simple and necessary so that you can define the order of execution of the decorators (if more than one). Add the following lines to beans.xml:

```
<decorators>
    <class>com.devchronicles.decorator.PriceDiscountDecorator</class>
</decorators>
```

Your work is done. You can now use your decorator.

```
@Any
@Inject
Product product;

public void createPriceList(){
    System.out.println("Label: " + product.generateLabel());
}
```

An instance of Table is injected into the *Product* member variable, and the generateLabel method is called. The output to the console will be as follows:

```
Label: 12.5, Dining Table (Discounted)
```

When a call is made to the generateLabel method of any Product instance, the container intercepts it. The call is delegated to the appropriate method of the PriceDiscountDecorator decorator, where it discounts the product's price and passes the call onto the original destination by calling the generateLabel method of the Table object.

A call chain is set up that includes all the decorators that are declared to decorate classes that implement the Product interface. The order in which the decorators are called is determined by the order in which they are declared in the bean.xml deployment descriptor.

You are going to see this in action in Listing 7-10, where you define another decorator. You create the BlackFridayDiscountDecorator decorator, implement the Product interface, and add the @Decorator and @Delegate annotations.

LISTING 7-10: The BlackFridayDecorator decorator

```
@Decorator
public class BlackFridayDiscountDecorator extends AbstractDiscountDecorator {

    @Any
    @Inject
    @Delegate
    private Product product;

    public String generateLabel() {
        product.setPrice(product.getPrice() * 0.25);
        product.setLabel(product.getLabel());
        return product.generateLabel();
    }

    // Not all methods shown

}
```

You must add the decorators to the `bean.xml` archive in the order that you want them to be invoked. Here, you declare that the `PriceDiscountDecorator` decorator should be invoked before the `BlackFridayDiscountDecorator` decorator.

```
<decorators>
    <class>com.devchronicles.decorator.PriceDiscountDecorator</class>
    <class>com.devchronicles.decorator.BlackFridayDiscountDecorator</class>
</decorators>
```

When the `generateLabel` method is invoked, a call chain is set up that includes the two decorators. The call to `generateLabel` is intercepted and delegated to the `generateLabel` method of the `PriceDiscountDecorator`. It calls `getPrice`, which will be intercepted and delegated to the `getPrice` method of `BlackFridayDiscountDecorator`, which in turn calls the `getPrice` method of its injected `Product` object. (This is the same instance that you injected into the `PriceDiscountDecorator` decorator.) This invocation is not intercepted because there are no more decorators declared for this interface, and it calls the `getPrice` method in the `Table` object. Once this call has finished, it returns down the call stack to the first `getPrice` method. This is called returning the price of the `Table`. The decorator reduces the price by 50 percent and calls the `setPrice` method. This call is delegated up the call chain until it reaches the `Table` object, where the new price is set. Then the call returns down the call chain.

The `getLabel` method is called and creates a call chain similar to that of the `getPrice` method.

Finally, the `generateLabel` method is invoked and intercepted by the `BlackFridayDiscountDecorator` decorator. The price is discounted by a further 25 percent, and a call chain similar to that set up by the `PriceDiscountDecorator` decorator is initiated.

The output to the console follows:

```
Label: 6.25, Dining Table (Discounted)
```

For the chain to continue unbroken, the `generateLabel` method must delegate to the `generateLabel` method of the delegate injected instance; otherwise, the chain is broken and only the first decorator is invoked.

All classes that implement the same interface as the one implemented by the delegate injection point are decorated, but only if those decorators are declared in `bean.xml`. This has two major implications:

➤ Decorators can be enabled and disabled at deployment time by editing the `bean.xml` file. This gives great flexibility over when and which decorators are invoked. For example, you can implement a price discount decorator only for the duration of the sales period and disable it when the period comes to an end. The flexibility of the deployment descriptor declaration means that this decorator can be easily enabled again if debugging information is later required.

➤ A decorator is automatically applied to classes that implement the same interface. This is efficient at the time of adding new classes because they are decorated with no additional coding. However, this could prove inconvenient if there is a requirement that not all classes of the same type are decorated. Luckily, there is a solution to this situation that involves using qualifiers to annotate only those classes that should be decorated.

To not decorate all classes of the same type, you need to create a custom qualifier and annotate the delegate injection point and the classes that you want decorated. You'll create a `Plate` product that implements the `Product` interface. Only this product must be discounted. To implement this requirement, you annotate it with a custom qualifier, thus excluding the other product from being decorated.

You create a custom qualifier and call it `@ClearanceSale`.

```
@Qualifier
@Retention(RUNTIME)
@Target({FIELD, PARAMETER, TYPE})
public @interface ClearanceSale {}
```

In Listing 7-11, you create the new implementation of the `Product` interface and annotate it with your custom qualifier.

LISTING 7-11: Class to be decorated is annotated with custom qualifier

```
@ClearanceSale
public class Plate implements Product {

    private String label = "Plate";
    private double price = 50.00;

    public void setLabel(String label) {
        this.label = label;
    }

    public void setPrice(double price) {
        this.price = price;
    }

    public String getLabel() {
        return label;
    }

    public double getPrice() {
        return price;
    }

    public String generateLabel() {
        return  price + ", " + label;
    }
}
```

Finally, you annotate the delegate injection point in the decorator that you want to invoke. In this case, choose the `PriceDiscountDecorator` decorator.

```
@ClearanceSale
@Any
@Inject
@Delegate
private Product product;
```

Only classes that are annotated with @ClearanceSale and implement the Product interface are injected into the delegate injection point of the PriceDiscountDecorator decorator; therefore, only your Plate class will be decorated. A delegate injection point can have as many qualifiers as is required, and it will only be bound to beans with the same qualifier.

Decorators Without XML Configuration

At deployment time, the CDI container scans all the JAR and WAR files in the application looking for bean.xml deployment descriptors. For those that it finds, it processes each one in turn, making the appropriate configurations. When it meets the <decorator/> descriptor, it enables the decorators for the archive in which the bean.xml file was found. It does not enable them for the whole application. This is a problem for developers who want the decorators to apply to all classes that implement the same interface regardless of where they are in the application. Since CDI 1.1,[4] it has been possible to enable decorators for the entire application by annotating the decorator class with @Priority and an Interceptor.Priority value. Here is an example of how to enable your two decorators for the whole application.

```
@Priority(Interceptor.Priority.APPLICATION)
@Decorator
public class PriceDiscountDecorator extends AbstractDiscountDecorator

@Priority(Interceptor.Priority.APPLICATION+10)
@Decorator
public class BlackFridayDiscountDecorator extends AbstractDiscountDecorator
```

Decorators annotated with a lower value priority are called first. In the preceding example, PriceDiscountDecorator is invoked before BlackFridayDiscountDecorator.

Decorators annotated with @Priority are called before decorators in the deployment descriptor. If a decorator is enabled in both, it is called twice. This may lead to undesirable results, so you need to ensure that decorators are enabled in only one way.

WHERE AND WHEN TO USE THE DECORATOR PATTERN

The decorator pattern dynamically adds behavior to an object at run time or when it is not possible or advisable to use subclassing (perhaps because it would create multiple subclasses). The pizza restaurant example shows how to add behavior to a pizza object at run time based on choices the customer made.

The functionality of an application programming interface (API) can be extended and improved by wrapping it in a decorator. Data streams are often decorated in this way. java .io.BufferedInputStream is a good example of a decorator wrapping a lower-level API and adding functionality to buffer an input stream.

In Java EE, decorators are implemented via Context Dependency Injection (CDI). You can use decorators to add new business behavior or any other functionality that can be wrapped around the original object. However, this design should be well documented and clearly implemented to allow for better maintainability.

The pluggability of decorators declared in the deployment descriptor makes it easy to enable and disable decorators without recompiling and redeploying. In a hot deployment environment, the server does not need to be restarted for the changes to the `bean.xml` to take effect. This makes it extremely easy to change the behavior of an application in a production environment with no interruption to service.

Qualifier use provides a finer grain of control over the execution of decorators than enabling/disabling them in the `bean.xml` deployment descriptor. You can use qualifiers to exclude certain implementations of an interface from being decorated or to apply different decorators to implementations of the same interface.

A decorator intercepts calls only to certain Java types. It is aware of all the semantics of that interface and can implement business logic. This makes it perfect for modeling business concerns that are identifiable for a certain interface type.

Decorators are often contrasted with interceptors. Interceptors intercept invocations of any Java type, but they are not semantically aware and therefore are not a suitable tool for modeling business concerns. Interceptors are used to implement cross-cutting concerns such as logging, security, and auditing that are not related to business logic.

The heavy use of decorators may introduce runtime bugs, a harder-to-understand code base, and a loss to the advantage of strongly typed static polymorphism. It may also introduce additional test cases. However, decorators can provide almost unlimited extensibility and a great interface for future implementations without breaking old code.

SUMMARY

In this chapter, you have seen how the implementation of the decorator pattern in Java EE is almost unrecognizable from its pre-Java EE ancestor. The object to be decorated is instantiated and injected by the container, and the decorators to be applied are determined by declarations made in the `bean.xml` deployment descriptor or via the strategic use of custom qualifiers.

The use of annotations and dependency injection has reduced the number of lines of code you must produce to implement a decorator solution and made it easier to introduce additional new classes, which are automatically decorated by virtue of the interface they implement.

You have seen how the decorator pattern has evolved into what is effectively a pluggable pattern that can be enabled and disabled while the application is in production with no loss to service. However, it maintains its original design principle of adding behavior or responsibilities to the objects it decorates.

EXERCISES

1. Extend the shop example given earlier by adding more discount decorators and introducing more qualifiers to gain finer control over which decorators are invoked for which concrete implementations.

2. Implement the decorator pattern on an existing API to add new functionality. For example: `java.io.FileInputStream`.

3. Create a decorator that adds behavior to a bank account system such that when the client withdraws more than a certain amount of cash, an SMS text message is sent to the client advising of the withdrawal.

NOTES

1. *Design Patterns: Elements of Reusable Object-Oriented Software* (Addison-Wesley, 1994): Erich Gamma, Richard Helm, Ralph Johnson, John Vlissides.
2. *Head First Design Patterns* (O'Reilly, 2004): Eric Freeman, Elisabeth Robson, Bert Bates, Kathy Sierra.
3. *Pyro:* `http://muse.com.tr/pyro.html`.
4. *CDI Specifications 1.1:* `http://docs.jboss.org/cdi/spec/1.1/cdi-spec.html#decorators`.

Aspect-Oriented Programming (Interceptors)

WROX.COM CODE DOWNLOADS FOR THIS CHAPTER

The wrox.com code download for this chapter is found at www.wrox.com/go/projavaeedesignpatterns on the Download Code tab. The code is in the Chapter 08 download and individually named according to the names throughout the chapter.

Aspect-oriented programming (AOP) is not a new concept. Its place in Java and third-party frameworks was secured from the early days of enterprise development. Despite this, it was not one of the classical design patterns listed in the GOF[1] book.

AOP introduced a new concept and paradigm to programming. The idea relies on basing the code execution order on aspects. Each aspect intercepts the program's execution and adds its own behavior before continuing with the call.

Aspects act like magic, adding further logic and behavior to the code at run time. However, this also brings an ambiguous and hard-to-follow code execution order that can often result in almost undebuggable code. AOP has many followers and fans, besides many haters.

Luckily, Java EE has a nice and clean implementation that can be helpful if it's used in the right way and context.

WHAT IS ASPECT-ORIENTED PROGRAMMING?

Aspect-oriented programming (AOP) aims to add behavior to existing code or applications to solve common concerns. It is fairly normal to receive a new logging or security request in the middle of the development cycle. Such requests may consume a huge amount of time in refactoring existing code even though the logging code is a bunch of repetitive lines. Such common concerns, whether they appear in the middle of the development cycle or in the design phase of the project, are called *cross-cutting concerns* and can be addressed with AOP.

AOP became a popular programming paradigm during the past decade. Although Java did not offer a full-fledged out-of-the-box solution, some well-implemented third-party frameworks offered AOP. AspectJ and Spring are widely accepted and have been used for a long time in Java-based projects. Java also had a similar but more basic approach with servlet filters, although it is limited to web requests. With servlet filters, any request or response can be intercepted, and any additional behavior can be added.

Java EE adopted AOP and introduced the *interceptor* concept. Each update to Java EE brought new functionalities and unleashed the full potential of AOP to the Java EE platform.

AOP is not classified as a design pattern but is accepted as a programming paradigm. Neither the GOF book nor *Head First Design Patterns*[2] discusses aspects. However, if either one did, an appropriate description would be "Provides a way to change execution behavior at run time (or compile time) to address cross-cutting concerns in the existing code base."

AOP relies on code injection during compile time or run time to add the desired behavior or functionality to each point of an existing code base that matches the given injection criteria. Frameworks that perform compile-time injection usually out-perform, but they produce class files that do not match the source code line by line because of the injected code. Runtime injection does not modify the source or class files and performs injection by intercepting calls and executing the desired code before or after the original execution order.

AOP can prove to be useful if it is necessary to add a repetitive action, such as logging or security, to a code base. The aspects can be turned on or off depending on the environment or phase of the project. Aspects can dynamically add the desired behavior to running code. They dynamically decorate the method calls just as the decorator pattern decorates objects.

WAR STORY

We had just finished development of a web application and were completing the final phase before going live. After completing functionality and user acceptance tests, we needed to submit the application to security trials. A team of security experts was hired to test our system for vulnerabilities. Because the application before ours was hacked and leaked important data, the security testing was taken very seriously.

We were pretty confident about our application, so we all grabbed some popcorn and watched the test phases. After a huge set of successful tests, one finally failed. The security guys had managed to capture the Hypertext Transfer Protocol (HTTP) request and change some parameters to get a response from the application. The issue was not huge because the middle tier had its own authorization system. Nevertheless, the tweaked request could access an authorized response.

To summarize, the client should call several services to access a resource. Let's say service A returns some IDs and Service B could be called with the IDs returned from Service A. Similarly, Service C could be called with one of the IDs returned from Service B. This means that an intruder could capture and insert a random B ID, which the user was authorized to query but didn't. In such a case, the client would bypass the standard call flow and access a resource.

Because the accessed information was a resource that the user authorized, the issue was not huge. Still, it was reported as a security flaw that bypassed regular flow; this got attention.

The application was already completed and tested, and we didn't really want to refactor the application. Instead, we came up with a brilliant idea: Because in each request the client needs to use an ID from the previous response, we could capture all returned IDs. If the requested ID was from the list of queried IDs, we could easily let it go or invalidate the session and force the user to log in again.

The idea was simple but effective, yet we didn't know how to implement it with minimal change. Because everything we wanted to do related to web requests, intercepting and validating them seemed like a good idea. Luckily, Java already offered a built-in solution, and we didn't need to use a fancy third-party framework.

The solution was to implement a servlet filter. This would cache the requested IDs in the response and check whether the next request had a valid ID from the list. We only needed to add a class file that acted as the servlet filter and an XML definition to put the servlet filter into action. The solution was pluggable and could be integrated with no problem. Also, it came with an option to turn it off in development environments.

The system not only passed all security tests, but it went beyond expectations. We could easily log and extract statistical data from request/response pairs. Best of all, the solution did not have an impact on the overall architecture and complexity of the system.

AOP can be a great tool to encapsulate common nonbusiness concerns. However, AOP can also be confusing if it adds behavior to business logic. Such implementations cause decentralized, distributed, and hard-to-test-and-debug business logic. The resulting code would be hard to maintain.

IMPLEMENTING AOP IN PLAIN CODE

Java SE does not offer out-of-the-box support for AOP. You can achieve plain AOP by using third-party frameworks such as AspectJ or Spring. Such frameworks used to depend on XML-only configuration; however, you can now achieve AOP through the use of annotations. Implementation and configuration of both frameworks are beyond the scope of this book, but they have a proven record and can easily be implemented. They both provide a valid alternative to the Java EE implementation.

However, Java web applications have the advantage of using servlets to intercept the request or the response, which works similarly to aspects. To implement a servlet filter, create a new class file and implement the servlet filter interface. Then provide an implementation of the doFilter() method, as shown in Listing 8-1.

LISTING 8-1: Simple implementation of a servlet filter

```
package com.devchronicles.interceptor.filter;

import java.io.IOException;
import java.util.ArrayList;
import java.util.List;

import javax.servlet.Filter;
import javax.servlet.FilterChain;
import javax.servlet.FilterConfig;
import javax.servlet.ServletException;
import javax.servlet.ServletRequest;
import javax.servlet.ServletResponse;
import javax.servlet.http.HttpServletRequest;
import javax.servlet.http.HttpServletResponse;

public class SecurityFilter implements Filter {

    @SuppressWarnings("unused")
    private FilterConfig filterConfig = null;

    @Override
    public void doFilter(ServletRequest request, ServletResponse response,
            FilterChain filterChain) throws IOException, ServletException {
        Log.info(((HttpServletRequest) request).getRemoteAddr());
        //perform some security check
    }

    @Override
    public void init(FilterConfig filterConfig) throws ServletException {
        this.filterConfig = filterConfig;
    }

}
```

The web container needs the configuration shown in Listing 8-2 to activate the servlet filter on given uniform resource locators (URLs). This is placed in the web application's web.xml file.

LISTING 8-2: Define the Servlet Filter

```xml
<?xml version="1.0" encoding="UTF-8"?>

<web-app xmlns:xsi="http://www.w3.org/2001/XMLSchema-instance"
xmlns="http://java.sun.com/xml/ns/javaee"
xmlns:web="http://java.sun.com/xml/ns/javaee/web-app_2_5.xsd"
xsi:schemaLocation="http://java.sun.com/xml/ns/javaee
http://java.sun.com/xml/ns/javaee/web-app_2_5.xsd" version="2.5">

<filter>
    <filter-name>LineSsoFilter</filter-name>
    <filter-class>com.devchronicles.interceptor.filter</filter-class>
</filter>

<filter-mapping>
    <filter-name>SecurityFilter</filter-name>
    <url-pattern>/*</url-pattern>
    </filter-mapping>

</web-app>
```

It is even easier to implement filters using Servlet 3.0 like in Listing 8-3 because it uses annotations and does not need XML configuration.

LISTING 8-3: Simple implementation of a servlet filter in Servlet 3.0

```java
package com.devchronicles.interceptor.filter;

import java.io.IOException;
import java.util.ArrayList;
import java.util.List;

import javax.servlet.ServletException;
import javax.servlet.ServletRequest;
import javax.servlet.ServletResponse;
import javax.servlet.http.HttpServletRequest;
import javax.servlet.http.HttpServletResponse;

import javax.servlet.Filter;
import javax.servlet.annotation.WebFilter;
import javax.servlet.annotation.WebInitParam;

@WebFilter(filterName = "TimeOfDayFilter", urlPatterns = {"/*"})
public class SecurityFilter implements Filter {

@Override
public void doFilter(ServletRequest request, ServletResponse response,
 FilterChain filterChain) throws IOException, ServletException {
    Log.info(((HttpServletRequest) request).getRemoteAddr());
    //perform some security check
 }

}
```

Servlet filters are easy-to-implement tools, but they're also powerful. However, the functionality is still limited to client server web requests. To intercept other method calls or to fine-tune the interception, you need a much more sophisticated approach.

ASPECTS IN JAVA EE, INTERCEPTORS

J2EE did not offer an out-of-the-box AOP solution but worked in harmony with third-party frameworks. Java EE 5 introduced interceptors, which resulted in an easy-to-use built-in aspect approach. However, the interceptor concept was limited to Enterprise JavaBeans (EJB) until Context and Dependency Injection (CDI) was introduced.

Interceptors in Java EE work in a similar way to aspects. Each interceptor addresses the concern and hosts the code block that contains the functionality to be added. The target to be decorated is called an *advice*. Each call to an advice within the scope of the interceptor is intercepted. The exact location of the aspect to be executed is called the *pointcut*.

Basic Java EE interceptors can only work on EJBs. Imagine an application consisting of hundreds of EJBs. The whole application can be configured to log all EJB calls by deploying an interceptor targeting all those EJBs.

Implementing interceptors in Java EE is straightforward. The first step is to create a new interceptor class and annotate it with the `@Interceptor` annotation. This class hosts the advice code. Any method annotated with `@AroundInvoke` is executed at the pointcut. However, there are some syntax rules regarding the pointcut method signature:

➤ Any pointcut method must return an object of type `Object` and have a parameter of type `InvocationContext`.

➤ Throw an exception.

You can use the `InvocationContext` parameter to access information about the current context as seen in Listing 8-4.

LISTING 8-4: Simple implementation of an interceptor

```
package com.devchronicles.interceptor;

import javax.interceptor.AroundInvoke;
import javax.interceptor.InvocationContext;

@Interceptor
public class SecurityInterceptor {

    @AroundInvoke
    public Object doSecurityCheck(InvocationContext context) throws Exception{

        //Do some security checks!

        Logger.getLogger("SecurityLog")
```

```
.info(context.getMethod().getName()+ "is accessed!");

        return context.proceed();
    }
}
```

To put the interceptor class into action, you must annotate the target advice with the
@Interceptors annotation as in Listing 8-5. The @Interceptors annotation would only be used in
an EJB or MDB (Message Driven Bean).

LISTING 8-5: Simple implementation of target advice

```java
package com.devchronicles.interceptor;

import javax.ejb.Stateless;
import javax.ejb.TransactionAttribute;
import javax.ejb.TransactionAttributeType;
import javax.enterprise.event.Event;
import javax.inject.Inject;
import javax.interceptor.Interceptors;


@Interceptors(SecurityInterceptor.class)
@Stateless
@TransactionAttribute(TransactionAttributeType.REQUIRED)
public class SomeBusinessService {

  public void startService(){
    //Complex business logic
    Logger.getLogger("AppLog").info("done...");
  }

  public void startAnotherService(){
    //Complex business logic
    Logger.getLogger("AppLog").info("done again...");
  }
}
```

The Interceptors annotation is flexible. You can also use it at both the class and the method
levels. The Interceptors annotation also supports multiple interceptor inputs, which enable
multiple interceptors on the target advice. Listing 8-5 uses class-level interceptors, which means
that the Security interceptor will intercept either of the service calls. If you do not want the
interceptor to cover all method calls in the class, you can use *method-level* annotations, as
shown in Listing 8-6.

LISTING 8-6: Implementation of class-level interceptors

```java
package com.devchronicles.interceptor;

import javax.ejb.Stateless;
import javax.ejb.TransactionAttribute;
```

continues

LISTING 8-6 *(continued)*

```java
import javax.ejb.TransactionAttributeType;
import javax.enterprise.event.Event;
import javax.inject.Inject;
import javax.interceptor.Interceptors;

@Stateless
@TransactionAttribute(TransactionAttributeType.REQUIRED)
public class SomeBusinessService {

    @Interceptors(SecurityInterceptor.class)
    public void startService(){
        //Complex business logic
        Logger.getLogger("AppLog").info("done...");
    }

    public void startAnotherService(){
        //Complex business logic
        Logger.getLogger("AppLog").info("done again...");
    }
}
```

This time only calls to the `startService()` method are intercepted, unlike in Listing 8-5, in which all methods of the class were intercepted. You should annotate each method separately.

Using `@Interceptor`, `@Interceptors` with `@AroundInvoke` unleashes a powerful tool that solves cross-cutting concerns in an AOP approach. Yet interceptors offer easy annotation-based implementation with no boilerplate code.

You can use the `InvocationContext` interface to extract information about the context or interact with the *advice* context. Following are some of the more useful methods:

METHOD	DESCRIPTION
`public Object getTarget();`	Return to the target advice.
`public Method getMethod();`	Return the executed method from the advice.
`public Object[] getParameters();`	Access target advice method's parameters.
`public void setParameters(Object[]);`	Set target advice method's parameters.
`public java.util.Map<String,Object> getContextData();`	Access context data.
`public Object proceed() throws Exception;`	Continue execution.

In Listing 8-7, you can access the method name. Also, you can check whether the interceptor had authorized the access before; if it has not, you can authorize the user for that method.

LISTING 8-7: Accessing information in the InvocationContext

```
package com.devchronicles.interceptor;

import javax.interceptor.AroundInvoke;
import javax.interceptor.InvocationContext;

@Interceptor
public class SecurityInterceptor {

  @AroundInvoke
  public Object doSecurityCheck(InvocationContext context) throws Exception{

    //Do some security checks!
    Logger.getLogger("SecurityLog").info(context.getMethod()
                            .getName()+ "is accessed!");
    String user = context.getContextData.get("user");

    if (user==null){
        user=(String)context.getParameters()[0];
        context.getContextData.put("user", user)'
    }

    return context.proceed();
  }

}
```

Interceptor Life Cycle

You can capture the interceptor's life-cycle phases easily with the help of life-cycle annotations. Unlike extending and overriding, using life-cycle annotations hooks any function to the appropriate phase. The available life-cycle annotations are @PostConstruct, @PrePassivate, @PostActivate, and @PreDestroy. Listing 8-8 shows how to hook up using interceptor life-cycle methods.

LISTING 8-8: Hooking the interceptor's life-cycle phases

```
package com.devchronicles.interceptor;

import javax.interceptor.AroundInvoke;
import javax.interceptor.InvocationContext;

@Interceptor
public class SecurityInterceptor {

    @AroundInvoke
    public Object doSecurityCheck(InvocationContext context)
                            throws Exception{
        //Do some security checks!
        Logger.getLogger("SecurityLog").info(context.getMethod()
                                .getName()+ "is accessed!");
```

continues

LISTING 8-8 *(continued)*

```
            String user = context.getContextData.get("user");
            if (user==null){
                user=(String)context.getParameters()[0];
                context.getContextData.put("user", user)'
            }

            return context.proceed();
        }

    @PostConstruct
    public void onStart(){
        Logger.getLogger("SecurityLog").info("Activating");
    }

    @PreDestroy
    public void onShutdown(){
        Logger.getLogger("SecurityLog").info("Deactivating");
    }
}
```

Because the hooks rely on annotations, method names do not make a difference; you can use any name.

Default-Level Interceptors

Marking the target advice with Interceptors annotation provides an easy implementation and setup, but the nature of AOP usually asks for more. Most scenarios require the interceptor to perform its operation targeting all advices. Imagine adding interceptors for logging or security—targeting only a subset of EJB wouldn't work. Also, annotating each EJB can become cumbersome and can easily lead to human error.

Java EE offers default-level interceptors to target all or subsets of EJB matching the naming scheme provided. Unlike in the previous example, to implement default-level interceptors, you need XML configuration:

```xml
<ejb-jar...>
  <interceptors>
      <interceptor>
          <interceptor-class>
              com.devchronicles.SecurityInterceptor
          </interceptor-class>
      </interceptor>
  </interceptors>
  <assembly-descriptor>
      <interceptor-binding>
          <ejb-name>*</ejb-name>
          <interceptor-class>
              <interceptor-class>
                  com.devchronicles.SecurityInterceptor
              </interceptor-class>
          </interceptor-class>
      </interceptor-binding>
  </assembly-descriptor>
</ejb-jar>
```

The first part of the XML file lists the interceptors; then the interceptor bindings need to be declared. This is done in the assembly description part, which can accept a wildcard (*) that applies to all or a specific name to create the binding between the interceptors and the EJB. The order of the interceptors listed also determines the execution order. The interceptors listed in the EJB-JAR file apply only to EJB in the same module.

Interceptor Order

If more than one interceptor has been defined for an advice, the order of the execution will be from the most general to the most specific case. This means that default-level interceptors will be executed before class-level interceptors, which will be followed by method-level interceptors.

This behavior is expected; nevertheless, the order of same-level interceptors can be a bit more confusing. If there is more than one default-level interceptor, the order in the EJB-JAR file determines the order of the execution of the interceptors.

```
<ejb-jar...>
  <interceptors>
    <interceptor>
      <interceptor-class>
        com.devchronicles.SecurityInterceptor
      </interceptor-class>
      <interceptor-class>
        com.devchronicles.AnotherInterceptor
      </interceptor-class>
    </interceptor>
  </interceptors>
  <assembly-descriptor>
    <interceptor-binding>
      <ejb-name>OrderBean</ejb-name>
      <interceptor-order>
        <interceptor-class>
          com.devchronicles.SecurityInterceptor
        </interceptor-class>
      </interceptor-order>
      <interceptor-class>
        com.devchronicles.AnotherInterceptor
      </interceptor-class>
    </interceptor-binding>
  </assembly-descriptor>
</ejb-jar>
```

When there is more than one class-level interceptor, the interceptors follow the order in which they are listed in the @Interceptors annotation:

```
@Interceptors(SecurityInterceptor.class, AnotherInterceptor.class)
@Stateless
@TransactionAttribute(TransactionAttributeType.REQUIRED)
public class SomeBusinessService {
    public void startService(){
    // ...
```

Finally, if more than one method-level interceptor is present, again, the interceptors follow the order they are listed in the `@Interceptors` annotation:

```
@Stateless
@TransactionAttribute(TransactionAttributeType.REQUIRED)
public class SomeBusinessService {
    @Interceptors(SecurityInterceptor.class, AnotherInterceptor.class)
    public void startService(){
    // ...
```

If you need to tweak the default ordering, you can do so by custom configuration within the EJB-JAR XML. The following overrides the interceptor order and provides a custom ordering:

```
<ejb-jar...>
  <interceptors>
      <interceptor>
          <interceptor-class>
              com.devchronicles.SecurityInterceptor
          </interceptor-class>
      </interceptor>
  </interceptors>
  <assembly-descriptor>
      <interceptor-binding>
          <ejb-name>OrderBean</ejb-name>
          <interceptor-order>
              <interceptor-class>
                  com.devchronicles.SecurityInterceptor
              </interceptor-class>
          </interceptor-order>
          <interceptor-class>
              com.devchronicles.AnotherInterceptor
          </interceptor-class>
          <method>
                  <method-name>startService</method-name>
          </method>
      </interceptor-binding>
  </assembly-descriptor>
</ejb-jar>
```

There might be exceptional cases in which the interceptors need to be disabled. You can disable interceptors with annotations as seen in Listing 8-9. Java EE offers two different annotations to disable default and class-level interceptors separately.

LISTING 8-9: Disabling the interceptors

```
package com.devchronicles.interceptor;

import javax.ejb.Stateless;
import javax.ejb.TransactionAttribute;
import javax.ejb.TransactionAttributeType;
import javax.enterprise.event.Event;
import javax.inject.Inject;
```

```
import javax.interceptor.Interceptors;

@ExcludeDefaultInterceptors
@ExcludeClassInterceptors
@Stateless
@TransactionAttribute(TransactionAttributeType.REQUIRED)
public class SomeBusinessService {

    public void startService(){
        //Complex business logic
        Logger.getLogger("AppLog").info("done...");
    }

    public void startAnotherService(){
        //Complex business logic
        Logger.getLogger("AppLog").info("done again...");
    }
}
```

Still, the example given is only valid in EJB and MDBs, which may not be enough for all cases. Thanks to CDI, it is not hard to achieve more.

CDI Interceptors

Before CDI, interceptors were applicable only for EJB and MDBs. CDI unleashed a huge power and transformed interceptors into an AOP-capable feature that works on any object.

Implementing CDI interceptors is straightforward and quite flexible. First, you need to specify a binding. A binding is a custom annotation annotated with @InterceptorBinding.

```
@InterceptorBinding
@Target({TYPE, METHOD})
@Retention(RUNTIME)
public @interface Secure {}
```

The @InterceptorBinding is used to bind interceptors with the target code. Next, you can implement and annotate the interceptor with the custom binding. CDI interceptors are implemented the same way as the EJB interceptors, the only significant difference being the use of the binding annotation which can be seen in Listing 8-10

LISTING 8-10: Binding an Interceptor with @Secure

```
package com.devchronicles.interceptor;

import javax.interceptor.AroundInvoke;
import javax.interceptor.InvocationContext;

@Secure
@Interceptor
public class SecurityInterceptor {

    @AroundInvoke
    public Object doSecurityCheck(InvocationContext context) throws Exception{
```

continues

LISTING 8-10 *(continued)*

```
        //Do some security checks!
        Logger.getLogger("SecurityLog").info(context.getMethod()
                                    .getName()+ "is accessed!");
        String user = context.getContextData.get("user");
        if (user == null){
            user = (String)context.getParameters()[0];
            context.getContextData.put("user", user)'
        }

        return context.proceed();
    }

    @PostConstruct
    public void onStart(){
        Logger.getLogger("SecurityLog").info("Activating");
    }
    @PreDestroy
    public void onShutdown(){
        Logger.getLogger("SecurityLog").info("Deactivating");
    }
}
```

Just like the EJB interceptors, the @Interceptor annotation needs to be used to promote the class file to an interceptor. The @Secure annotation binds the interceptor. Finally, the @AroundInvoke annotation marks the method to be executed during intercepted calls.

The next step is to implement the annotation on an advice, as shown in Listing 8-11.

LISTING 8-11: Implementing the @Secure on an advice

```
package com.devchronicles.interceptor;

import javax.interceptor.Interceptors;

@Secure
public class SomeBusinessBean {

    public void startService(){
        //Complex business logic
        Logger.getLogger("AppLog").info("done...");
    }

    public void startAnotherService(){
        //Complex business logic
        Logger.getLogger("AppLog").info("done again...");
    }
}
```

CDI interceptors require one additional step of declaring the interceptors in the `beans.xml` file. This is one of the rare cases in which you need to use XML configuration; it's used to determine the execution order of the interceptors.

Interceptor bindings can include other interceptor bindings that wrap multiple bindings together. The CDI container is not started if the `beans.xml` file is missing:

```
<beans xmlns="http://java.sun.com/xml/ns/javaee"
xmlns:xsi="http://www.w3.org/2001/XMLSchema-instance"
xsi:schemaLocation=" http://java.sun.com/xml/ns/javaee
http://java.sun.com/xml/ns/javaee/beans_1_0.xsd">
   <interceptors>
       <class> com.devchronicles.interceptor.SecurityInterceptor</class>
       <class> com.devchronicles.interceptor.SomeOtherInterceptor</class>
   </interceptors>
</beans>
```

Although the declaration order of the binding annotations may imply a sense of execution order, in reality it has no effect. The execution order of the interceptor depends on the declaration order in the `beans.xml` file.

Mixing CDI and EJB interceptors may create ambiguity in the ordering. As a rule, EJB interceptors execute before CDI interceptors do.

Intercepting methods creates complexity, but creating multiple bindings and mixing CDI and EBJ interceptors brings this complexity to the next level. Complex interceptor structures may expose a complex application architecture for developers who are not familiar with the code.

WHERE AND WHEN TO USE INTERCEPTORS

AOP is a popular programming paradigm that can help to implement and encapsulate cross-cutting concerns. In many cases, AOP can really shine. Logging, auditing, security, and other repeating nonbusiness behavior are good candidates.

Interceptors in Java EE are powerful tools that allow you to implement AOP without the need for a third-party framework. With the introduction of CDI interceptors, Java EE has become more complete and capable. Implementing an interceptor may require some XML configuration, unlike other patterns listed in this book. However, the configuration is only limited to provide ordering, which other patterns such as decorators may also require.

Interceptors can address many cross-cutting concerns. They provide a clean implementation while encapsulating the common concern. However, interceptors can be troublesome if they change business behavior. If this happens, the business logic is distributed between the class and the interceptor. The business method becomes unreadable and misleading because it doesn't expose the whole logic. Additionally, it unnecessarily complicates the architecture and application flow. Besides, debugging is almost impossible and complicated.

Readability and self-documenting code is an important aim, and misuse of interceptors can cause great harm if it consists of business logic. However, using interceptors for nonbusiness and repeating behavior can simplify the business methods and help greatly.

As a general rule, avoid using interceptors for injecting business logic or changing the execution behavior. Interceptors are great when you need repetitive work that covers some methods or classes.

SUMMARY

AOP is a popular subject that has many supporters but also many enemies. As expected, it is not a panacea that solves all problems. Aspects can greatly reduce code readability and complicate the overall application flow if not used properly.

However, aspects can be magical tools that implement additional behavior to the existing code base with minimal effort. You can easily turn them on or off depending on the running time environment. For example, you can turn off a logging aspect during development and put it into action in the test environment.

Java EE offers simple interceptors that support annotations and need little XML configuration, except in special cases. You can use interceptors both in EJB and MDB contexts either at the class or the method levels. You can also declare interceptors at a default level, which targets all EJBs matching the given criteria. The default level and ordering needs some configuration to be done in the EJB-JAR XML file.

CDI adds great extensibility and functionality to interceptors. You can easily customize CDI interceptors and use them in a cleaner way with the `@InterceptorBinding` annotation. You can use interceptor bindings to wrap other interceptor bindings, forming a chain of interceptors to execute. CDI interceptors do need minimal XML configuration to help the CDI container determine the execution order.

EJB and CDI interceptors work alone or together in harmony. They offer all the functionality needed to implement AOP without a third-party framework.

The proper use of interceptors creates beautifully crafted applications with magical execution flow. When it is time to decide to implement interceptors, make sure they don't change business flow and contain application logic.

NOTES

1. *Design Patterns: Elements of Reusable Object-Oriented Software* (Addison-Wesley, 1994): Erich Gamma, Richard Helm, Ralph Johnson, John Vlissides.
2. *Head First Design Patterns* (O'Reilly, 2004): Eric Freeman, Elisabeth Robson, Bert Bates, Kathy Sierra.

Asynchronous

WROX.COM CODE DOWNLOADS FOR THIS CHAPTER

The wrox.com code download for this chapter is found at www.wrox.com/go/
projavaeedesignpatterns on the Download Code tab. The code is in the Chapter 09
download and individually named according to the names throughout the chapter.

Although asynchronous programming is not always listed as a design pattern, it has been
a popular and important programming model for the past decade. The asynchronous
programming model relies on multithreading and executing the given functionality in a
separate thread. Not only do multithreaded environments and programming languages take
advantage of asynchronous programming techniques, but single-threaded platforms, such
as the popular server-side JavaScript platform NodeJS, make good use of asynchronous
programming principles.

> **NOTE** *The asynchronous pattern is also referred to as* nonblocking method
> execution *because the invoked method does not block the caller.*

Java was designed to support multiple threads from its start. However, it failed to provide a simple approach to making asynchronous calls. The `Future<T>` interface, which was introduced in Java 5, was Java's first attempt at implementing asynchronous programming, but it was cumbersome and tricky to use. Subsequent versions of Java introduced the `@Asynchronous` annotation. The asynchronous servlet provided a much better set of tools to aid in asynchronous programming.

WHAT IS ASYNCHRONOUS PROGRAMMING?

The asynchronous programming pattern is a special and well-integrated case of multiple threads. Due to the nature of threads, multithreading models tend to need notification systems and depend on boilerplate code to initiate threads.

Asynchronous calls are used even in single-threaded environments like Node.JS. Almost all user interface (UI) frameworks use asynchronous execution to keep UI active and responsive. The first "A" of AJAX,[1] which powered the Web 2.0 movement, stands for asynchronous.

However, asynchronous programming can be useful in places other than user interfaces, typically on the sever side. Neither J2SE nor J2EE offered a built-in easy implementation for asynchronous programming. With Java 5, the Concurrency Framework, based on JSR166, was released. JSR166 included many utilities that made asynchronous programming possible, easier, and better controlled. The `Future<V>` interface also provided a way to help developers to implement asynchronous method execution.

Meanwhile, Spring offered asynchronous method calls, which are enabled with annotations. Java EE did not include such a convenient solution until version 6.0. The `@Asynchronous` annotation was introduced with Java EE 6 and offered an easy way to implement asynchronous method execution.

Asynchronous Pattern

Asynchronous programming is not listed as a design pattern in either the GoF[2] book or in the *Head First Design Patterns*[3] book. If it was, its description might be "Provides a way to invoke a method without blocking the invoker."

The nature of method execution is to block the caller until the called method finishes its execution. This behavior is straightforward and expected but may not be desired in all cases. Almost all UI frameworks and web platforms rely on nonblocking requests.

> **WAR STORY**
>
> I was given the task of developing the customer services web portal for a telecommunications company. We had implemented a detailed logging infrastructure while developing the portal. We did not log to a database to ensure

that the logging was fast and failsafe in moments when the database was not available. We were successful in developing a system that had fast response times and was reliable. We were pleased with what we had achieved.

Then we were asked to log each user's actions to a database table along with some specific user-related data. The database we were asked to use had a reputation for being slow and for regularly crashing and restarting. This was bad news for our fast and reliable logging system. We now had to refactor our system, taking into consideration the unreliability of the database. Imagine what would happen if a user interaction was being logged at the same time the database went down. The synchronous call to the logging system would block the response to the user until it either regained connection or timed out. The user would have to wait, which was unacceptable.

We did not want the user to wait for the database to respond and expose a database error to the front end, especially considering that we were only logging statistics. After implementing and testing all the DAO classes, we added the @Asynchronous annotation and prepared to go live.

As usual, we were confident in our well-tested deployment package, so we decided to go home to sleep rather than spending the night with the server administrators who were doing the deployment. The next morning we received an e-mail advising us that the application was live.

Soon we discovered that our server's log files were full of errors, showing that the database connection had been unavailable. We contacted the server administrators and quickly discovered that the database admins had forgotten to create the log tables in the live database. The tables were quickly created, and all was well until the database started to suffer from performance-related issues and had frequent server restarts (as was expected given its reputation).

Our application had failed to persist some noncritical logs but never faltered in its performance. Every time there was a problem with the database and the logging failed, the user had already finished what he was doing and didn't notice that the logging had failed, thanks to the use of asynchronously calling the logging functionality.

Asynchronous programming is a great tool to use when separating tasks that do not need to interact with each other.

The asynchronous pattern relies on the fire and forget approach where an operation is done in parallel or in a way not blocking the executor thread, and the result is checked when it is ready. Usually the asynchronous approach makes use of parallel execution. It may not be accurately reflected with a class diagram but may be better shown with a flow diagram. Figure 9-1 demonstrates several asynchronous execution flows.

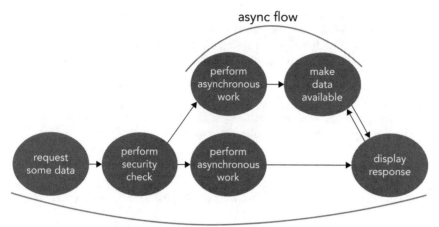

classic asynchronous request/response flow

FIGURE 9-1: Asynchronous flow diagram

IMPLEMENTING ASYNCHRONOUS PATTERN IN PLAIN CODE

Java has supported threads that you can easily use for asynchronous code execution from its initial design:

```
public class AsyncRunnable implements Runnable {

    public void run() {
        System.out.println("Running!");
    }
}
```

To execute the `Runnable` class, initialize it in a thread and invoke the `run` method by calling the `start()` method on the newly created thread:

```
(new Thread(new AsyncRunnable())).start();
```

Although the preceding example is the preferred way to start a thread process, another approach is to extend the `thread` class and override the `run()` method:

```
public class AsyncThread extends Thread {

    public void run() {
        System.out.println("Running!");
    }

}
```

To execute the class, instantiate it and then call the `start()` method:

```
(new HelloThread()).start();
```

Two essential operations are commonly used when dealing with threads: `sleep()` and `join()`. Both operations throw an `InterruptedException`.

The `sleep()` method lets the thread sleep for a specified period, given in milliseconds. The following code snippet puts the current thread into the sleep state for one second:

```
Thread.sleep(1000);
```

The `join()` method makes one thread wait for another thread's execution to finish. Consider a thread, t1, that needs a resource from another thread, t2. To make t1 wait for t2 to finish, join t1 to t2, as shown in the following code snippet:

```
t2.join();
```

One of the most well-known and widely used approaches to programming asynchronously in Java is using the `Future<V>` interface. This interface enables the use of a proxy object, which offers a reference for the future object. Because the concurrency framework does not offer annotation-based support for asynchronous execution, the `Future` interface is mostly coupled with an `ExecutorService`, which is part of the concurrency framework.

The following example uses an executor service to complete a task while it returns a reference to the `Future` interface with the appropriate generic type:

```
ExecutorService executor = Executors.newSingleThreadExecutor();

Future<String> reference = executor.submit(
    new Callable<String>() {
        public String call() {
            return "Hello!!";
        }
    }
);
//..
if (reference.isDone())
    System.out.println(reference.get());
```

The `FutureTask` class is an implementation of the `Future<T>` interface, which implements the runnable interface and can be executed directly:

```
FutureTask<String> reference = new FutureTask<String>(
    new Callable<String>() {
        public String call() {
            return "Hello!!";
        }
    }
);

executor.execute(reference);
```

You can cancel this execution by calling the `cancel(boolean mayInterruptIfRunning)` method. If the `mayInterruptIfRunning` parameter is set to `true`, calls to the method `SessionContext.wasCancelled()` return true. Otherwise, a call to the `SessionContext.wasCancelled()` method returns `false`. To check the status of cancelation, you can use the `isCancelled()` method, which returns `true` if a cancelation is successful.

The concurrency framework JSR-133 offers great tools for threads and concurrent programming, such as `BlockingQueues`. These topics are beyond the scope of this chapter. See the book *Java Concurrency in Practice*[4] for further reading. The Fork/Join Framework, which was introduced in Java 7, also offers a huge change in favor of asynchronous and parallel programming in Java.

ASYNCHRONOUS PROGRAMMING IN JAVA EE

Because J2EE failed to offer built-in support for the asynchronous programming paradigms (except for Timer), third-party frameworks, such as Spring and Quartz, stepped in to fill this gap. This deficit was corrected in Java EE 5; it was the first Java version to support the asynchronous programming pattern out of the box.

Asynchronous Beans

Java EE supports asynchronous programming in several ways. The simplest way to implement the asynchronous pattern in Java EE is, not surprisingly, via the application of an annotation. Annotating a method with `@Asynchronous` is enough to advise the Java EE container to asynchronously execute the invoked method in a separate thread. To see the asynchronous annotation in action, go back to the singleton logging bean example in Chapter 4, "Singleton Pattern" and add the asynchronous annotation to change its default behavior. Listing 9-1 shows an example of an asynchronous bean.

LISTING 9-1: An example of an asynchronous bean

```
package com.devchronicles.asynchronous;

import javax.annotation.PostConstruct;
import javax.ejb.Singleton;
import javax.ejb.Startup;
import java.util.logging.Logger;
import javax.ejb.Asynchronous;


@Startup
@Singleton
public class MyLoggingBean {

    private Logger logger;

    @PostConstruct
    public void start(){
        logger = Logger.getLogger("MyGlobalLogger");
        logger.info("Well, I started first!!!");
    }


    public void logInfo(String msg){
```

```
        logger.info(msg);
    }

    @Asynchronous
    public void logAsync(String msg){
        logger.info(msg);
    }
}
```

The `logAsync()` method, unlike its `logInfo()` counterpart, is executed asynchronously. To observe asynchronous behavior, add `Thread.sleep()` calls:

```
public void logInfo(String msg) {
  logger.info("Entering sync log");

  try {
      Thread.sleep(1000);
  } catch (InterruptedException e) {}

  logger.info(msg);
}


@Asynchronous
public void logAsync(String msg {
  logger.info("Entering async log");

  try {
      Thread.sleep(13000);
  } catch (InterruptedException e) {}

  logger.info(msg);
}
```

Finally, create a new bean to call both functions in order, as shown in Listing 9-2.

LISTING 9-2: Refactor of Listing 9.1 to include both functions

```
package com.devchronicles.asynchronous;

import javax.annotation.PostConstruct;
import javax.ejb.Singleton;
import javax.ejb.Startup;


@Startup
@Singleton
public class TestLogging {

    @EJB
    MyLoggingBean logBean;

    @PostConstruct
```

continues

LISTING 9-2: *(continued)*

```
public void testLoggers(){

    System.out.println("call async");
    logBean.logAsync("Log Async");

    System.out.println("call sync");
    logBean.logInfo("Log Sync");

    System.out.println("finished");

    }
}
```

A typical console output would be as follows:

```
> call async

> Entering async log

> call sync

> Entering sync log

> Log Sync

> finished

> Log Async
```

After you execute the `testLoggers()` method, call the `logAsync()` and `logSync()` methods. Both methods let their execution thread sleep for the given length of time. As can be seen from the console output, the `async()` method was called and went into a long sleep but did not lock the execution of the `sync()` method. The `sync()` method sleeps for a while but returns control to the caller method and prints `finished`. Finally, the `async()` method wakes up and finishes logging by printing `Log Async` to the console.

This example clearly shows that the asynchronous call does not stop the caller thread, nor does it stop the `sync()` method. However, when the `sync()` method goes into the sleep state, the caller method waits until the sleep ends. The `@Asynchronous` annotation is an easy way to implement asynchronous behavior and can be added to almost any method at any time during and after development.

Asynchronous Servlets

So far, you have seen that you can convert any method of a bean to an asynchronous method. Now you'll look at how to make a servlet act asynchronously. Without asynchronous support in servlets, it is hard to respond to the asynchronous web challenge.

The Servlet 3.0 specification (JSR 315) made huge improvements to the Java web application programming interfaces (APIs). With JSR 315, the servlet specification was updated (after a long wait) to support an asynchronous execution model, easy configuration, pluggability, and other minor enhancements.

Asynchronous servlets rely on a basic improvement in Hypertext Transfer Protocol (HTTP) 1.1, which enabled persistent connections. In HTTP 1.0, each connection is used to send and receive only a single request and response couple; however, HTTP 1.1 allowed web applications to keep the connection alive and to send multiple requests. On a standard implementation, the Java back end would need a separate thread constantly attached to the HTTP connection. However, Java nonblocking I/O (NIO) APIs recycle threads between active requests, thanks to the new NIO capability. Today all web servers compatible with the Servlet 3.0 specification have built-in support for Java NIO. Why do you need such behavior from servlets? The nature of back-end systems involves lengthy operations such as connecting to other servers, performing complex calculations, and making transactional database operations. However, the nature of web pages requires quite the opposite. Web users expect fast response times and a functional UI even if back-end operations are completed. AJAX addressed this issue for the browser and started the Web 2.0 revolution.

Servlet 3.0 introduced the `startAsync()` method, which enabled asynchronous operations. Listing 9-3 shows an example.

LISTING 9-3: An example of the startAsync() method

```
package com.devchronicles.asynchronous;

import java.io.*;
import javax.servlet.*;
import javax.servlet.annotation.*;
import javax.servlet.http.*;

@WebServlet(urlPatterns={"/async"}, asyncSupported=true)
public class AsyncServlet extends HttpServlet {

@Override
protected void doGet(HttpServletRequest req, HttpServletResponse res)
                    throws IOException, ServletException {

    final AsyncContext asyncContext = req.startAsync();
    final String data;

    asyncContext.addListener(new AsyncListener() {

        @Override
        public void onComplete(AsyncEvent event) throws IOException {
            AsyncContext asyncContext = event.getAsyncContext();
            asyncContext().getWriter().println(data);
        }

        @Override
        public void onTimeout(AsyncEvent event) throws IOException {
            // Code not shown for brevity
        }

        @Override
        public void onError(AsyncEvent event) throws IOException {
            // Code not shown for brevity
        }
```

continues

LISTING 9-3: *(continued)*

```java
        @Override
        public void onStartAsync(AsyncEvent event) throws IOException {
            // Code not shown for brevity
        }
    });

    new Thread() {
        @Override
        public void run() {
            asyncContext.complete();
        }
    }.start();


    res.getWriter().write("Results:");
    //Read data from database
    data = "Queried data…";
    //sleep thread for some time…
    }
}
```

This servlet prints `Results:` and later prints retrieved data from the database, which is a simple string in this scenario. You need to initialize a separate thread. AsyncListener's `onComplete` method is executed only when the execution completes. Several other life cycle methods exist in the AsyncListener:

➤ **onStartAsync**—executes when the asynchronous context starts

➤ **onTimeOut**—executes only if a timeout occurs

➤ **onError**—executes only if an error is received

The Servlet 3.1 specification provided an easier way to implement asynchronous servlets by using managed thread pools and the executor service. The example in Listing 9-4 uses a `ManagedThreadFactory` to create a new thread.

LISTING 9-4: An example that uses ManagedThreadFactory

```java
package com.devchronicles.asynchronous;

import java.io.*;
import javax.servlet.*;
import javax.servlet.annotation.*;
import javax.servlet.http.*;

@WebServlet(urlPatterns="/async", asyncSupported=true)
public class AsyncServlet extends HttpServlet {

    @Resource
    private ManagedThreadFactory factory;

    @Override
```

```
    protected void doGet(HttpServletRequest req, HttpServletResponse res)
                        throws ServletException, IOException {

        final AsyncContext asyncContext = req.startAsync();
        final PrintWriter writer = res.getWriter();

        Thread thread = factory.newThread(new Runnable() {

            @Override
            public void run() {
                writer.println("Complete!");
                asyncContext.complete();
            }
        });

    thread.start();
    }
}
```

This example creates a new thread that hosts the time-consuming process and finally calls a complete function from `asyncContext`. `ManagedThreadFactory` serves as an available thread from the pool that you need to start explicitly.

Another approach is to submit the asynchronous runnable to `ManagedExecutorService` instead of creating and starting the thread in the servlet. Delegating threading issues to `ExecutorService` provides cleaner code, as you'll see in Listing 9-5.

LISTING 9-5: An example that delegates to the ExecutorService

```
package com.devchronicles.asynchronous;

import java.io.*;
import javax.servlet.*;
import javax.servlet.annotation.*;
import javax.servlet.http.*;

@WebServlet(urlPatterns="/async", asyncSupported=true)
public class AsyncServlet extends HttpServlet {

    @Resource
    private ManagedExecutorService executor;

    @Override
    protected void doGet(HttpServletRequest req, HttpServletResponse res)
    throws ServletException, IOException {

        final AsyncContext asyncContext = req.startAsync();
        final PrintWriter writer = res.getWriter();

        executor.submit(new Runnable() {
          @Override
```

continues

LISTING 9-5: *(continued)*

```
        public void run() {
          writer.println("Complete!");
          asyncContext.complete();
        }
      });
    }
  }
```

Although it's just one line less than the previous listing, Listing 9-5 delegates the creation and starting of the thread to the `ExecutorService` and only deals with servlet-specific code.

Asynchronous servlets are easier to understand and code and have an immediate effect on runtime behavior because it directly switches to the asynchronous execution model. Asynchronous servlets provide a clean implementation without a lot of boilerplate code.

WHERE AND WHEN TO USE ASYNCHRONOUS PROGRAMMING

You can use the asynchronous pattern almost anywhere where it is required to return a response before all the execution is complete. This approach can vary from executing the less important functions of the application asynchronously, such as logging or keeping the user informed about a time-consuming operation. Asynchronous programming makes the critical execution path shorter while delegating subtasks to other threads. The result is better response times.

Asynchronous annotation is a simple way to implement asynchronous methods or convert existing ones. Each method marked with the asynchronous annotation runs in a separate thread without locking the current thread's execution. This behavior is a perfect match for conditions that do not affect the main execution cycle but need to be performed on the back end. Examples include logging and maintenance resources.

You can use asynchronous servlets in almost all modern web apps. Asynchronous servlets provide nonblocking asynchronous behavior without a special need for AJAX. Asynchronous servlets can help when a server-based push operation is needed, such as updating information or delivering a message.

Because each asynchronous execution requires a new thread, the Java Virtual Machine (JVM) needs to perform more context switches as more asynchronous methods are implemented. A large number of context switches cause thread starvation and result in poorer performance than a synchronous implementation.

Imagine that you are reading one book. Between reads, you must remember the story, the characters, and the last page you've read. If you're reading two books at the same time, you may finish the second shorter book without needing to finish the longer one you started. The time spent changing context from one book to the other is acceptable.

Reading six books in parallel would be challenging. It may require so many context changes that you may not be able to finish any of the books in the expected time and end up changing from one book to the other without making much progress in any of them.

Asynchronous programming radically modifies the execution order and therefore debugging. Because debugging relies on suspending the execution and then stepping line by line through it, it is more difficult to understand the execution behavior and to mimic what is really happening. The JVM determines the execution order of threads at run time. It is almost impossible to simulate the same behavior because of very different available resources on test and development environments. If you don't need it, asynchronous execution adds undesired complexity.

Threading and asynchronous execution can be a great tool only if used properly without starving resources. It is a good idea to run nonblocking parts asynchronously, but not on every method.

SUMMARY

In the age of multicores and web 2.0, asynchronous programming uses computing resources, delegates nonblocking tasks, and results in faster and more responsive user interfaces. Even if your application does not implement the asynchronous pattern, most application servers and JVMs use asynchronous execution internally via thread pools for many operations. Using those available threads and resources greatly affects your application's efficiency and responsiveness.

Threading has been a first-class citizen from the early days of Java, but using threads to run asynchronous tasks was complicated and wasn't always safe in server-managed containers. With the release of the Concurrency Framework, Java unleashed a huge set of tools into the hands of Java developers.

Java EE followed this trend by providing an easy-to-use and implement annotation-based asynchronous programming model. Adding the `@Asynchronous` annotation tells the container to execute the function asynchronously.

The servlet API introduced important changes in release 3.0 and further improvements in release 3.1. The new servlet API uses the new nonblocking Java I/O to support asynchronous web programming in an efficient way. Although previous approaches needed a request/response couple to be bound to a thread, the new model can use or release threads using the internal thread pool that the container provides.

Today Java EE offers all the needed tools to run asynchronous code without the need for a third-party framework such as Spring or Quartz. This makes the asynchronous pattern a great tool to implement if you want to execute nonblocking code asynchronously with almost no boilerplate code.

EXERCISES

1. Create an implementation of a session bean that has an asynchronous method.

2. Develop simple functionality that uses asynchronous methodology to persist application log data to a database.

3. Use the asynchronous feature of Servlet 3.0 to design an asynchronous web service.

NOTES

1. "AJAX (Asynchronous JavaScript and XML): A New Approach to Web Applications." Jessie James Garret. `http://www.adaptivepath.com/ideas/ajax-new-approach-web-applications/`.

2. *Design Patterns: Elements of Reusable Object-Oriented Software* (Addison-Wesley, 1994): Erich Gamma, Richard Helm, Ralph Johnson, John Vlissides.

3. *Head First Design Patterns* (O'Reilly, 2004): Eric Freeman, Elisabeth Robson, Bert Bates, Kathy Sierra.

4. *Java Concurrency in Practice* (Addison-Wesley Professional, 2006): Brian Goetz, David Holmes, Doug Lea, Tim Peierls, Joshua Bloch.

10

Timer Service

WHAT'S IN THIS CHAPTER?

➤ Advancements made in the timer service

➤ Automatic timers

➤ Programmatic timers

➤ Setting the schedule with schedule expressions

➤ Timers and transactions

WROX.COM CODE DOWNLOAD FOR THIS CHAPTER

The wrox.com code download for this chapter is found at www.wrox.com/go/ projavaeedesignpatterns on the Download Code tab. The code is in the Chapter 10 download and individually named according to the names throughout the chapter.

Business applications need to perform tasks based on either calendar events or a timed schedule, whether it is to generate weekly user activity reports, repopulate a cache, or send a client a reminder e-mail. There are many use case scenarios. The timer service enables you to program timer events at specific times or regular intervals.

This chapter shows you how to configure the timer service using both automatic and programmatic techniques and how to schedule tasks using the cron-like schedule expressions.

WHAT IS THE TIMER SERVICE?

Can you imagine needing to wake up every morning to check the clock to see if it is time to get up? Probably not. Even before the invention of the alarm clock, people used sunlight or roosters to wake up. But roosters and the sun are not customizable. This lack of customization led to the invention of one of the most important devices of modern life: the alarm clock. Today even basic cell phones and fitness trackers offer alarms that you can adjust to different times and different days and even offer snooze options.

For a long time, neither Java SE nor Java EE offered a built-in solution for time-based operations. This lack of support was filled with community-led open source.

Traditionally, timer-based tasks would have been scheduled using a third-party tool such as Quartz,[1] but such a tool tends to be tricky to use. Third-party tools require you to download and install a library, implement interfaces, and configure XML files. They're anything but straightforward.

Fortunately for you and partly because of the difficulty faced by developers trying to use third-party libraries, a scheduling facility was introduced into the EJB 2.1 specification. This timer service satisfied the simplest use case scenarios. And for those complicated cases, there was still Quartz. Indeed, Quartz almost became the de facto standard of time-based operations in Java.

There is no default implementation for timers in Java SE. You can use Quartz in both Java SE and Java EE, but Quartz usage is a separate topic beyond this book. So this chapter skips the Java implementation and moves on to Java EE.

Advancements were made in the EJB 3.2 specification (the latest release) to the timer service. Introduced were the @Schedule and @Schedules annotations and cron-like calendar expressions. Now all but the most exceptional use case scenarios are satisfied. The timer service runs in the container as a service and registers Enterprise JavaBeans (EJB) for callbacks. It tracks the timers that exist and their schedules, and it even takes care of persisting the timer in case a server shuts down or crashes. The only thing the developer needs to do now is schedule the timer.

The timer service has been through a long development cycle. An overview of the advancements is summarized in Table 10-1.

TABLE 10-1: Timer Service Development

EJB AND JAVA VERSION	DEVELOPMENT
EJB 2.1 Java 1.4 (November 2003)	The ejbTimer implements the TimedObject interface. The TimerService is accessed through the EJBContext method. The business logic must be in the ejbTimeout method.
EJB 3.0 Java 5 (May 2006)	The TimerService object is injected via direct injection using the annotation @Resource. The business logic must be placed in a method annotated with @Timeout. Schedule set by specifying a date, duration, or ScheduleExpression object or an XML configuration file. Referred to as programmatic timers in Java EE 6.

EJB 3.1 Java 6 (December 2009)	The container sets the `TimerService` object automatically; no injection is required.
	The business logic must be placed in a method annotated with `@Schedule` or `@Schedules`.
	The schedule is set in the annotations attributes and bycalendar-based EJB timer expressions.
EJB 3.2 Java 7 (June 2013)	This extended the EJB Lite group to include the nonpersistent EJB timer service.
	Includes enhancements to the `TimerService` API that allows access to all active timers in the EJB module.
	Restrictions on `Timer` and `TimerHandle` that obliged references to be used only inside a bean have been removed.

WAR STORY

Recently, I was brought in to consult on a web project that was suffering from intermittent performance issues. These issues had only appeared recently—just as the site's visitor numbers started to accelerate.

The developers had chosen to use a No-SQL database to persist GPS data regarding the location of the site's visitors. This was a good decision because this particular No-SQL data store was adept at geospatial queries.

Queries were regularly run against the database, which collated data from the location collection and aggregated it to generate reports. These reports generated daily visitor statistics and were executed every day by a junior staff member.

After some investigating, I discovered that the performance issues the application was having coincided with the time the reports were being run. The extra hit to the database caused by running the reports was responsible for the deterioration in performance.

The solution was quite simple. Run the reports when the database was experiencing lower use. After reviewing the database usage reports, I determined that the optimal time to run the reports was 03:00 GMT. Clearly, I couldn't ask the junior member of the staff to start work at 3:00 in the morning, so I decided to automate the generation of the reports and configured the `timerservice` to launch the report generation.

Many tasks are best run in off hours for the same reason as spelled out here. Repopulating data caches is a common example of a heavy process that should be run when the effect on site performance is minimal.

IMPLEMENTING A TIMER IN JAVA EE

There are two types of timers in Java EE 7: automatic and programmatic. Automatic timers are set upon the deployment of an enterprise Java bean (EJB) that contains a method annotated with either `@Schedule(...)` or `@Schedule(...)`. The annotated method is invoked by the container's scheduler at the specified times, or time intervals defined within the arguments of the annotations. Such methods are referred to as callback methods. The timer starts ticking as soon as the EJB is deployed. A programmatic timer is set at run time by a method called from within the business logic. The time can be configured on the fly and invoked at anytime (or not at all). The timer start ticking when the programming logic determines that it should start.

> ### TIMER SERVICE IMPLEMENTATION
>
> The EJB container implements the timer service. An enterprise bean can access this service in three ways: by means of dependency injection, through the EJBContext interface, or through lookup in the Java Naming and Directory Interface (JNDI) namespace. This book only examines the way by means of dependency injection, because it's the newest and most efficient.

Automatic Timers

The container invokes any method appropriately annotated with `@Schedule` and applies the schedule configuration specified in the annotation's attributes. The attributes of the annotation are set following the calendar-based timer attributes in the "Timer Expression" section that follows. Here is a simple example:

```
@Schedule(second="*/1", minute="*", hour="*")
public void executeTask(){
    System.out.println("Task performed");
}
```

In this code snippet, the method `executeTask` is annotated `@Schedule`; this indicates to the container to set a timer upon deployment based on the time values specified in the annotations attributes. In this example the container invokes the `executeTask` method once every second.

By default, all timers are persisted and restored after a server shutdown or crash. If you set the optional attribute *persistent* to `false`, the timer is reset on server restart. You can set two additional attributes: *info* and *timezone*. If you set *timezone*, that time zone is respected when executing the timer; otherwise, the server time zone is used. The info attribute allows a developer to provide a description of the time that you can retrieve by calling the `getInfo` method of the `Timer` interface.

```
@Schedule(hour = "23", minute = "59", timezone = "CET",
          info = "Generates nightly
report")
public void executeTask(){
    System.out.println("Task performed");
}
```

In the preceding code snippet, the `executeTask` method is invoked at 23:59 Central European time regardless of the time zone of the server on which it is deployed. A call to the method `getInfo` returns the text `Generates nightly report`.

You can configure more complex timers using `@Schedules` (note the pluralization) with multiple timer expressions.

```
@Schedules({
    @Schedule(dayOfMonth = "1"),
    @Schedule(dayOfWeek = "Mon,Tue,Wed,Thu,Fri", hour = "8")
})
public void executeTask() {
    System.out.println("Task performed");
}
```

This timer fires on the first of every month and every work day at 08:00. Listing 10-1 shows a complete example of an automatic timer.

LISTING 10-1: The simplest implementation of an automatic timer

```
package com.devchronicles.timer;

import javax.ejb.Schedule;
import javax.ejb.Schedules;

public class PeriodicTimer {

    @Schedules({
        @Schedule(dayOfMonth = "1"),
        @Schedule(dayOfWeek = "Mon,Tue,Wed,Thu,Fri", hour = "8")
        })
    public void executeTask() {
        System.out.println("Task performed");
    }

}
```

One drawback of the automatic timer is that its schedule is set at deployment time and cannot be changed while the application is executing. Fortunately, there is a solution to this situation in the form of the programmatic timer, which you can set at any moment during run time.

Programmatic Timers

Programmatic timers are created at run time by invoking one of the create methods of the `TimerService` interface. Here is a simple example:

```
public void setTimer(){
    timerService.createTimer(30000, "New timer");
}
```

When the application code invokes the `setTimer` method, it creates a single-action timer that calls a "timeout" method in the same bean after the specified duration of 30,000 milliseconds. A "timeout" method is identified by the annotation `@Timeout` and must conform to certain requirements. It must not throw exceptions or return a value. It's also exempt from needing to take a parameter, but if it does, it must be of type `javax.ejb.Time`. There can be only one "timeout" method.

```
@Timeout
public void performTask() {
    System.out.println("Simple Task performed");
}
```

The Context Dependency Injection (CDI) container injects a reference to the `TimerService` into an instance variable annotated `@Resource`. Here the container injects the instance variable `timerService`.

```
@Resource
TimerService timerService;
```

 If you put together the previous three code snippets into a single bean and the application code calls the `setTimer` method, you create a timer that, after 30 seconds, calls the "timeout" method `performTask`. Listing 10-2 shows the simplest possible implementation of the programmatic timer in Java EE 7.

LISTING 10-2: The simplest implementation of a programmatic timer

```
package com.devchronicles.timer;

import javax.annotation.Resource;
import javax.ejb.Timeout;
import javax.ejb.TimerService;

public class SimpleProgrammaticTimer {

    @Resource
    TimerService timerService;

    public void setTimer(){
        timerService.createTimer(30000, "New timer");
    }

    @Timeout
    public void performTask() {
        System.out.println("Simple Task performed");
    }
}
```

There are four timer creation methods in the `TimerService` interface with ten signatures. Table 10-2 shows an example of each one:

TABLE 10-2: Examples of the Four Timer Creation Methods

METHOD	EXAMPLE
`createIntervalTimer(new Date(), 10000, new TimerConfig());`	This creates a timer that fires at the given date and then every ten seconds thereafter.
`createSingleActionTimer(1000, new TimerConfig());`	This creates a timer that fires after one second.
`createTimer(30000, "Created new programmatic timer");`	This creates a timer that fires after 30 seconds.
`createCalendarTimer(new ScheduleExpression().second("*/10").minute("*").hour("*"));`	This creates a timer that fires every ten seconds.

All methods apart from the `createCalendarTimer` method can take as the first parameter either duration in milliseconds or a date. This sets up the point at which the timer is triggered. Here is an example:

```
SimpleDateFormat formatter = new SimpleDateFormat("dd/MM/yyyy 'at' HH:mm");
Date date = formatter.parse("26/01/2015 at 17:56");
timerService.createSingleActionTimer(date, new TimerConfig());
```

In this code snippet, the "timeout" method is triggered at 17:56 on January 26, 2015.

If a scheduled timer is required, you can use the `createCalendarTimer` method. This method takes a `ScheduleExpression` object in which a schedule is set using the values described in the "Timer Expression" section that follows.

```
ScheduleExpression expression = new ScheduleExpression();
expression.second("*/10").minute("*").hour("*");
timerService.createCalendarTimer(expression);
```

In this code snippet, the schedule is set to trigger every ten seconds of every minute of every hour.

All the creation methods return a `Timer` object that represents the timer. This object has the method `getHandle`, which returns a serializable handle to the timer. The handle object can be persisted in a database or memory.

Later you can retrieve the handle object and return a reference to the timer by invoking the `getTimer` method. With this object in hand, you can retrieve useful information about the timer.

It's easy to obtain information about the behavior of the timer. You can retrieve details regarding the timer's schedule by calling the method `getSchedule`. This returns a `ScheduleExpression` object that has a `getter` method for each attribute. For example, `getMinute()` returns the value set for the minute attribute. The `getNextTimeout` method gets the point when the timer fires next, whereas the method `getTimeRemaining` returns the milliseconds before the timer expires.

The `isCalendarTimer` method returns `true` if the timer was set by constructing a `ScheduleExpression` object. You must call it before the `getSchedule` method to determine if the timer was set this way; otherwise, `isCalendarTimer` throws an `IllegalStateException` exception.

You can determine information about the timer's persistent state by using the `isPersistent` method. Similarly, you can obtain information about the time by calling the `getInfo` method.

Timers are automatically cancelled when they expire. The container cancels the single-event timers, and you can cancel scheduled timers by calling the `cancel` method on the `Timer` object.

Timer Expression

Both programmatic and automatic timers can use calendar-based timer attributes. Table 10-3 shows the range of timer attributes that are used to set the timers. For automatic calendar-based timers, you set the calendar attributes in the annotation, whereas programmatic calendar-based timers use methods of the `ScheduleExpression` class to set the calendar attribute values.

TABLE 10-3: Calendar-Based Expressions

ATTRIBUTE	DESCRIPTION	PERMITTED VALUES
second	One or more seconds within a minute	0 through 59
minute	One or more minutes within an hour	0 through 59
hour	One or more hours within a day	0 through 23
dayOfWeek	One or more days within a week	0 through 7 (0 and 7 refer to Sunday) Sun through Sat
dayOfMonth	One or more days within a month	1 through 31 –7 through –1 (days from end of month) Last 1st, 2nd, 3rd - nth Sun through Sat
month	One or more months within a year	1 through 12 Jan through Dec
year	A particular calendar year	2014, 2015, etc.

It's worth noting that the default value for the time attributes is 0 (zero) and for the non-numerical values it is * (asterisk).

This table has been appropriated from the Oracle's Java EE 7 tutorial.[2] The syntax is cron-like and should be familiar to most programmers. There are a few interesting characteristics worth pointing out.

The asterisk character is a placeholder for all possible values for the given attribute. For example, to set a schedule to trigger every hour, you would use the expression hour="*" for annotation-configured timers. For programmatic timers, you would invoke the method hour("*")on an instance of the ScheduleExpression class.

You can express values for each attribute as a list or a range. For example, the expression dayOfMonth="1, 15, last" sets the timer to trigger on the first, fifteenth, and last day of every month, whereas the expression hour="8-18" represents every hour from 08:00 until 18:00.

You can specify intervals and augment them with a starting point. The expression hour="8/1" triggers every hour starting from 08:00, whereas the expression hour="*/12" triggers every 12 hours. However, you can only set intervals for seconds, minutes, and hour attributes.

Table 10-4 offers a few examples of the calendar-based schedule in action.

TABLE 10-4: Examples of Expressions in Action

Expression	Action
Second="10"	Every ten seconds
hour = "2",	Every two hours
minute = "15"	Every 15 minutes
dayOfWeek="Mon, Fri"	Every Monday and Friday at midnight
dayOfWeek="0-7", hour="8"	Every day at 8 a.m.
dayOfMonth="-7"	Five days before the end of every month at midnight
dayOfMonth="1st Mon", hour="22"	First Monday of every month at 10 p.m.
Month="Mar", dayOfMonth="15"	The 15th of the following March
year="2015", month="May"	May 1, 2015 at midnight

New in the EJB 3.2 implementation is an enhancement to the timer service API that allows access to all active timers in the EJB module. These include both programmatically and automatically created timers.

LISTING 10-3: All timers can be retrieved and manipulated

```
package com.devchronicles.timer;

import java.util.Collection;
import javax.annotation.PostConstruct;
import javax.annotation.Resource;
import javax.ejb.Singleton;
import javax.ejb.Startup;
```

continues

LISTING 10-3: *(continued)*

```
import javax.ejb.Timer;
import javax.ejb.TimerService;

@Singleton
@Startup
public class AllTimers {

    @Resource
    TimerService timerService;

    @PostConstruct
    public void manageTimer(){

        Collection<Timer> timers = timerService.getAllTimers();

        for(Timer t : timers){
            System.out.println("Timer Info: " + t.getInfo());
            System.out.println("Time Remaining: " + t.getTimeRemaining());
            t.cancel();
        }
    }
}
```

In Listing 10-3, the bean is instantiated at start-up, and the manageTimer method is called. You retrieve a collection of all the active timers and iterate over the collection, printing out the timer info and the number of milliseconds that will elapse before the next scheduled timer expiration. Finally, you cancel the timer.

Transactions

Beans create timers within a transaction that the container manages. If this transaction is rolled back, so is the timer. If this transaction is rolled back then the timer is also rolled back. This means that its creation is rolled back and if it were canceled the cancellation would be undone and the timer reinstated. In listing 10-4 we show an example of a timer method marked with a transaction annotation.

LISTING 10-4: A timer can set a transaction attribute

```
package com.devchronicles.timer;

import javax.annotation.Resource;
import javax.ejb.Timeout;
import javax.ejb.TimerService;

public class SimpleProgramaticTimer {

    @Resource
```

```
    TimerService timerService;

    public void setTimer(){
        ScheduleExpression expression = new ScheduleExpression();
        expression.second("*/10").minute("*").hour("*");
        timer = timerService.createCalendarTimer(
                new ScheduleExpression().second("*/10").minute("*").hour("*"));
    }

    @Timeout
    @TransactionAttribute(TransactionAttributeType.REQUIRED)
    public void performTask() {
    System.out.println("Simple Task performed");
    }
}
```

Beans that use container-managed transactions set the transitions attribute on the method annotated `@Timeout`. Transactions are designated `Required` or `RequiresNew`. The transaction is started before the method is called. If the transaction is rolled back, the `@Timeout` method is called again.

SUMMARY

In this chapter, you have seen how to create automatic and programmatic timers and how they behave within a transaction. Timers can be quite useful when a cron-like job needs to run without disturbing the main business logic. You can see examples of timers in many projects and in almost all programming languages. The automatic timer is created by annotating a method with either `@Schedule` or `@Schedules` and hard-coding timer values as attributes of the annotations by declaring them in the `ejb-jar.xml` deployment descriptor. Programmatic timers are created by the application code and can change their values at run time.

The timer type you choose to solve your problem will depend largely on whether the frequency of the event will change based on business logic (client services) or technical requirements (repopulating a cache). The latter would best be served with a programmatic timer, whereas the former would benefit most from an automatic timer.

Timers are persisted by default to guard against server shutdowns and crashes and can be serialized in a database and later retrieved. Timers take part in a transaction and are fully rolled back with the transaction. It became a little easier to manage timers in EJB 3.2; you can retrieve all active timers in a collection and call timer methods on each instance.

With the new achievements on Java EE, timers became solid and capable, leaving most third-party frameworks obsolete.

EXERCISES

1. Write a cache that repopulates a map from a database. Set the timer service to fire at 3 a.m., calling the repopulate method of the cache.

2. Develop a programmatic timer that sends a notification to a client when his subscription is up for renewal.

NOTES

1.   Quartz Job Scheduler: `http://www.quartz-scheduler.org/`.
2.   Oracle's Java EE 7 tutorial: `http://docs.oracle.com/javaee/7/tutorial/doc/ejb-basicexamples004.htm#GIQLY`.

11

Observer Pattern

WHAT'S IN THIS CHAPTER?

➤ How to implement the observer pattern in plain code

➤ How the observer pattern works in the real world

➤ How to implement the observer pattern using @Observes and Event firing

➤ How to use qualifiers to gain fine-grain control over observers

➤ How to implement transaction-sensitive observers and rollbacks

WROX.COM CODE DOWNLOAD FOR THIS CHAPTER

The wrox.com code download for this chapter is found at www.wrox.com/go/ projavaeedesignpatterns on the Download Code tab. The code is in the Chapter 11 download and individually named according to the names throughout the chapter.

The observer pattern is one of the most widely used and accepted design patterns in modern programming languages, software, and user interface (UI) frameworks. Most programming languages use observers within their internal application programming interfaces (APIs), and Java is no exception. But Java EE goes further than most and provides a default implementation of the observer pattern, so developers can use this pattern without implementing it from scratch. This chapter focuses on Java's default implementation of the observer pattern: where it is used, how observers are implemented via annotations in Java EE, and how observers can be made transaction sensitive.

WHAT IS AN OBSERVER?

The idea behind the observer pattern is that an object that changes its state can inform other objects that a change has occurred. In the language of the design pattern, the object that changes its state is called the *subject*, whereas those objects that receive notification of the change are called the *observers*. The relationship is one to many, with the subject having many observers.

Imagine a chat application that automatically refreshes every second so it can check for new messages. Also imagine that it has a chat room feature allowing many people to chat together. Each of these chat clients regularly checks with the server to see if there has been a new message posted by one of the other clients. As you can imagine, this is not very performance friendly. Would it not make much more sense if the newly sent message was "pushed" to all subscribed clients? It would certainly be more efficient. The observer pattern can solve this problem. Here, the observer would be the chat server, and each client would be a subject. The server would be registered with each client, and when the client posts a new message (a change in state of the subject), the subject would call a method on the server to notify it of the new message. Then the server would call a method on all its registered clients and send the message to each one.

> **NOTE** *The observer pattern is also referred to as the* Hollywood principle, *whose motto is "don't call us; we'll call you." This is not surprising; most Hollywood agents would prefer to call clients for a new role rather than being hounded by clients calling them. This system works well because there's never a perfect time to call an agent to check about an available job. You'll likely either miss out on a job if jobs arrive more frequently than you're calling, or you'll be seen as obnoxious if you're calling more often than jobs arrive.*
>
> *With the help of the observer pattern, an agent calls appropriate clients just as a new job opens, without losing time or wasting resources.*

Description

The GoF[1] book states that the observer pattern "defines a one-to-many dependency between objects so that when one object changes state, all its dependents are notified and updated automatically." The *Head First Design Patterns*[2] book gives the example of a weather monitoring application that sends a notice when temperatures change. The observer pattern is based on the principle of inheritance and is one of the behavioral design patterns.

To be an observer, each concrete observer implementation needs to share a similar interface. The subject lets each observer add itself to a registry. When the subject changes, the observer calls each subject's registered implementation to notify the observer about the changes.

This is an efficient implementation because only one call happens for each observer at the time of the change. A naive solution such as regularly checking the subject may produce an unlimited number of calls from different observers even though there had been no change to the object observed.

The observer pattern is not that different from a news subscription. Objects that want to subscribe to changes on another object register themselves to receive news of those changes. Rather than checking the target object, these objects are called when there is a change.

UI Frameworks are another place where observers are heavily used, although this is more related to desktop applications, not enterprise applications. In the context of UI frameworks, the observer pattern is often referred to as the listener pattern. Essentially, these patterns are the same. Button click listeners, drag drop handlers, and value change listeners all rely on an implementation of the observer pattern.

Almost all web frameworks are built on the model-view-controller pattern, which also uses the observer pattern internally. See Chapter 14, "Model View Controller Pattern," for more details.

WAR STORY

For a long time, part of my daily job has been to mentor interns and fresh graduates. This war story goes back to a talented intern I had the chance to work with. This bright electronics graduate had more experience with hardware and structural programming than object-oriented languages; therefore, she had little knowledge of design patterns. She had just completed a successful Arduino-based project.[3]

We started developing an Android application that used Android's built-in face detection feature to detect whether the user was in front of the device. Coming from an Arduino project, the intern's first approach was to create a loop to query the camera and see if it had detected a new face. This loop was running in the main application thread, so it was blocking on the application.

After realizing that she had locked the UI thread, she decided to create a separate thread to perform the face detection job. She was using the "if the only tool you have is a hammer, every problem looks like a nail" approach.[4] We chatted for a while about how the Arduino application was structured. On the Arduino, the whole application was a loop that we wanted to keep running until we stopped it, and all program features were handled in that loop. However, our Android application had a different structure. The application needed to be informed of when there was a face detected rather than querying the camera to see if a face had been detected. Once this graduate understood how observers work, she didn't have much difficulty implementing the pattern because the Android system was already built on the observer pattern. All she needed to do was add the appropriate listener class and perform whatever function she needed when a face was detected.

Observer Class Diagram

As can be seen from Figure 11-1, the observer pattern introduces an `Observer` interface that all concrete observers must implement. This interface has just one method that is called by the subject to notify the observers that there has been a change in state. Each subject holds a list of registered observers and calls the `notifyObservers` method to inform the registered observers about any updates or changes in the subject. It has methods for registering and unregistering observers.

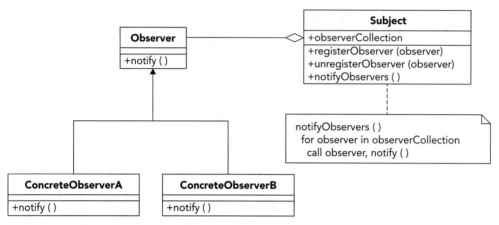

FIGURE 11-1: Class diagram of the observer pattern

IMPLEMENTING THE OBSERVER PATTERN IN PLAIN CODE

Java provides an out-of-the-box implementation of the observer pattern. By implementing the `Observer` interface and extending the `Observable` class, developers can easily implement the observer pattern.

The first thing you need to do is create a class that extends the `Observable` class. In Listing 11-1, a news agency informs several types of subscribers when a new story is published. The subscriber may introduce its own behavior after receiving an update. Listing 11-2 provides an interface for publishing the observable class.

LISTING: 11-1: The news agency implementing the observable interface

```
package com.devchronicles.observer;

import java.util.ArrayList;
import java.util.List;
import java.util.Observable;
import java.util.Observer;

public class NewsAgency extends Observable implements Publisher {

    private List<Observer> channels = new ArrayList<>();

    public void addNews(String newsItem) {
        notifyObservers(newsItem);
    }

    public void notifyObservers(String newsItem) {
        for (Observer outlet : this.channels) {
            outlet.update(this, newsItem);
        }
```

```
    }

    public void register(Observer outlet) {
        channels.add(outlet);
    }
}
```

LISTING: 11-2: The Publisher interface

```
package com.devchronicles.observer;

public interface Publisher {}
```

Next, you need to create the class that observes the `NewsAgency` for changes. This observer must implement the `Observer` interface as in Listing 11-3.

LISTING: 11-3: Concrete observer

```
package com.devchronicles.observer;

import java.util.Observable;
import java.util.Observer;

public class RadioChannel implements Observer {

    @Override
    public void update(Observable agency, Object newsItem) {
        if (agency instanceof Publisher) {
            System.out.println((String)newsItem);
        }
    }
}
```

Finally, you must register the `RadioChannel` observer with the `NewsAgency` observable and create some news.

```
// Create the observer and subject
NewsAgency newsAgency = new NewsAgency();
RadioChannel radioChannel = new RadioChannel();

// Register the observer with the subject
newsAgency.register(radioChannel);

// Now add some news headlines
newsAgency.addNews("Breaking news: Life found on Mars");
newsAgency.addNews("Update: Earth invasion imminent");
newsAgency.addNews("Just in: Hail to our new Martian overlords");
```

The output in the console should be as follows:

```
Breaking news: Life found on Mars
Update: Earth invasion imminent
Just in: Hail to our new Martian overlords
```

Notice that you can register many observers with the NewsAgency and receive updates. Perhaps a TVChannel observer or an InternetNewsChannel observer can register to receive updates from the NewsAgency. In addition, you can have other Publishers (or any other type of object that implements Observable) issue updates to any observer that wants to register itself to receive news. These observers can check the type of the Observable and process the update according to its source.

One significant drawback of implementing the observer pattern in this way is that you have to extend the Observable class. This forces the use of a class hierarchy that might not be desirable. Because you cannot extend more than one class in the single-inheritance world of Java, this way of implementing the observer pattern restricts the inheritance design. You can't add the Observable behavior to an existing class that already extends another superclass, thus restricting its reuse potential.

But don't despair. You can also implement the observer pattern by "hand," without using the internal Observer and Observable interfaces, by following the given class diagram. However, because this book is focused on Java EE, this implementation is left for you to play with.

IMPLEMENTING THE OBSERVER PATTERN IN JAVA EE

Although Java had built-in support for the observer pattern from inception, Java EE offers an easier implementation via the @Observes annotation and javax.enterprise.event.Event<T> interface. Any method annotated with @Observes listens for events of a certain type. When it "hears" such an event, the parameter of the observer method receives an instance of the type and then executes the method.

The @Observes annotation lets any method listen for any event to be fired with the marked object type. Listing 11-4 is a simple example of a bean that fires an event of type String and another bean that listens for events of that type from our bean.

LISTING 11-4: The observable service bean

```
package com.devchronicles.observer;

import javax.ejb.Stateless;
import javax.ejb.TransactionAttribute;
import javax.ejb.TransactionAttributeType;
import javax.enterprise.event.Event;
import javax.inject.Inject;

@Stateless
@TransactionAttribute(TransactionAttributeType.REQUIRED)
public class EventService {

    @Inject
    private String message;

    @Inject
    Event<String> event;

    public void startService(){
        event.fire("Starting service " + message);
    }
}
```

The container injects an Event object of type String into the event instance variable of the EventService class. This forms part of the message when the to fire String object is fired. This instance variable Message object is a String which may be produced by a factory. (See Chapter 6, "Factory Pattern," for more information about the factory design pattern injected to the EventService class.) To make this example work without creating a factory even simpler, you can just define any String constant to the variable called message and remove the @Inject annotation as follows.

```
private String message = "produced message";
```

Now the observable part is completed, so it is time to create an observer that listens for your String events. The addition of the @Observes annotation to the method signature marks the method as an observer of events of the type it precedes. In this case, the @Observes annotation precedes the type String and thus listens for events of that type. The @Observes annotation followed by an object type does the magic and lets the annotated method observe the fired event of the given type.

In Listing 11-5, the @Observes annotation has been added to the serviceTrace method signature, which marks the method as an observer for String events. When an event of type String occurs, the serviceTrace method receives the object that the event produced via its parameter. serviceTrace can then manipulate the String object as it wants. In this case, it prints the message to the console.

LISTING 11-5: The observer bean

```
package com.devchronicles.observer;

import javax.ejb.Stateless;
import javax.enterprise.event.Observes;

@Stateless
public class TraceObserver {

    public void serviceTrace(@Observes String message){
        System.out.println("Service message: " + message);
    }
}
```

If you run the server and invoke the start service method, you will realize how magically a string will be injected to the EventService class, and then a String event is fired "where it will be coughed (observed)" by the serviceTrace method of the TraceObserver class, and a message is printed to the console. Surprisingly, this is all that you need to implement the observer pattern in Java EE without further configuration.

Although in real-world scenarios you probably wouldn't be firing and observing plain strings but rather your own objects that would be observed by their type, it is still quite easy to differentiate between the same object types of objects and set up different observers to listen for them.

You are now going to look at an example in which you use *Qualifiers* to disambiguate String objects. You have seen how this can be effective when implementing a factory pattern that produces different implementations of the same type of object.

In Listing 11-6, you start with the code that disambiguates your `Strings`.

LISTING 11-6: The annotation Qualifier interface

```
package com.devchronicles.observer;

import java.lang.annotation.ElementType;
import java.lang.annotation.Retention;
import java.lang.annotation.RetentionPolicy;
import java.lang.annotation.Target;
import javax.inject.Qualifier;

@Qualifier
@Retention(RetentionPolicy.RUNTIME)
@Target({ElementType.FIELD,ElementType.PARAMETER})
public @interface MessageEvent {

    Type value();

    enum Type{ SERVICE, PARAMETER }
```

The interface preceding class defines a `MessageEvent` qualifier and two enum types (`SERVICE` and `PARAMETER`) that you will use to act as annotation to mark the strings to be fired by the event instances.

```
import com.devchronicles.observer.MessageEvent.Type;

@Stateless
@TransactionAttribute(TransactionAttributeType.REQUIRED)
public class EventService {

    @Inject
    private String message;

    @Inject @MessageEvent(Type.SERVICE)
    Event<String> serviceEvent;

    @Inject @MessageEvent(Type.PARAMETER)
    Event<String> parameterEvent;

    public void startService(){
        serviceEvent.fire("Starting service "+message);
        parameterEvent.fire("-d -p");
    }
```

To use the *Qualifiers*, you just add the `MyEvent` annotation to the relevant injected instance with the desired enum type in parenthesis. Then you later fire the events from within the `startService` method, just as you did before in the previous example. The bold parts code lines are all you have added to the previous example in the previous listing.

Now you'll add the annotations to the observer part. As you did before, you just have to add the *Qualifiers* to the relevant `@Observes` annotation.

```
import com.devchronicles.observer.javaee.MessageEvent.Type;

@Stateless
public class TraceObserver {

    public void serviceTrace(
            @Observes @MessageEvent(Type.SERVICE) String message) {
        System.out.println("Service message: " + message);
    }

    public void parameterTrace(
            @Observes @MessageEvent(Type.PARAMETER) String message) {
        System.out.println("with parameters: " + message);
    }
}
```

Firing and observing your own object types is even simpler. The object type is unique, and it's not necessary to create your own annotation qualifiers; you can use the object instead.

Observable events are transactional and are delivered in the transactional phase that you define for that event. That may be before or after the transaction has completed or after a successful or unsuccessful transaction.

Now you'll see this in action. In Listing 11-7, you define three observer methods that specify a transaction phase during which the observers listen for events of type String.

LISTING 11-7: The Transaction event observer

```
package com.devchronicles.observer;

import javax.enterprise.event.Observes;
import javax.enterprise.event.TransactionPhase;

public class TransactionEventObserver {

    public void onInProgress(@Observes String message) {
        System.out.println("In progress message: " + message);
    }

    public void onSuccess(
            @Observes(during = TransactionPhase.AFTER_SUCCESS) String message) {
        System.out.println("After success message: " + message);
    }

    public void onFailure(
            @Observes(during = TransactionPhase.AFTER_FAILURE) String message) {
        System.out.println("After failure message: " + message);
    }

    public void onCompletion(
            @Observes(during = TransactionPhase.AFTER_COMPLETION) String message) {
        System.out.println("After completion message: " + message);
    }

}
```

There are five transitional phases: BEFORE _ COMPLETION, AFTER _ COMPLETION, AFTER _ SUCCESS, AFTER _ FAILURE, and the default IN _ PROGRESS. In Listing 11-7, we have not implemented BEFORE _ COMPLETION. In Listing 11-8 we implement a class that demonstrates event firing in successful and failure scenarios.

LISTING 11-8: Provoke success and failure scenarios

```java
package com.devchronicles.observer;

import javax.annotation.Resource;
import javax.ejb.SessionContext;
import javax.ejb.Stateless;
import javax.ejb.TransactionAttribute;
import javax.ejb.TransactionAttributeType;
import javax.enterprise.event.Event;
import javax.inject.Inject;

@Stateless
@TransactionAttribute(TransactionAttributeType.REQUIRED)
public class Children {

    @Resource
    SessionContext sc;

    @Inject
    Event<String> message;

    int[] children = new int[3];

    public void getSixthChild() {
        try {
            int sixthChild = children[5]; // Throws an IndexOutOfBounds Exception
        } catch (Exception e) {
            message.fire("Rollback event occurred.");
            System.out.println("Exception caught.");
            sc.setRollbackOnly();
        }
    }

    public void getThirdChild() {
        int thirdChild = children[2]; // Succeeds
        message.fire("Successful event");
    }

}
```

The Children class simulates a successful transaction in the getThirdChild method and an unsuccessful transaction in the getSixthChild method by causing an IndexOutOfBoundsException.

You'll examine each method to see how the events are observed. The getThirdChild method fires a String event, passes it the message Successful event, and then finishes successfully. The output from calling this method follows:

```
In progress: Successful event
After completion message: Successful event
After success message: Successful event
```

The onInProgress method is invoked immediately when the event is fired and while the transaction is still in flight. The other two methods—onCompletion and onSuccess—must wait until the transaction reaches the *AFTER _ COMPLETION* and *AFTER _ SUCCESS* phases, respectively, before they can execute.

Next you'll look at the getSixthChild method, which fails by causing an IndexOutOfBoundsException. The output that results from calling this method follows:

```
In progress: Rollback event occurred.
Exception caught.
After completion message: Rollback event occurred.
After failure message: Rollback event occurred.
```

As before, the onInProgress method is invoked immediately, and the onCompletion and onFailure methods must wait until the method completes. Once the onInProgress method outputs the message Exception caught and the transaction is marked for rollback by calling the SessionContext method setRollbackOnly, the onInProgress method completes, and you can execute your observers. The onCompletion method is executed, followed by the OnFailure method.

The setRollbackOnly method marks the current transaction for rollback, so it can never be committed. This action triggers the transaction into the AFTER _ FAILURE phase and invokes the onFailure method.

Observers can also be given conditional behavior, although it's limited to being notified if an instance of the bean that defines the observer method already exists in the current context. The observer method is called only if an instance exists. To define an observer method as conditional, add notifyObserver = Reception.IF _ EXISTS as an argument to the @Observes annotation.

```
import javax.enterprise.event.Reception;

public void addMember (
        @Observes(notifyObserver = Reception.IF_EXISTS) String message){
  // Implementation code.
}
```

The default behavior is to create an instance if it does not exist.

WHERE AND WHEN TO USE THE OBSERVER PATTERN

The observer pattern, which can unleash huge performance gains, is an effective way to promote loose coupling and change the direction of calling/listening.

When designing your application or refactoring another's code, watch out for unnecessary and time interval-based method executions, which can be good candidates for implementing the observer pattern.

In the Java EE realm, you can migrate existing code to the observer pattern without too much hassle. Java EE observers are usually accompanied by dependency injection, which uses @inject, and factories, which use @produces.

The observer pattern's greatest strength, the decoupling of classes, is also its greatest weakness. As control of the observable moves to the observer, you lose track of the application's workflow. Vision becomes obscured as one event triggers another. A complicated implementation of the observer pattern can be a nightmare to debug, so it is recommended that you keep the implementation simple. Avoid multiple layers of observers; using just one layer (or a few) is ideal.

To help future and present developers determine the purpose of your code, the name of an observer should reflect its purpose. In addition, you should incorporate the reason for the observation into the name of its methods, expressing the purpose of the class.

In the Java EE realm, existing code can be migrated to the observer pattern without much hassle. Java EE observers are usually accompanied by dependency injection (@inject) and factories (@produces). The heavy and unnecessary use of observers may introduce hard to follow and debug systems. However, since most developers are used to observers from UI or web frameworks, they usually have an instinct to use in the right context most of the time.

Whenever you see a resource subject to change and callers trying to capture the data from subject, never hesitate to use the observer pattern. Transaction-sensitive observers offer functionality that was not easily available in earlier versions. In the BEFORE _ COMPLETION phase, you can cancel the current transaction by invoking the setRollbackOnly method, thus allowing nontransactional operations to be performed within a transactional phase. If an exception is thrown, the entire transaction can be rolled back.

During the IN _ PROCESS phase, which spans the entire transaction, observable events can be fired and observed immediately. This can be implemented as a type of progress monitor or logger.

A call to an observer method blocks the event emitter and is synchronous but can be made asynchronous by annotating the observer method @Asynchronous. (See Chapter 9, "Asynchronous," for more information about how to use this annotation.) You should take care when making observers of the BEFORE _ COMPLETION phase asynchronous because the setRollbackOnly method is ineffective, and the transaction will not be rolled back. The asynchronous method occurs in a new transaction.

SUMMARY

You have seen how Java's core observer pattern's implementation has advanced in Java EE 7 and how it can be made sensitive to the transactional phase of the events that it observes. Its implementation completely decouples business logic from the observer, leaving only the event type and qualifier to connect them. This has raised the concern that vision over the relationship is lost, although this can be mitigated by appropriately naming the class and methods and illustrating the relationship in the class's documentation.

The transactional phase sensitivity has added another dimension to the observer pattern. It provides integration between the observer methods and the transaction, allowing rollbacks to be invoked.

EXERCISES

1. List as many implementations of the observer pattern as you can that you would find in the Java language.

2. Create an example that uses `notifyObserver = Reception.IF_EXISTS` as an argument to the `@Observes` annotation.

3. Use the observers transitional sensitivity to monitor the progress of a transaction and log the result of the transaction (success or failure).

NOTES

1. *Design Patterns: Elements of Reusable Object-Oriented Software* (Addison-Wesley, 1994): Erich Gamma, Richard Helm, Ralph Johnson, John Vlissides.
2. *Head First Design Patterns* (O'Reilly, 2004): Eric Freeman, Elisabeth Robson, Bert Bates, Kathy Sierra.
3. A small hardware board for maker projects: `http://www.arduino.cc`.
4. Abraham Maslow (1908–1970) American Psychologist.

12

Data Access Pattern

WROX.COM CODE DOWNLOADS FOR THIS CHAPTER

The wrox.com code download for this chapter is found at www.wrox.com/go/ projavaeedesignpatterns on the Download Code tab. The code is in the Chapter 12 download and individually named according to the names throughout the chapter.

It is unimaginable to think of an enterprise application that does not in some way interact with a data source. The data source may be a relational, object-oriented or NoSQL database, a Lightweight Directory Access Protocol (LDAP) repository, a file system, a web service, or an external system. From whatever source the data comes, the enterprise application must interact with it and perform basic create, retrieve, update, and delete (CRUD) operations. Almost all servers use such data sources to persist sessions or long-running processes seamlessly.

The way in which you use data sources can vary substantially, and their implementation can differ widely. There are different SQL dialects, such as Postgre SQL and Oracle. The simple objective of the data access object (DAO) pattern is to encapsulate access to the data source by providing an interface via which the various layers can communicate with the data source.

This chapter discusses the original problem that the DAO solved and its relevance in modern Java EE applications. Also examined are the role of the related data transfer object (DTO) and how it and the factory pattern fit together with the DAO. In addition, this chapter covers the use of the JPA and ORM in the context of the DAO. You'll see an implementation of the DAO and how to improve it by using generics. Finally, you will read about the changed role of the pattern and why it is still a valid design pattern.

WHAT IS A DATA ACCESS PATTERN?

The original solution that the DAO pattern proposed was defined in the book *Core J2EE Patterns: Best Practices and Design Strategies*[1] as follows:

> *Use a data access object (DAO) to abstract and encapsulate all access to the data source. The DAO manages the connection with the data source to obtain and store data.*

The problem that was solved with the abstraction and encapsulation of the data source was to guard against the application being dependent on the data source implementation. This decoupled the business layer from the data source. It was thought that if the data source changed, the decoupling would reduce or negate any impact. However, in reality, the data source rarely changed—not even between vendors of the same source type such as between Postgre and MS SQL. It is hard to imagine that a decision would be made to migrate an SQL data source to an XML flat file system, LDAP repository, or web service. This simply didn't happen. So what value does the DAO pattern have in modern Java EE? Do you really need this pattern?

The DAO pattern is still a valuable pattern, and its original solution is still valid, although the motivation for its implementation has changed in its emphasis. Rather than guarding against the impact of an unlikely change in the data source type, the value is in its mockability and testability and its use in structuring the code and keeping it clean of data access code. There is still value in using it as a way to encapsulate legacy data storage systems and to simplify access to complex implementations of data sources. However, these are more likely to be corner and exceptional cases.

The DAO pattern encapsulates CRUD operations in an interface that is implemented by a concrete class. This interface can be mocked and therefore easily tested, avoiding a connection to the database. Testing is improved because writing tests using mocks is easier than integrating tests with a live database. The DAO's concrete implement uses low-level APIs such as JPA and Hibernate to perform the CRUD operations.

Data Access Class Diagram

Figure 12-1 shows the class diagram of the DAO, demonstrating the interaction between the client and the DAO and the DTO. Not shown is the optional factory that produces the DAO instance.

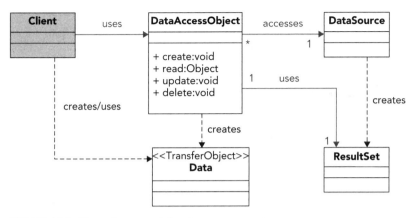

FIGURE 12-1: Class diagram of the data access pattern

OVERVIEW OF THE DATA ACCESS PATTERN

The implementation of the DAO pattern involves several components:

➤ The DAO interface

➤ The concrete implementation of the DAO interface

➤ The DAO factory

➤ The DTO

The factory, interface, and DTO are optional components, not required components, but you will see these two patterns used with the DAO pattern. The factory pattern is discussed in further detail in Chapter 6, "Factory Pattern."

Data Transfer Object Pattern

The DTO carries the data retrieved from or persisted to the database across logical layers. For example, to transfer a list of User objects retrieved from the data access layer to the web layer, the service layer would be responsible for transferring from a DAO to a DTO.

> **NOTE** *The DTO is also referred to as the Value Object.*

The solution that the DTO pattern proposes is defined in *Core J2EE Patterns: Best Practices and Design Strategies* as follows:

Use a Transfer Object to carry multiple data elements across a tier.

The DTO reduces remote requests across the network in applications that make many method calls to enterprise beans, resulting in improved performance. Sometimes not all the data retrieved from the database is required on the web layer or whatever other layer requires the use of data. So the

DTO reduces to just the essential data that the layer requests, thereby optimizing the transfer of data across tiers. This chapter does not go into detail regarding the DTO. It's recommended that you read the DTO chapter in the *Core J2EE Patterns: Best Practices and Design Strategies* book.

Java Persistence Architecture API and Object Relational Mapping

The Java Persistence API (JPA) manages the application's interactions with the data source. It specifies how to access, persist, and manage data between the application's objects and the data source. JPA itself cannot perform CRUD or other data-related operations; it's just a set of interfaces and implementation requirements. However, a compliant Java EE application server must provide support for its use.

The JPA specification replaces the EJB 2.0 Container-Managed Persistence (CMP) entity beans specification, which was heavyweight and complex. CMP received an adverse reaction from many in the developer community that resulted in the wide adoption of proprietary solutions such as Hibernate and TopLink. This prompted the development of JPA (released with EJB 3.0), which aimed to bring together CMP, Hibernate, and TopLink and seems to have been largely successful.

At the heart of JPA is the concept of an entity. For those of you familiar with CMP, this is what was referred to as an *entity bean*. An *entity* is a short-lived object that is capable of being persisted in a database—not as a serialized object but as data. It is a Plain Old Java Object (POJO) whose members are annotated and mapped to a field in the data source. To better understand how this is represented in code, you'll go through a code snippet.

In the following snippet, you represent a `Movie` entity class as a POJO that's appropriately annotated:

```
@Entity
public class Movie {

    @Id @GeneratedValue
    private Long id;
    private String title;
    private String description;
    private Float price;
    public Movie(){}
    // For brevity, the getters and setters have been left out.

}
```

As you can see, this is a simple class with just three annotations. The `@Entity` class level annotations indicate that this class should be treated as an entity class, and the `@Id` and `@Generated` annotations mark the `id` member as an auto-generated identification field. This means that when the entity is persisted, the `id` field is automatically generated according to the rules of auto-generated fields laid down by the data source. If the data source is a database, then all fields in this entity are persisted to a table called `Movie`. No other annotations are necessary to indicate which fields are persisted. It is convention over configuration that all fields are persisted unless otherwise annotated. This mapping is referred to as *Object Relational Mapping* (ORM). It is beyond the scope of this chapter to discuss in detail JPA and ORM, so it is recommended that you read *The Java EE 7 Tutorial: Part VIII Persistence*.[2]

IMPLEMENTING THE DATA ACCESS PATTERN IN JAVA EE

Now you'll go through an example to see how to implement the DAO in Java EE. You are going to use the movie rental domain and a relational database as the data source. You'll start by creating a movie entity class and annotating it with appropriate JPA annotations, as shown in Listing 12-1.

LISTING 12-1: The movie entity class

```java
package com.devchronicles.dataaccessobject;

import java.io.Serializable;
import javax.persistence.Entity;
import javax.persistence.Id;
import javax.persistence.NamedQuery;

@Entity
public class Movie implements Serializable {
    private static final long serialVersionUID = -6580012241620579129L;

    @Id @GeneratedValue
    private int id;
    private String title;
    private String description;
    private int price;
    //Some runtime value which
    //does not need to be persisted
    @Transient
    private int runtimeId;

    public Movie() {}

    public int getId() {
        return this.id;
    }

    public void setId(int id) {
        this.id = id;
    }

    public String getTitle() {
        return this.title;
    }

    public void setTitle(String title) {
        this.title = title;
    }

    public String getDescription() {
        return this.description;
```

continues

LISTING 12-1 *(continued)*

```
    }

    public void setDescription(String description) {
        this.description = description;
    }

    public int getPrice() {
        return this.price;
    }

    public void setPrice(int price) {
        this.price = price;
    }

    public int getRuntimeId() {
        return this.runtimeId;
    }

    public void setRuntimeId(int runtimeId) {
        this.runtimeId = runtimeId;
    }

}
```

The class in Listing 12-1 is a simple POJO with appropriate JPA annotations. As briefly mentioned earlier, the `@Entity` class level annotation indicates that this class should be treated as an entity class and should be managed by the persistence provider. The entity class must have a no-arg constructor that has to be public or protected, although it may have other constructors. It must be a top-level class, which means that it cannot be an enum or an interface, and it must not be final. Also, none of the persistent instance variables or setter/getter methods of the entity class can be final. The entity class must implement the `Serializable` interface.

You have annotated the `id` member with `@Id` and `@GeneratedValue`, which marks the `id` member as an auto-generated primary key. All entities must have a primary key, which can be a single member or a combination of members.

The primary key can be one of the following types:

➤ **Primitive Java types**—`byte`, `char`, `short`, `int`, `long`

➤ **Wrapper classes of primitive Java types**—`Byte`, `Character`, `Short`, `Integer`, `Long`

➤ **Arrays of primitive or wrapper types**—`long[]`, `Long[]`, and so on

➤ **Java types**—`String`, `BigInteger`, `Date`

All members of the entity class are automatically mapped to fields of the same name in the `movie` table unless they're annotated with `@Transient`. This means that the `id` member maps to the `id` field in the `movie` table, the `title` member maps to the `title` field in the `movie` table, and so on.

Next, in Listing 12-2, you create the DAO interface. This should define the basic CRUD methods and any other methods that might prove useful.

```
package com.devchronicles.dataaccessobject;

import java.util.List;

public interface MovieDAO {
    public void addMovie(Movie movie);
    public Movie getMovie(int id);
    public void deleteMovie(int id);
    public void updateMovie(Movie movie);
    public List<Movie> getAllMovies();
}
```

Now for the concrete implementation of the DAO interface shown in Listing 12-3. Here you implement the CRUD operations. Notice that the constructor accepts an instance of the `EntityManager`. This instance is associated with a persistence context that is defined in `persistence.xml`. The `EntityManager` API provides create, remove, and persistence functionality as well as the ability to create queries. Any transient field would not be saved or retrieved from the database so expect the data on the transient field to be reset each time the object is re-created.

```
package com.devchronicles.dataaccessobject;

import java.util.List;
import javax.persistence.EntityManager;

public class MovieDAOImpl implements MovieDAO{

    private EntityManager em;

    public MovieDAOImpl(EntityManager em) {
        this.em = em;
    }

    @Override
    public void addMovie(Movie movie) {
        em.persist(movie);
    }

    @Override
    public Movie getMovie(int id) {
        return getAllMovies().get(id);
    }

    @Override
    public void deleteMovie(int id) {
        em.remove(getMovie(id));
```

continues

LISTING 12-3 *(continued)*

```
    }

    @Override
    public void updateMovie(Movie movie) {
        em.merge(movie);
    }

    @Override
    public List<Movie> getAllMovies() {
        return em.createQuery("SELECT m FROM Movie m", Movie.class)
        .getResultList();
    }
}
```

In Listing 12-4, you create the DAO factory. The `EntityManager` is created and injected into this class and then passed as a constructor argument to the `createMovieDAO` method that creates the DAO object. The factory pattern is discussed in more detail in Chapter 6, so please refer to it for more information.

LISTING 12-4: The DAO Factory

```
package com.devchronicles.dataaccessobject;

import javax.enterprise.context.ApplicationScoped;
import javax.enterprise.inject.Produces;
import javax.persistence.EntityManager;
import javax.persistence.PersistenceContext;

@ApplicationScoped
public class MovieDAOFactory {

    @PersistenceContext(unitName="moviePU")
    private EntityManager em;

    @Produces
    public MovieDAO createMovieDAO() {
        return new MovieDAOImpl(em);
    }

}
```

The list of entities in your application is called a *persistence unit*, and the application's persistence unit is defined in the `persistence.xml` configuration file. This file should reside in your application's META-INF directory. The significant elements of `persistence.xml` follow:

➤   **Persistence unit name**—You can give the persistence unit a name so that you can define several persistence units and then select them at run time.

➤ **Persistence unit transaction type**—In a Java SE application, the default transaction type is *RESOURCE_LOCAL*, while in a Java EE environment, the transaction type is *JTA*. This means that the entity manager participates in the transaction.

➤ **Provider**—This element identifies the class that provides the factory for creating the EntityManager instance.

➤ **Class**—The entity classes used in the application should be listed in the class element.

➤ **Property**—Additional properties can be specified, such as database connection properties and persistence provider properties like options to drop-create new tables.

The EntityManager is associated with a persistence context that is defined in the persistence.xml in Listing 12-5.

LISTING 12-5: The persistence.xml

```xml
<?xml version="1.0" encoding="UTF-8"?>
<persistence version="2.1"
    xmlns="http://xmlns.jcp.org/xml/ns/persistence"
xmlns:xsi="http://www.w3.org/2001/XMLSchema-instance"
    xsi:schemaLocation="http://xmlns.jcp.org/xml/ns/persistence
http://xmlns.jcp.org/xml/ns/persistence/persistence_2_1.xsd">
    <persistence-unit name="moviePU" transaction-type="JTA">
    <provider>org.eclipse.persistence.jpa.PersistenceProvider</provider>
        <jta-data-source>jdbc/sample</jta-data-source>
        <class>com.devchronicles.dataaccessobject.Movie</class>
    </persistence-unit>
</persistence>
```

The specific data source is defined in this persistence.xml file. In this case, you have defined a Derby database using the eclipse link provider. You have defined the transaction type as JTA because this is a Java EE application implementation, and you have specified the class entity to be *com.devchronicles.dataaccessobject.Movie*.

Finally, you need to inject the DAO that you have created and use it. The client in Listing 12-6 gets an instance of the DAO injected and uses it to retrieve all movies.

LISTING 12-6: The client

```java
package com.devchronicles.dataaccessobject;

import javax.ejb.Stateless;
import javax.inject.Inject;
import java.util.List;

@Stateless
public class Client {

    @Inject
```

continues

LISTING 12-6 *(continued)*

```
    MovieDAO movieDAO;

    public List<Movie> getAllMovies() {
        return movieDAO.getAllMovies();
    }

}
```

The preceding implementation of the DAO is simplistic and can be improved upon in several ways.

Type-Safe DAO Implementation

One way to improve upon the DAO implementation is to make the DAO interface type-safe. This allows a type-safe DAO that a subinterface can implement for each entity type you want to persist. A base DAO might look like the code in Listing 12-7.

LISTING 12-7: Type-safe base DAO

```
    package com.devchronicles.dataaccessobject;

    import java.util.List;

    public interface BaseDAO<E, K> {
        public void create(E entity);
        public Movie retrieve(K id);
        public void update(E entity);
        public void delete(K id);
    }
```

The first type parameter, E, is used to represent the entity, whereas the K type parameter is used as the key. A subinterface that would define methods specific to that entity could then extend the BaseDAO interface.

In Listing 12-8, you create an interface that extends the BaseDAO and defines a method that returns a list of all movies.

LISTING 12-8: Specific movie implementation of the base DAO

```
    package com.devchronicles.dataaccessobject;

    import java.util.List;

    public interface MovieDAO extends BaseDAO<Movie, Integer>{

        public List<Movie> findAllMovies();

    }
```

A concrete class would implement this interface and provide code for each method.

WHERE AND WHEN TO USE THE DATA ACCESS PATTERN

Some have argued that the DAO is no longer a useful pattern because you can easily invoke the `EntityManager` directly. This is a reasonable argument because the `EntityManager` provides a clean API that abstracts away the underlying data access layer. It is also reasonable to suggest that the likelihood of a change in the data provider is remote, which makes the abstraction that the DAO provides less purposeful. Although these arguments have merit, it is still arguable that the DAO has its place in a well-designed Java EE application. (The place might not be where it was originally intended, though.)

The value of extending the `BaseDAO` as shown in Listing 12-7 for each entity type is in the extensibility of each implementation. Methods that are specific to an entity can be written while maintaining a common interface. You select the DAO implementation once for each entity rather than choosing the right `EntityManager` method each time it is required to persist or retrieve data.

Named queries can be located within the entity to which they relate. This keeps the queries in a logical place, making maintenance easier. The DAO allows for a uniformed and controlled data access strategy because all access to the entity's data is required to go via the entity's DAO. It maintains the principle of single responsibility because only the DAO accesses and manipulates the application's data.

Don't forget that even though it's remote, the data source might change. If it does, you'll be glad that there is an abstraction on the data layer.

SUMMARY

The DAO has its fans and detractors. The decision of whether to use the pattern in your application should be based on the design requirements of the application. Like all patterns, its use for use's sake is potentially dangerous and could cause more confusion because over abstract obscures the purpose of the code. Ensure that you understand well the various implementations of the pattern and how it interacts with the DTO and factory pattern.

EXERCISES

1. Write an interface and its implementation for a movie order DAO. You can use the examples in the text as a starting block.

2. Write a service façade and a DTO that uses the MovieDAO.

NOTES

1. *Core J2EE Patterns: Best Practices and Design Strategies* (Prentice Hall/Sun Microsystems Press, 2003): Deepak Alur, John Crupi, and Dan Malks.
2. *The Java EE 7 Tutorial: Part VIII Persistence.*
   http://docs.oracle.com/javaee/7/tutorial/doc/.

13

RESTful Web Services

WROX.COM CODE DOWNLOADS FOR THIS CHAPTER

The wrox.com code download for this chapter is found at www.wrox.com/go/projavaeedesignpatterns on the Download Code tab. The code is in the Chapter 13 download and individually named according to the names throughout the chapter.

There is little doubt that you will have heard the term REST. What is less certain is that you will understand exactly what it means and how it is implemented. Many people who know nothing or very little about REST will tell you that your site must be REST "compatible" and that, without REST, your site cannot possibly survive. REST is a buzzword to these people, but for those who know what REST is and what benefits it can offer, it's much more than just another buzzword. So what does REST really mean, and where does it come from?

REST means REpresentational State Transfer and is an architectural style of representing and transferring data. It consists of a set of six constraints placed on data, components, and their interactions within a distributed hypermedia system (the Internet). It is not tied to a protocol (although in almost all cases it is used with Hypertext Transfer Protocol [HTTP]), and it does not have a World Wide Web Consortium (W3C) standard. It is a set of conventions, styles, and approaches that have been agreed upon over time by use and convention.

The term *REST* was coined by Roy Fielding in his 2000 doctoral dissertation titled "Architectural Styles and the Design of Network-Based Software Architectures."[1] Since then, the REST concept has been widely adopted by developers and architects such that it has become an integral part of many languages and frameworks. For example, Ruby provides a natural way to use RESTful routes, and the Spring framework provides a simplified way to implement Hypermedia As The Engine Of Application State (HATEOAS), which is level 3 of the Richardson Maturity Model of REST support (more on this later).[2]

REST is usually referred to as an architectural approach rather than a design pattern. However, REST was developed against common problems faced in enterprise app, which is the same idea behind the design patterns.

WHAT IS REST?

REST means many things to many people, and discussions can become quite theoretical. This chapter discusses it from the perspective of a developer who wants to implement a RESTful application programming interface (API) for a forum site discussing movies.

IN THE WORDS OF ROY FIELDING

REST emphasizes scalability of component interactions, generality of interfaces, independent deployment of components, and intermediary components to reduce interaction latency, enforce security, and encapsulate legacy systems.

The most practical way of thinking about REST is as a style for formatting URIs that represents resources (data) your application can provide and resources that it can store. What is meant by resources? In a forum website, you have many resources, such as the site's users and the users' posts. These resources are represented by nouns and combined with an HTTP method to form a RESTful uniform resource identifier (URI). For example, you can represent an account resource with the URI /accounts and combine it with the HTTP GET method such that a request to this URI would return all accounts. Likewise, you can represent an identifiable account resource by appending the post's ID to the URI like so: /accounts/:id. A GET request to this URI returns the details of the account with the given ID. Not only can you get resource representations by using a RESTful URI, you can create resources. To do this, you would create a URI using the HTTP POST method. For example, to create a new account resource, you would send a POST request to the URI /accounts with a payload in the HTTP body containing the data necessary to create the resource.

As you have gathered, a URI represents a resource on a remote server, and the method of requesting the resources (the HTTP method) implies certain actions on that resource.

It is tempting to map HTTP methods to create, retrieve, update, and delete (CRUD) actions (for example, POST to Create and GET to Read).[3] However, this is not in the spirit of REST and does not help in the understanding of resource representations. In fact, it's more akin to a remote procedure call (RPC) pattern implementation, which is at level 0 on the Richardson Maturity Model. You are only interested in implementing REST at the highest level: level 3, please refer to the section, "Richardson Maturity Model of REST API" for full details.

A RESTful API is not about actions; it's about nouns. These nouns represent resources. So you'll learn about a post resource, a user resource, and an address resource as opposed to verbs such as `getUser`, `addPost`, and `deleteAddress`. REST is different from simple object access protocol (SOAP) and RPC, which are about the actions you want to perform on the application's data. In a RESTful sense, you would call a URI with an appropriate HTTP method.

Each resource is identified by a URI. There may be multiple ways to refer to the same resources, so you might be able to access the same resource from different starting points. For example, you can obtain the resource that represents a user by accessing the user directly via the URI `GET /users/:id` or by going from one user to the list of users who follow that user and then to the user `GET /user/:id1/followers/:id1`. The representation of the resource is not the actual resource itself; it's a representation of the resource, and it is perfectly valid for the same resource to be represented in different ways.

The resource representation flow is bidirectional between client and server and represents at least part of the resource state. When that happens, it contains just enough data to create, modify, or delete that resource on the server.

Resource representations are typically JavaScript Object Notation (JSON) or Extensible Markup Language (XML), but they can be any format, including a custom representation.

THE SIX CONSTRAINTS OF REST

According to Roy Fielding's dissertation, a truly RESTful architecture conforms to all but one of the stated constraints. This group of constraints is called the REST style.

Client-Server

The client-server constraint is based on the separations of concerns principle and defines clearly the separation between the client and the server. The constraint is simple and requires a client to send a request and a server to receive that request. The server may respond to the client's request.

Uniform Interface

This constraint defines the interface between the client and the server, stating that it should be as generic and simple as possible. You have already learned that a resource is a representation of the data, and the client does not have direct access to the data. This constraint defines how that resource is represented by nouns and that the interface is maintained by the creator of the actual data system. This is to ensure some degree of constancy of the interfaces over time. The constraint does not specify that the implementation should use the HTTP protocol, but it is almost always based on HTTP. As you have already seen, if you use the HTTP specification, the URI is constructed from the resource nouns and the HTTP verbs.

Stateless

The server should not maintain client state. In other words, each message/request is self-descriptive; it has enough information or context for the server to process that message. This implies that if there is state, it is maintained on the client side. The advantage of this constraint is that it increases scalability, reliability, and visibility. The disadvantage is that it decreases performance because messages need to be larger to maintain stateless communication.

Cacheable

The server responses must be cacheable. The RESTful interface should provide a mechanism for marking messages as cacheable or noncacheable. This can be implicit, explicit, or negotiated and allows the client to reissue a message if necessary.

Layered System

The client cannot assume direct access to the server. The response may be a cached response, or it may retrieve the resource directly from the server. This improves scalability because there might be software or hardware between the client and the server.

Code on Demand

This constraint defines a REST architecture as consisting of hierarchical layers that are limited to communicating with their immediate neighbors. This separation of concerns simplifies the architecture and isolates disparate and legacy components. The principle benefit you receive is an increase in scalability because new components can be easily introduced and obsolete ones retired or replaced. The drawback of this constraint is a reduction in the system's performance resulting from the increased indirection related to the multiple layer structure.

This constraint allows a client to download and execute code from the server, which enables the server to temporarily extend the client by transferring logic. This may be in the form of a JavaScript snippet. The code on demand constraint is the only optional one.

Violating any of these constraints (except code on demand) means that the service is not strictly RESTful. A constraint violation does not mean the service is not a viable and useful implementation, however.

RICHARDSON MATURITY MODEL OF REST API

You have already read about how a truly RESTful API achieves level 3 of the Richardson Maturity Model. Now you'll look a little deeper and examine each level on the model.

The model, developed by Leonard Richardson, attempts to classify an API according to its adherence to the constraints imposed by REST. The more compliant your implementation, the better it fares. There are four levels. The bottom is level 0, which designates the less compliant implementation, and the top is level 3, which is the most compliant and therefore the most RESTful.[4]

Level 0: The Swamp of POX (Plain Old XML)

This model uses HTTP as a transport protocol to invoke remote interactions. It does not use the protocol to indicate an application state; it is usually just used to tunnel requests and responses on one URI, such as /getUser, using only one HTTP method. This is a classic example of an RPC model and is more akin to SOAP and XML-RPC than REST.

Level 1: Resources

This is where the model starts to be able to distinguish between different resources. It will talk to different end points because each end point represents a different resource. It uses a URI like POST resources/123, but it still uses just one HTTP method.

Level 2: HTTP Verbs

At this level, you implement full use of the HTTP verbs and combine them with your resource nouns to provide the type of REST that has been discussed so far in this chapter. You take full advantage of the features that HTTP offers to implement your RESTful API. However, you still have not reached the level of a truly RESTful API.

Level 3: Hypermedia Controls

At this level, the model uses HATEOAS (Hypermedia As The Engine Of Application State) to direct the application state. The objective of hypermedia controls is to advise the client of what can be done next and to supply the URIs necessary to perform the next action. You will see how this works and how to implement HATEOAS later in this chapter.

DESIGNING A RESTFUL API

A well-designed RESTful API means a well-defined uniform interface. For this, a thorough understanding of the HTTP methods and response codes is important, and a complete knowledge of the data structure of your application is needed. The objective is to combine them into a simple, clean, and beautiful resource URI.

WAR STORY

One of the companies I worked for had a tradition that once a team completed a project, it presented its project to the other teams. It was at about the same time that REST was getting popular. One of the teams decided to build a REST back end to serve both the mobile and the web clients. We were thrilled and listened intently to how they successfully built a beautifully designed REST back end and how it was able to serve data for both systems. As the team's lead started to give technical details about the system, we realized they were maintaining the client state on the server side. Not at all RESTful.

continues

continued

I raised the issue and asked if that design was really following RESTful principles. Of course, my words offended the project architect, and he started showing us the REST API docs and how each client would work with OAuth and passing parameters via uniform resource locators (URLs). Nevertheless, the system was relying on preserving the state rather than transferring it.

Just like fashionistas, developers and system designers love trends and want to look trendy. However, without understanding the underlying principles and determining whether they really address your concerns and problems, you may end up being the weird-looking guy who wanted to be trendy but failed to fully understand the technology. In their case, they had built a representative state preserving (RESP?) back end instead of REST.

You will soon learn the elements that make up a URI.

Resource Naming

RESTful APIs are written for clients and should have meaning for the clients of those APIs. When choosing nouns to name the resources, you should be familiar with the structure of the application's data and how your clients are likely to use them. There are no defined rules as to how you should name your resources, but there are conventions that, if followed, can help you create a set of self-descriptive resource names that others intuitively understand.

Nouns Not Verbs

You must name the resources after nouns, not verbs or actions. The purpose of the resource name is to represent the resource. The HTTP method describes the action to be performed. The next section covers the HTTP method in more detail. To represent a single user resource, you would use the noun *users* to represent all users and the user's ID to identify the specific user, like so: `users/123456`. An example of a non-REST and badly formed URI would be `users/123456/update`, or it would include the action in a query string such as `users/123456?action=update`.

The nature of data is that it is hierarchical. So imagine that you want to represent all the posts of the user with ID `123456`. You would use the noun *posts* to represent all posts and create the URI `users/123456/posts`. Earlier, it was mentioned that the representation of the resource is not the actual resource itself, but a representation of the resource, and the same resource can be represented in different ways. To represent all posts by a specified user, you can use the URI `posts/users/123456`. Once you have a representation of a resource, you can decide what you want to do with it by using one of the four HTTP methods. To retrieve a resource, you use the `GET` method, and to create a resource, you use the `POST` method. More on this in the next section.

Self-Descriptive

As you have seen, the nouns chosen should reflect the resource they represent. Combining these representations with identifiers makes the URI easy to interpret and intuitive to understand. If you read a URI in combination with its HTTP method and it is not immediately obvious what resource it represents, it has failed as a RESTful URI.

Plural Not Singular

Resource names should be plural because they represent collections of data. The resource name *users* represents a collection of users, and the resource name *posts* represents a collection of posts. The idea is that plural nouns represent a collection in the service, and the ID refers to one instance within that collection. It may be justifiable to use a singular noun if there is only one instance of that data type in the entire application, but this is quite uncommon.

HTTP Methods

There are eight HTTP methods defined in Hypertext Transfer Protocol 1.1; however, only four are commonly used when designing RESTful APIs. They are GET, POST, PUT, and DELETE. These methods have specified meanings and usages within the context of REST. The concept of idempotency is especially important when considering the HTTP method. The meaning of idempotency from a RESTful API point of view is that a call repeatedly made by a client to the same URI will always produce the same result. So making one request produces the same outcome, on the server, as the request made multiple times. (This assumes that a different and separate operation has not changed the resource's state.)

Only one of the four most commonly used methods is idempotent: GET. This means that any resource URI that is executed with this method cannot effect change on the server. You cannot use it to create, update, or delete a resource. The HTTP 1.1 specification refers to this method as safe because it "should not have the significance of taking an action other than retrieval." In the context of REST, this method is used for getting a resource's representation from the server. It must never be used to make changes to data.

The other three methods—POST, PUT, and DELETE—are not idempotent methods and are expected to effect change on the server. You'll learn about each method and how to use it in the context of a forum site. You'll also learn about the HTTP response codes (http://www.w3.org/Protocols/rfc2616/rfc2616-sec10.html) that can be returned, along with the responses to the client and what they mean.

GET

You use this method to get resource representations from the service. You should never use it to update, delete, or create a resource. Calling it once should have the same effect as calling it 100 times. If the resource requested is successful, the representation of the resource is returned in the body of the HTTP response in the requested data format, which commonly is either JSON or XML. The HTTP response code returned is 200 (OK). If the resource is not found, it should return 404 (NOT FOUND), and if the resource request is badly formed, it should return 400 (BAD REQUEST). A well-formed URI that you might use in your forum application could be GET users/123456/followers, which represents all the followers of the user 123456.

POST

You use the POST method to create a new resource within the given context. For example, to create a new user, you would post to the *users* resource the data necessary for a new user to be created. The service takes care of creating the new resource, associating it to the context, and assigning an

ID. On successful creation, the HTTP response is 201 (CREATED), and a link to the newly created resource is returned either in the Location header of the response or in the JSON payload of the response body. The resource representation may be returned in the response body. This is often preferable to avoid making an additional call to the API to retrieve a representation of the data that had been just created. This reduces the chattiness of the API.

In addition to the HTTP response codes to a GET request, a POST can return 204 (NO CONTENT) if the body of the request is empty. A well-formed URI that you might use in your forum application could be POST users, with a request body containing the new user's details or POST users/123456/ posts to create a new post for the user 123456 from the data in the request body.

PUT

The PUT method is most commonly used to update a known resource. The URI includes enough information to identify the resource, such as a context and an identifier. The request body contains the updated version of the resource, and if the update is successful, it returns the HTTP response code 200. A URI that updates a user's information is PUT users/123456. Less commonly, you can use the PUT method to create a resource if the client creates the identifier of the resource. However, this way of creating a resource is a little confusing. Why use a PUT when a POST works just as well and is commonly known? An important point to note about updating a resource is that the entire representation of the resource is passed to the service in the HTTP body request, not just the information that has changed.

DELETE

Surprisingly, you use this method to delete a resource from a service. The URI contains the context and the identifier of the resource. To delete a user with the ID 123456, you use the URI DELETE users/123456. The response body may include a representation of the deleted resource. A successful deletion results in a 200 (OK) HTTP response code being returned; if the resource is not found, a 400 code is returned.

REST IN ACTION

You are going to design the RESTful API for a forum site using what you have learned so far.

You start by examining the data structure of the site and identifying the data domains. The two main domains are users and posts. Users can be further analyzed into followers, and posts are often organized under topics. So with these domains, start thinking about the URI you need to represent these resources.

The *users* noun

To create a new user, you know that you must use POST and the *users* context, so a URI that creates a user would look like this:

```
POST /users
```

The body of the request contains all that you need to create the new user. The response includes the URI to the representation of the user. This is a GET method request, like so: GET /users/123456. This requests details of the user with ID 123456.

If you want to update the user, you need to use the PUT method like so: PUT /users/123456.

And if you want to delete the user, you use the DELETE method, like so: DELETE /users/123456.

If you want to do a batch delete, it is acceptable to pass all the IDs of the users you want to delete in the body of a call to DELETE /users. This would be far less chatty than multiple calls to each user's resource.

You might want to get all users in the service like so: GET /users. This call would, of course, be restricted by security so that only the users that the caller is authorized to view would be returned.

That is all for the user's context. Now you'll look at the *follower's*. A follower is a user who follows another user because he is interested in that person's posts.

To get all the followers for a given user, use the GET method, like so:

```
GET /users/123456/followers
```

To create a new follower of a user, you pass the ID of that follower in the body of a request to POST /users/123456/followers. You can get the details of the follower in one of two ways:

```
GET /users/123456/followers/456789
```

or

```
GET /users/456789
```

This is an example of how you can represent a resource in two different ways. To delete a follower of a given user, you can do this:

```
DELETE /users/123456/followers/456789
```

This action removes user 456789 as a follower of user 123456 but does not actually delete the user. However, the following deletes the user:

```
DELETE /users/456789
```

You have read about the followers context. Now you'll look at the topics and posts.

The *topics* noun and the *posts* noun

You have already seen how to create a user by using the POST method. The same is true when creating a topic and a post.

To create a topic, use:

```
POST /topics
```

To create a post under a topic, use:

```
POST /topics/123/posts
```

Note that you cannot create a post by doing this:

```
POST /posts
```

because you have no context. There is not enough information for the service to create a post because you don't know to which topic the post should be associated.

To get a topic and a post, use:

```
GET /topics/123
```

To get a specific post under a topic, use:

```
GET /topics/123/posts/456
```

or

```
GET /posts/456
```

To delete a topic or a post, use:

```
DELETE /topics/123
```

To delete a post, use:

```
DELETE /topics/123/posts/456
```

or

```
DELETE /posts/456
```

To amend a post or a topic, use can any of the following three methods:

```
PUT /topics/123
PUT /topics/123/posts/456
```

or

```
PUT posts/456
```

Now that you have the simplest URIs and contexts defined, you can start to have some fun and combine the users, topic, and post to make them more complicated.

To retrieve a representation of all topics posted by a given user, use this:

```
GET /users/123456/posts
```

To get all posts under a given topic for a given user, use this:

```
GET /users/123456/topics/123/posts
```

To get all posts by a follower of a given user of a given topic, use this:

```
GET /users/123456/followers/456789/topics/123/posts
```

You can be creative with your combinations of resource. Despite the seemingly complicated nature, you must never forget that the clients of the RESTful API use the URIs, so the URIs should be easy to understand, and nesting should be kept to a minimum. If you feel that your URI is so complicated that it should be accompanied by an explanation, you should consider refactoring it.

An example of a well-designed and thought out RESTful API has been implemented by the cloud storage company Sugarsync (https://www.sugarsync.com/developer). I recommend that you review their resource reference to see how they clearly define the folder, address, and workspace resources. Note how the HTTP methods are used to create, read, and delete resources.

IMPLEMENTING REST IN JAVA EE

This chapter has discussed at length the theory behind a well-designed RESTful API. Now that you have seen how you might style the URIs, you can jump in and see how all this looks in code.

Java EE 7 provides some helpful annotations that make the job of constructing a RESTful API straightforward. The most useful is the `@Path` annotation. This annotation defines the context URI and the class or method that will process requests made on that URI. Additionally, there are annotations for each HTTP method: `@GET`, `@POST`, `@PUT`, `@DELETE`, and so on. These annotations mark methods that will process requests made with the stated HTTP method.

Your application can have more than one RESTful context. To take care of this case, the `@ApplicationPath` annotation takes a parameter that denotes the space in which your RESTful API will exist. With just these two types of annotations, you have all you need to implement a simple RESTful API.

Now in Listing 13-1 you'll implement the URI `GET /users`.

LISTING 13-1: Simplest implementation of a RESTful API in Java EE

```
package co.uk.devchronicles.forum;

import javax.ws.rs.ApplicationPath;
import javax.ws.rs.GET;
import javax.ws.rs.Path;
import javax.ws.rs.core.Application;

@ApplicationPath("/")
@Path("users")
public class Users extends Application{

    @GET
    public String getUsers(){
        return "Here we return a representation of all users";
    }
}
```

If you have this application deployed on your local machine and your application is called `forum`, you can test this URI by visiting `http://localhost/forum/users`. You should notice the text message `Here we return a representation of all users` displayed in the browser window.

Note in Listing 13-1 how you can annotate the class with the `@Path` annotation and pass it the users context. The string that you pass does not have to be preceded by a forward slash or be followed by a trailing slash. The space in which the RESTful interface will exist has been defined as the root ("/") of the application. The method that is called when a `GET` request is made to the URI users is annotated with the `@GET` annotation. In this simple example, a string is returned, but the real goal is to send back the data retrieved for the database in a JSON or XML format along with an HTTP status code. This is what occurs in Listing 13-2.

LISTING 13-2: Responding to the client with a JSON payload

```java
package co.uk.devchronicles.forum;

import java.util.ArrayList;

import javax.json.Json;
import javax.json.JsonArrayBuilder;
import javax.ws.rs.ApplicationPath;
import javax.ws.rs.GET;
import javax.ws.rs.Path;
import javax.ws.rs.Produces;
import javax.ws.rs.core.Application;
import javax.ws.rs.core.MediaType;
import javax.ws.rs.core.Response;

@ApplicationPath("/")
@Path("users")
public class Users extends Application{

    @GET
    @Produces(MediaType.APPLICATION_JSON)
    public Response getUsers(){

        ArrayList<User> allUsers = this.findAllUsers();
        JsonArrayBuilder jsonArrayBuilder = Json.createArrayBuilder();

        for(User user : allUsers){
            jsonArrayBuilder.add(
                Json.createObjectBuilder()
                    .add("id", user.getId())
                    .add("firstname", user.getFirstname())
                    .add("lastname", user.getLastname())
            );
        }

        return Response.ok(jsonArrayBuilder.build()).build();
    }

    public ArrayList<User> findAllUsers(){
        ArrayList<User> allUsers = new ArrayList<>();
        allUsers.add(new User(123456, "Alex","Theedom"));
        allUsers.add(new User(456789, "Murat","Yener"));
        return allUsers;
    }

}
```

Listing 13-2 generates a JSON object from the user data that's in the database (for brevity, a method is used to return the user data) and sends it back to the client with a 200 HTTP response code. The first thing you will notice is that the getUsers() method is now annotated with @Produces(MediaType.APPLICATION _ JSON); this specifies the MIME type that this method can produce and returns to the client. The javax.json.Json and javax.json.JsonArrayBuilder classes are used to build the JSON and wrap it as a javax.ws.rs.core.Response object before returning it to the client. If all goes well, you should see the following output in the browser:

```
[
    {"id":123456,"firstname":"Alex","lastname":"Theedom"},
    {"id":456789,"firstname":"Murat","lastname":"Yener"}
]
```

So far, you have seen how to retrieve a resource representation of all users in the system, but what if you only want one user and you know the user's identification number? Well, this is just as simple. In the URI, you pass the user's ID number like so:

```
GET /users/123456
```

and in the REST controller class, you recuperate the ID number by referencing the REST path and using a URI variable to pass the ID to the method. You annotate the method that will consume the RESTful API call with @Path("/{id}"), and in the signature of the method, you annotate the argument to which the ID value should be passed.

```
@GET
@Path("/{id}")
@Produces(MediaType.APPLICATION_JSON)
public Response getUser(@PathParam("id") String id){
    User user = this.findUser(id);
    JsonArrayBuilder jsonArrayBuilder = Json.createArrayBuilder();
    jsonArrayBuilder.add(
                    Json.createObjectBuilder()
                                    .add("id", user.getId())
                                    .add("firstname", user.getFirstname())
                                    .add("lastname", user.getLastname())
    );

    return Response.ok(jsonArrayBuilder.build()).build();
}

public User findUser(String id){
    return new User("123456", "Alex","Theedom");
}
```

As you can see in the previous code snippet, the ID string parameter is annotated with @PathParam("id") so that the ID recuperated from the URI by the @Path("/{id}") annotation is passed into the method. It is not necessary to include the full path of the URI in the @Path annotation because the base URI is set in the @Path annotation on the class. All paths set on methods are relative to the base path set on the class.

The URI variable can be a regular expression. For example, the path annotation @Path("/{id: [0-9]*}") will match only IDs that are numbers. Any IDs that don't match will result in a 404 HTTP response being returned to the client.

You have seen some simple URI constructions that consist of one resource noun and a URI variable. How do you deal with a more complicated URI, such as GET /users/123456/followers/456789? You do it in the same way as before, just with a slightly more complicated @Path and @PathParam.

```
@GET
@Path("/{user_id}/followers/{follower_id}")
@Produces(MediaType.APPLICATION_JSON)
public Response getUser(
@PathParam("user_id") String user_id,
@PathParam("follower_id") String follower_id)
```

You have looked in detail at the GET HTTP method. What about the POST, PUT, and DELETE methods? To write a method that responds to an HTTP POST request, you do almost the same as you would with GET, but you change two elements. You annotate the method with @POST instead of @GET and @Consumes in place of @Produces. Here's a simple example:

```
@POST
@Consumes(MediaType.APPLICATION_JSON)
@Path("/{user_id}/followers/")
public Response createUser(@PathParam("user_id") String user_id, String body)
```

This example works in the same way as for the GET methods, but notice that there is no explicit mapping of the HTTP request body to a method parameter. The mapping is implicit. The content of the HTTP body is passed to the only unannotated parameter that it finds in the method signature. No more than one is allowed to avoid confusion.

The PUT and DELETE HTTP methods operate in a similar way to the POST method.

Your URI may contain query parameters. You can retrieve these from the URI by annotating a parameter in the method signature with @QueryParam("page"). This annotation retrieves the page query parameter from the URI /users?page=10.

There are many more annotations in the JAX-RS API that facilitate the design of a good RESTful API. It's recommended that you familiarize yourself with all of them.

HATEOAS

As has already been discussed, HATEOAS is at the highest level of REST implementation in the Richardson Maturity Model and should be considered the nirvana of RESTfulness.

Imagine that a client requests a resource that represents all the posts in the system that the user has permission to view. The URI would be GET /posts, and the response, if successful, might return with the following HTTP body:

```
{
  "posts": [
    {
      "id": 71892,
      "title": "Best movie of 2015",
      "content": "I think the best movie of 2015 is the Golden Egg of Siam.",
      "links": [
        {
```

```
             "rel": "self",
             "href": "http://localhost:8080/rest/posts/71892",
             "method": "GET"
          },
          {
             "rel": "replies",
             "href": "http://localhost:8080/rest/posts/71892/posts",
             "method": "GET"
          },
          {
             "rel": "follower",
             "href": "http://localhost:8080/rest/posts/71892/followers",
             "method": "GET"
          },
          {
             "rel": "owner",
             "href": "http://localhost:8080/rest/posts/71892/users",
             "method": "GET"
          }
        ]
      },
      {
        "id": 71893,
        "title": "Worst movie of 2015",
        "content": "The worst movie has gotta be Just Being Me.",
        "links": [
          {
             "rel": "self",
             "href": "http://localhost:8080/rest/posts/71893",
             "method": "GET"
          },
          {
             "rel": "owner",
             "href": "http://localhost:8080/rest/posts/71893/users",
             "method": "GET"
          }
        ]
      }
    ]
  }
```

There's a lot going on here. The response is in JSON format and is formed of one JSON object named post that contains an array of posts:

```
{
  "posts": [
    {
      ... element one in the array
    },
    {
      ... element two in the array
    }
  ]
}
```

In the example, there are only two elements to the array representing two posts. Each post is a JSON object that follows the same format:

```
{
    "id": 71892,
    "title": "Best movie of 2015",
    "content": "I think the best movie of 2015 is the Golden Egg of Siam.",
}
```

As can be seen from the JSON snippet it contains an ID that identifies the post resource followed by the post's title and content. This is the minimum that you would expect to see in a response to a request for a post resource regardless of the maturity of the rest interface. What makes this response special is the links element.

```
"links": [
    {
      "rel": "self",
      "href": "http://localhost:8080/rest/posts/71892",
      "method": "GET"
    },
    ...
]
```

This is where HATEOAS comes to life. There are three parts to each link in the link array. The rel is the relation that the href link has to the current resource. The href is a link to more resources, and the method is the method that must be used to obtain the resource. The rel element can have any value and does not have to follow a convention, although it is customary for 'self' rel to refer to a link that represents more information about the current resource. In this example, it just refers to itself. The other links refer to other users' responses to the post (replies or responses), the users who follow the post (followers), and the user who posted the post (owner). Any resource that relates to the principle post resource can be represented by a link in the link array.

As you can see from the example, the first post in the array has four links in its links array, whereas the second has only two. This is because the second post does not have users following it or any responses.

Providing links in this way gives the client the information it needs to navigate to further resources and allows you to easily extend and grow the API with relatively little pain.

A good example of a well-designed implementation of HATEOAS is the one implemented by Paypal .com (https://developer.paypal.com/webapps/developer/docs/integration/direct/paypal-rest-payment-hateoas-links/). They have used HATEOAS to allow you to build an API that interacts with their payment system simply by following the links provide in the links array.

WHERE AND WHEN TO USE REST

REST is an easy and well-established approach that is not constrained by standards. Some may argue that this is a distinct disadvantage when compared to SOAP, which is an industry standard with its own well-defined protocol and implementation rules. However, its ease of implementation and use by others outweighs any difficulty created by a lack of a standard. Making a RESTful resource for consumption is as simple as providing a URI, and using the HTTP protocol cross-language communication is easy. The common language is HTTP, the language of the web, which is simple and understood by all.

Bandwidth limitation situations prove no problem for REST's lightweight approach and are especially attractive on mobile devices. It costs little to make a request for a resource from a RESTful API. Remember that it is just an HTTP request and that the data returned can be in any appropriate format. The format does not have to be JSON or XML; it can be Atom Syndicate Format (ATOM) or some custom format. The flexibility afforded by using just a simple URI to represent a resource allows the client developer to be imaginative. You can use Asynchronous Javascript and XML (AJAX) to call one or more URIs, perhaps from different REST providers. You can combine the responses to these calls to provide rich content for the site's visitors.

If your implementation of REST uses the HTTP protocol (which it most probably will), you receive the bonus feature of free caching. The HTTP protocol incorporates a cache as a core feature that you can exploit in your application by setting appropriate HTTP header values.

SUMMARY

Your application's REST API should be simple and intuitive for other developers to use, and it is your responsibility as a developer to design an API that fits the requirement of your application while ensuring that the API's users can access the resources required for the proper function of their application.

In this chapter we have touched upon the basics of a good RESTful API design. There are many more considerations that we have not even mentioned, such as security, the use of query strings, and how to provoke server side tasks.

Luckily REST is ubiquitous, and resources to help you develop a truly RESTful API are plentiful. Just search the Internet and you will not be at a loss for articles, forums, and books devoted to the topic of REST.

EXERCISES

1. Search the Internet for public RESTful APIs, and write some simple code that consumes them.

2. Implement the URI for the forum site detailed in the preceding text, and write a front end client that consumes them.

3. Develop one journey through the site using a fully HATEOAS-style approach.

NOTES

1. "Architectural Styles and the Design of Network-Based Software Architectures," Roy Fielding, 2000. Chapter 5: `www.ics.ucl.edu/~fielding/pubs/dissertation/rest_arch_style.htm`.
2. Leonard Richardson explained the model of RESTful maturity during a QCon talk in 2008. `www.crummy.com/writing/speaking/2008-QCon/act3.html`.
3. The HTTP/1.1 RFC standard defines the following methods: OPTIONS, GET, HEAD, POST, PUT, DELETE, TRACE, and CONNECT.
4. Martin Fowler provides a good overview on his website: `www.martinfowler.com/article/richardsonMaturityModel.html`.

14

Model View Controller Pattern

WHAT'S IN THIS CHAPTER?

➤ An introduction to the MVC pattern

➤ The MVC pattern's origins

➤ How to implement the MVC pattern using compound patterns

➤ Implementing the MVC pattern In Java EE

➤ When and where to use the MVC pattern

WROX.COM CODE DOWNLOADS FOR THIS CHAPTER

The wrox.com code download for this chapter is found at www.wrox.com/go/ projavaeedesignpatterns on the Download Code tab. The code is in the Chapter 14 download and individually named according to the names throughout the chapter.

The model view controller (MVC) pattern is one of the most ubiquitous architectural design patterns in modern application development that is listed in the book from the Gang of Four. It is built on the philosophy of separation of concerns and encapsulates the processing of application data from the presentation of the data. Not encapsulating the processing of data from the presentation of data leads to highly coupled systems that are hard to maintain and extend. The separation of concerns that the MVC pattern provides makes modifications to both the business logic and the user interface much easier and more independent.

The MVC pattern is not much different than buying a subscription from a cable provider and a TV set from an electrical store. One provides the content, and the other makes sure you view it in the right way. Neither worries about the changes in the technology on the field. You can always buy a new TV set when better panels are released or subscribe to more channels without buying new hardware.

Developers of web applications use the MVC pattern extensively, and it is within this context that its implementation will be discussed.

WHAT IS THE MVC DESIGN PATTERN?

In MVC, the *model* represents the application's data and related business logic. The model may be represented by one object or a complex graph of related objects. In a Java EE application, the data is encapsulated in domain objects often deployed in an EJB module. Data is transported to and from the database access layer in data transfer objects (DTOs) and accessed via data access objects (DAOs). See Chapter 12, "Data Access Pattern."

The *view* is the visual representation of the data contained in the model. A subset of the model is represented in a single view; thus, the view acts as a filter to the model data. The user interacts with the model data via the view's visual representation and invokes business logic that in turn acts upon the model data.

The *controller* links the view to the model and directs application flow. It chooses which view to render to the user in response to the user's input and the business logic that's processed. The controller receives a message from the view, which it forwards to the model. The model in turn prepares a response and sends it back to the controller where the view is chosen and sent to the user.

The MVC pattern logically spans the client and middle tier of a multitier architecture. In a Java EE environment, the model is located in the business layer, normally in the form of an Enterprise JavaBeans (EJB) module. The controller and view are located in the web tier. The view is likely to be constructed from JavaServer Faces (JSF) or JavaServer Pages (JSP) with the help of Expression Language (EL). The controller is normally a servlet that receives Hypertext Transfer Protocol (HTTP) requests from the user. See Chapter 2, "Basics of Java EE" for a discussion of multitier architecture and the different application layers.

Often the MVC pattern is combined with other patterns, such as the command (or action), strategy, composite, and observer patterns. This chapter doesn't delve into the depths of these patterns, but it does touch on the action pattern in the example that follows.

BACKGROUND

The first mention of this pattern occurred before the invention of the modern-day Internet in a paper published by the SmallTalk programmer Trygve Reenskaug in December 1979 while he was working at Xerox Parc.[1]

Even though the MVC elements of this pattern were defined more than 30 years ago, they are surprisingly relevant to their current use in a web application.

Figure 14-1 shows the user making a request to the controller. The controller handles the request by updating the model and rendering a new view, which is then sent to the user.

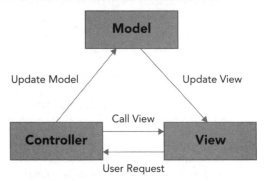

FIGURE 14-1: Diagram of the model view controller pattern

> **WAR STORY**
>
> Back when JSP was all the rage and the Y2K bug had not brought on the worldwide nuclear destruction that we had been promised, I was working for a small web start-up. Our start-up was composed of just a few JSP/Java developers and some flash designers. We wanted to build a website portal that would serve dynamic content that depended on the specific needs of the client that had contracted us.
>
> So we jumped into the project with 100 percent enthusiasm and developed a highly dynamic website that displayed different features for different clients. We were truly proud of our creation, and so were the many clients who bought our wonderful site. In fact, we were becoming quite successful, and rather quickly, too. It seemed that everyone was really happy with our product, and we were happy with our success. But that happiness was short lived. As more and more clients bought our product, the site became increasingly difficult to manage. What we had done was mix the business logic with the view logic, so for each new client, we had to amend all the JSP in the site. Soon the JSP became a horrible mishmash of business and display logic, and we ended up with unmanageable spaghetti code. It became a nightmare, so we had no choice but to rewrite the entire application, but this time implementing the MVC pattern.
>
> We did rewrite the application, and it became manageable, but only after many late nights and a lot of weekends spent in the office. The moral of this story is that the MVC pattern is good, not only for your application's maintenance and extensibility, but for your life-work balance.

MVC Types

The MVC pattern comes in many different forms. The two most recognized are referred to as Type I and Type II.

> ➤ **MVC Type I**—This type is a page-centric approach in which the view and the controller exist as one entity referred to as the view-controller. With this approach, the controller logic is implemented within the view, such as in a JSF. All the tasks that the controller performs, including retrieving HTTP request attributes and parameters, invoking the business logic, and managing the HTTP session, are embedded in the view using scriptlets and tag libraries. Type I highly couples the view generation with the application flow, making maintenance troublesome.

> ➤ **MVC Type II**—The maintenance problems with Type I are overcome in Type II by moving the controller logic out of the view and into a servlet, leaving the JSF to concern itself with the rendering of the data for the view.

> ### ALTERNATIVE TO MVC—MEET MVP
>
> Sorry for the disillusion, but MVP does not stand for most valuable pattern. MVP is the abbreviation for model view presenter, which is an alternative to model view controller. Instead of creating a triangular relationship between controller, view, and model like MVC, MVP offers one way of communication to each party—the presenter takes charge of all communication between the view and model. It is pretty popular in .NET, Silverlight, Google Web Toolkit, and Vaadin.

The principle difference between Type I and Type II is where the controller logic is located: in Type I it is in the view, and in Type II it is in a servlet.

Many frameworks, such as Spring MVC, Struts, Grails, and Wicket, implement their own version of the Type II MVC pattern. For example, Spring MVC includes the concept of the Dispatcher servlet that interacts with the HTTP requests and delegates to the controller, view (and view resolver), and handlers. Figure 14-2 shows a diagram of Spring's implementation of the MVC pattern.

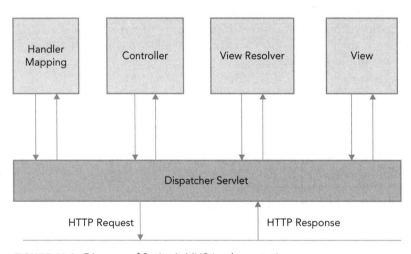

FIGURE 14-2: Diagram of Spring's MVC implementation

IMPLEMENTING THE MVC PATTERN IN PLAIN CODE

You are going to implement the MVC pattern with the help of the action pattern. This pattern takes on the responsibility of determining where to redirect the user based on the user's request. It helps maintain the single responsibility of the controller.

You'll start with the controller class. In Listing 14-1, you have implemented a simple controller that responds to any HTTP GET request made to the /users/* path. The mapping of this relationship is defined in the web.xml file:

```
<servlet>
    <servlet-name>FrontController</servlet-name>
    <servlet-class>com.devchronicles.mvc.plain.FrontController</servlet-class>
</servlet>
<servlet-mapping>
    <servlet-name>FrontController</servlet-name>
    <url-pattern>/users/*</url-pattern>
</servlet-mapping>
```

In the listing, you map the controller class com.devchronicles.mvc.plain.FrontController to the request URL /users/*. Therefore, for every request made to this URL, it is directed to the FrontController class for processing.

SERVLETS 3.0

Alternatively, you can annotate the controller class with the request URL like so: @WebServlet({"/users/*"}). This annotation removes the need to define the servlet mapping in the web.xml.

The doGet() method is invoked for such requests, and an Action object is retrieved from the AbstractActionFactory, which determines the location of the view that should be returned to the user.

LISTING 14-1: The refactored UserService class

```
package com.devchronicles.mvc.plain;

import java.io.IOException;
import javax.servlet.ServletException;
import javax.servlet.annotation.WebServlet;
import javax.servlet.http.HttpServlet;
import javax.servlet.http.HttpServletRequest;
import javax.servlet.http.HttpServletResponse;

public class FrontController extends HttpServlet {

protected void doGet(HttpServletRequest request, HttpServletResponse response)
                throws ServletException, IOException {

    Action action =
        AbstractActionFactory.getInstance().getAction(request);
    String view = action.execute(request, response);
        getServletContext().getRequestDispatcher(view).forward(request,
        response);
    }

}
```

Listing 14-2 has two classes: AbstractActionFactory and ActionFactory. The
AbstractActionFactory class creates an instance of the ActionFactory class. The Action Factory's
getAction method accepts an HttpServletRequest object, which contains a reference to the URI
of the requested location. The factory uses the URI to determine which Action object to return to
the controller. You maintain a map of URI request paths and Action objects in the action Map. An
Action object is chosen from the map based on the URI request path and returned to the controller.

LISTING 14-2: The Factory class

```
package com.devchronicles.mvc.plain;

public class AbstractActionFactory {

    private final static ActionFactory instance = new ActionFactory();

    public static ActionFactory getInstance() {
        return instance;
    }
}

package com.devchronicles.mvc.plain;

import java.util.HashMap;
import java.util.Map;
import javax.servlet.http.HttpServletRequest;

public class ActionFactory {

    private Map<String, Action> actions = new HashMap<>();
    private Action action;

    public ActionFactory() {
        actions.put("GET/users", new HomeAction());
        actions.put("GET/users/listusers", new ListUsersAction());
    }

    public synchronized Action getAction(HttpServletRequest request) {
        String path = request.getServletPath() + request.getPathInfo();
        String actionKey = request.getMethod() + path;
        System.out.println(actionKey);
        action = actions.get(actionKey);
        if(action == null){
            action = actions.get("GET/users");
        }

        return action;
    }
}
```

What is important in the Action object is that the concrete implementation provides an
implementation of the execute() method. This method performs business-specific logic required
to generate the page that the user requested. It may query a database to obtain data, perform
calculations, or generate a file.

In Listing 14-3, the `ListUserAction`'s execute method constructs a list of users that it adds as an attribute to the request object; then it returns the location of the view to render and display to the user. The data now stored in the request object is accessed by the `listuser.jsp` page and displayed.

For brevity, a `List` object has been populated and returned, but in a real application, this is where you would use EJB or other data objects that connect to a database.

LISTING 14-3: The Action class

```
package com.devchronicles.mvc.plain;

import java.util.ArrayList;
import java.util.List;
import javax.servlet.http.HttpServletRequest;
import javax.servlet.http.HttpServletResponse;

public class ListUsersAction implements Action {
    public String execute(HttpServletRequest request, HttpServletResponse
                          response) {

        List<String> userList = new ArrayList<>();
        userList.add("John Lennon");
        userList.add("Ringo Starr");
        userList.add("Paul McCartney");
        userList.add("George Harrison");
        request.setAttribute("listusers", userList);
        return "/WEB-INF/pages/listusers.jsp";
    }
}
```

The `Action` object returns to the controller, which receives the location of the page to which it should dispatch the request and response objects.

```
String view = action.execute(request, response);
getServletContext().getRequestDispatcher(view).forward(request, response);
```

In Listing 14-4, the JSP accesses the page's `requestScope` variable and retrieves the `userList` list object created in `ListUserAction`. It then iterates over the collection and displays the usernames.

LISTING 14-4: The listuser.jsp access generates the page the user requested

```
<%@ page language="java" contentType="text/html; charset=ISO-8859-1"
pageEncoding="ISO-8859-1"%>
<%@ taglib uri="http://java.sun.com/jsp/jstl/core" prefix ="c" %>
<!DOCTYPE html PUBLIC "-//W3C//DTD HTML 4.01 Transitional//EN"
"http://www.w3.org/TR/html4/loose.dtd">
<html>
<head>
<meta http-equiv="Content-Type" content="text/html; charset=ISO-8859-1">
```

continues

LISTING 14-4 *(continued)*

```
<title>List of users</title>
</head>
<body>
<h1>Our users are:</h1>
<c:forEach items="${requestScope.listusers}" var="listusers">
    <br> ${listusers}
</c:forEach>
</body>
</html>
```

The example that's been demonstrated is a simple implementation of the MVC pattern. You'll continue by looking at how you would implement the same application but using the advantages of Java EE 7.

IMPLEMENTING THE MVC PATTERN IN JAVA EE

The plain code implementation of the MVC pattern required you to write the controller logic, map the URLs to controller classes, and write a lot of plumbing code. However, in the latest release of Java EE, the plumbing code has been done for you. You only need to concentrate on the view and the model. The FacesServlet takes care of the controller implementation.

THE FACESSERVLET

The FacesServlet takes control of managing user requests and delivering the view to the user. It manages the life cycle for web applications that use JSF to construct the user interface. All user requests go through the FacesServlet. The servlet is integral to JSF and can be configured if nonconventional behavior is required. However, thanks to the concept of convention over configuration, you will find that for all but the most complex web applications, it is not necessary to change the default configurations.

CONFIGURING THE FACESSERVLET

If you do need to change the FacesServlet configuration, you must amend the `faces-config.xml` file.

Since JSF 2.2, you can perform the most common configurations by using annotation, further reducing the need to touch the `faces-config.xml` file.

MVC USING THE FACESSERVLET

You are going to rewrite the preceding example using the FacesServlet servlet and JSF. The view declaration language for JSF is called facelets. Facelets are the replacement for JSPs and are written in XHTML using cascading style sheets (CSS).

JSF includes the concept of backing beans. These are Plain Old Java Objects (POJOs) annotated with the `@Named` and the `@RequestScope` annotations. These beans are accessible by the

JSF page for the duration of the HTTP request. You can refer to their methods directly in the JSF. In Listing 14-5, you rewrite `ListUsersAction.class` to make it a backing bean.

LISTING 14-5: The ListUserAction class rewritten as a backing bean

```java
package com.devchronicles.mvc.javaee;

import java.util.ArrayList;
import java.util.List;
import javax.enterprise.context.RequestScoped;
import javax.inject.Named;

@RequestScoped
@Named
public class ListUsersAction {

    private List<String> userList = new ArrayList<>();
        public List<String> getUserList() {
        return userList;
    }

    public String execute() {
        userList.add("John Lennon");
        userList.add("Ringo Starr");
        userList.add("Paul McCartney");
        userList.add("George Harrison");
        return "/WEB-INF/pages/listusers.xhtml";
    }
}
```

Because all backing beans are annotated with at least `@Named` and `@RequestScope`, there is a *Stereotype* annotation you can use that gives it all the behavioral characteristics of a backing bean when it's applied. This annotation is the `@Model` annotation.

Next, you need to create an `index.xhtml` file. This replaces `home.jsp` and is called directly from the browser. The purpose of this JSF is to call the `execute` method on `ListUsersAction` that prepares the data for the view `listusers.xhtml`.

Listing 14-6 shows how this method is provoked.

LISTING 14-6: The home page to the simple MVC example

```html
<!DOCTYPE html PUBLIC "-//W3C//DTD XHTML 1.0 Transitional//EN"
"http://www.w3.org/TR/xhtml1/DTD/xhtml1-transitional.dtd">

<html xmlns="http://www.w3.org/1999/xhtml"
xmlns:h="http://java.sun.com/jsf/html">

<h:head><title>Welcome</title></h:head>

<h:body>
```

continues

LISTING 14-6 *(continued)*

```
<h1>Welcome to our site</h1>
<h:form>
    <h2>Click to see a <h:commandLink value="list of users"
        action="#{listUsersAction.execute}"/>.</h2>
</h:form>
</h:body>
</html>
```

You use the `h:commandLink` tag and reference the backing bean and the `execute()` method in the action element. The `execute()` method is called directly from the JSF; it generates the user list, returns the location of the view that will render the list, and then invokes the `getUserList()` method and displays the user list. Listing 14-7 demonstrates this.

LISTING 14-7: The view that renders the model data

```
<!DOCTYPE html PUBLIC "-//W3C//DTD XHTML 1.0 Transitional//EN"
"http://www.w3.org/TR/xhtml1/DTD/xhtml1-transitional.dtd">

<html xmlns="http://www.w3.org/1999/xhtml"
    xmlns:ui="http://java.sun.com/jsf/facelets"
    xmlns:h="http://java.sun.com/jsf/html">

<head>
<title>List of users</title>
</head>
<body>
    <h1>Our users are:</h1>
    <ui:repeat value="#{listUsersAction.userList}" var="listusers">
        <h:outputText value="#{listusers}" />
        <br/>
    </ui:repeat>
</body>
</html>
```

In the backing bean, the action class is referred to as `listUsersAction` starting in lowercase, and the method `getUserList()` omits the word `get`. If a method starts with `get`, you can omit it.

When you deploy this application, the `index.xhtml` view renders the link, which when clicked will display a list of users as follows:

```
Our users are:
John Lennon
Ringo Starr
Paul McCartney
George Harrison
```

You have now successfully built an MVC-style website using the latest features of Java EE 7.

WHERE AND WHEN TO USE THE MVC PATTERN

The most prolific use of the MVC pattern is in web applications, although you can use it anywhere there is a benefit to separating the view logic from the business logic. In fact, the use of the MVC pattern in web application architecture is so ubiquitous that any suggestion *not* to use it would be met with derision and disdain.

There is no doubt that the two principle benefits of using the pattern are strong. Its separation of concerns makes for a flexible and adaptable web application, and its separation of production allows different parts of the application to be developed virtually independently of each other. For example, one team can work on the display logic while separately another team can work on the business logic and domain objects.

SUMMARY

The MVC pattern has many commentators offering their point of view on its use, implementation, and even validity. You will read my interpretations of this pattern and see many implementations. It can be confusing to see the real benefits of this pattern.

You should go back to the essence of the MVC pattern: the separation of the display logic from the business logic. If you implement code that stays true to this objective, you have successfully implemented the MVC pattern.

The concept behind a separation of presentation and business logic is to maintain a clear divide between domain objects that model your problem and the presentation of that logic. This separation allows the business data to be presented in any number of different ways, simultaneously and without the need for the domain object to know anything about the way it is being displayed. It could be displayed on the screen in a variety of formats or as Word or Excel files.

EXERCISES

Develop the example in the chapter further by adding different views to display the user list.

NOTE

1. Professional website of Trygve M. H. Reenskaug: `http://heim.ifi.uio.no/~trygver/themes/mvc/mvc-index.html`.

15

Other Patterns in Java EE

WHAT'S IN THIS CHAPTER?

➤ WebSockets

➤ Message-oriented middleware

➤ Microservices versus monoliths

WROX.COM CODE DOWNLOADS FOR THIS CHAPTER

The wrox.com code download for this chapter is found at www.wrox.com/go/ projavaeedesignpatterns on the Download Code tab. The code is in the Chapter 15 download and individually named according to the names throughout the chapter.

This chapter discusses some of the things that are benefits of Java EE and development. You might think of this chapter as containing all the topics that are important to know but don't fit in any of the other chapters.

This chapter introduces web sockets, which is an exciting new feature of Java EE. Then it introduces message-orientated middleware before moving on to the related topic of microservice architecture.

Enjoy this eclectic bag of tech goodies!

WHAT ARE WEBSOCKETS?

WebSockets might be the most interesting improvement on the web since the introduction of Asynchronous JavaScript And XML (AJAX). It has been popular since the emergence of HTML5 and is supported by many web frameworks. However, it took quite a long time to have a stable and compatible specification for WebSockets.

The Hypertext Transfer Protocol (HTTP) model was designed long before the Internet was popular, and it relied on simple specification and design. In the traditional HTTP model, a client opens a connection to the back-end server, sends an HTTP request of type[1] GET, POST, PUT, or DELETE, and the HTTP server returns an appropriate response. There have been several attempts to hack and communicate over standard HTTP, such as AJAX, as well as design a new model such as SPDY.

The traditional HTTP model has been cumbersome for almost any application that goes beyond the simple get-and-submit-content data model. Think about a chat client, in which the participants can send messages in any order, and hundreds can be chatting at the same time. The standard request-response approach would be too limiting for such purposes. Some early approaches to get past this limitation were AJAX and Comet. Both relied on long polling: opening an HTTP connection and keeping it alive (maintaining the connection open) by not finalizing the response.

With WebSockets, the client can initiate a raw socket to the server and execute full-duplex communication. WebSockets support was introduced with JSR-356. The package javax.websocket and its server subpackage contain all classes, interfaces, and annotations related to WebSockets.

To implement WebSockets in Java EE, you need to create an endpoint class with the WebSocket life-cycle methods shown in Listing 15-1.

LISTING 15-1: An example of an endpoint

```java
package com.devchronicles.websockets;
public class HelloEndpoint extends Endpoint {

    @Override
    public void onOpen(final Session session, EndpointConfig config) {

        session.addMessageHandler(new MessageHandler.Whole<String>() {

            @Override
            public void onMessage(String msg) {
                try {
                    session.getBasicRemote().sendText("Hello " + msg);
                } catch (IOException e) { }
            }
        });
    }
}
```

The Endpoint class introduces three life-cycle methods: onOpen, onClose, and onError. At least the extending class needs to implement the onOpen method.

You can deploy this endpoint in two different ways: either by configuration or programmatically.

To programmatically deploy the code in Listing 15-1, your application needs to invoke the following:

```java
ServerEndpointConfig.Builder.create(HelloEndpoint.class, "/hello").build();
```

The deployed WebSocket is available from `ws://<host>:<port>/<application>/hello`. However, a better way is to use annotation configuration. Therefore, the same endpoint becomes Listing 15-2.

LISTING 15-2: An example of an endpoint with annotations

```
package com.devchronicles.websockets;

@ServerEndpoint("/hello")
public class HelloEndpoint {

    @OnMessage
    public void onMessage(Session session, String msg) {
        try {
            session.getBasicRemote().sendText("Hello " + msg);
        } catch (IOException e) { }
    }
}
```

This approach lets you use annotations and keep up with the Plain Old Java Object (POJO) approach because you are not extending a base class. The annotated endpoint has the same life-cycle methods as the one in Listing 15-2, but it introduces an additional `onMessage` life-cycle method. Rather than implementing `onOpen` and adding the `onMessage` handler, it's enough to implement an annotated `onMessage` method in the annotation-based approach. You can annotate several methods with `@OnMessage` to receive different types of data, such as `String` or `ByteBuffer` for binary.

The client-side implementation of WebSockets depends on the web frameworks in use. However, a simple JavaScript version is shown in the following snippet.

```
var webSocket = new WebSocket('ws://127.0.0.1:8080/websockets/hello');
webSocket.send("world");
```

A better example is to send a complex object in JavaScript Object Notation (JSON) format, which can be marshaled to an object, as in the following code snippet.

```
var msg = {
    type: "message",
    text: "World",
    date: Date.now()
};

webSocket.send(JSON.stringify(msg));

webSocket.onmessage = function(evt) { /* Expect to receive hello world */ };
```

WebSockets are great for building web applications that need persistent and asynchronous messaging between the client and the server. Java EE offers an easy implementation of WebSockets. They have far more configurations and implementation options than discussed here. If we have sparked your interest in WebSockets we suggest you visit Oracle's Java EE Tutorial,[2] which explains in more details how to program WebSockets using the Java API.

WHAT IS MESSAGE-ORIENTATED MIDDLEWARE

The communication between components in a Java EE system is synchronous. A call chain is started from the calling Enterprise JavaBean (EJB) to a data access object (DAO) to the entity, and so on to the final target. All components of the call chain must be available and ready to receive the call, and the calling component must wait for a response before proceeding. The success of the invocation depends on the availability of all components. As you saw in Chapter 9, "Asynchronous," an invocation of an asynchronous method does not require the calling object to wait for a response. It can continue with the normal flow of execution, while the asynchronous method sets up its own call chain.

Message-oriented middleware (MOM) provides a type of buffer between systems that allows the communication to be delayed if a component is not up and running. Messages are delivered as soon as all components are available. Invocations are translated into messages and sent via a messaging system to a target component that processes the message and may respond. If the target component is not available, the messages are queued waiting for the system to become available. When the component is available, the messages are processed.

At one end of the chain is a producer that translates the call into a form that can be transmitted as a message, and at the other end is a consumer who receives the message. The consumers and producers are highly decoupled, because they don't know anything about each other. They don't even have to be written in the same language or be hosted on the same network; they may even be distributed over several external servers.

A MOM system is composed of four players: messages, consumers, producers, and brokers. Producers generate the messages and send them to brokers, who distribute the messages to destinations where they're stored until a consumer connects and processes them.

There are two architectural implementations of MOM: point-to-point and publish/subscribe.

In the point-to-point implementation, the producer sends a message to the destination, which is called a *queue*. In the queue, the message waits for a consumer to pick it up and confirm that it has been processed successfully. If it has, the message is then removed from the queue. Figure 15-1 shows the producer putting the message M1 onto the queue and then the consumer picking up the message from the queue and processing it. In this implementation the message is only processed by one consumer.

FIGURE 15-1: Point-to-point implementation

In the publish/subscribe implementation, the destination is called a *topic*. A producer publishes a message to a topic, and all consumers who subscribe to the topic receive a copy of the message. This is shown in Figure 15-2, where messages M1 and M2 are published to the topic T1 and consumed by consumer C1 and C2, and message M3 is published on topic T2 and consumed by consumers C2 and C3.

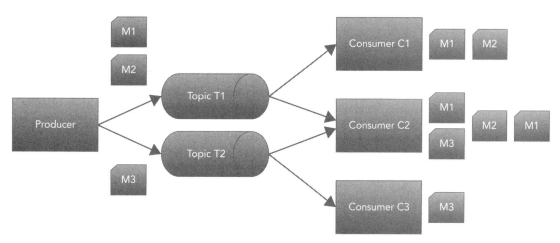

FIGURE 15-2: Publish/subscribe implementation

Java EE provides a convenient application programming interface (API) that deals with these implementations and is called the Java Message Service (JMS). It is a set of interfaces that describe the creation of messages, providers, and consumers. When implemented in an EJB container, message-driven beans (MDBs) act as listeners for JMS messages being invoked asynchronously.

WHAT IS THE MICROSERVICE ARCHITECTURE?

Over the past few years, the microservice architecture pattern has become a hotly discussed and popular pattern. The idea behind it is to design a large distributed scalable application that consists of small cohesive services that are able to evolve or even be completely rewritten over the life of the application.

This is not a new idea, and it is similar to the Service Orientated Architecture (SOA) pattern that has been in use for a long time. The essence of the microservice is the idea that each service should be small—perhaps as small as only a few hundred lines of code. The objective is to decompose a large, monolithic application into much smaller applications to solve development and evolutionary problems.

This chapter discusses the reasons for following the microservice path, its disadvantages and benefits, and how it compares to the more established and familiar monolithic architecture.

Monolithic Architecture

The most common way to develop and package a web application has always been to collect all the resources, components, and class files into a single Web application ARchive (WAR) or Enterprise ARchive (EAR) file and deploy it to a web server. A typical application for a bookstore might include components that manage the user's accounts, process payment, control stock, administer customer services, and generate front-end views. All this is developed in one monolithic application and then packaged and deployed to a web server. Figure 15-3 shows a simplified representation of a monolithic application.

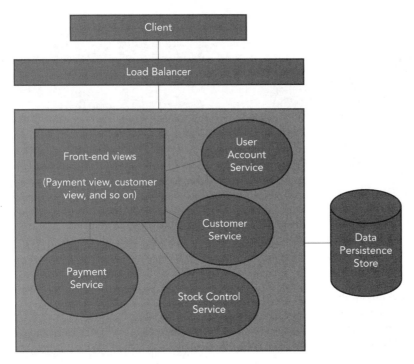

FIGURE 15-3: Monolithic architecture

The components are packaged together in a logical modular form and deployed as one single monolithic application. It's a simple way to develop and deploy an application because there's only one application to test. Integrated Development Environments (IDEs) and other development tools are designed with the monolithic architecture in mind. Despite these benefits of monolithic architecture, applications built to this design are often very large.

A small application is easy for developers to come to grips with, to understand, and maintain, but a large monolithic application can be difficult, especially for those developers who have recently joined the team. They may take many weeks or months to thoroughly understand the application.

Frequent deployments are not practical because they require the coordination of many developers (and perhaps other departments). It may take hours or days to arrange a deployment, hindering the testing of new features and bug fixes. A significant drawback to the monolithic design is that it's difficult to change the technology or framework. The application was developed based on technology decisions made at the beginning of the project. You are stuck with these decisions; if a technology is found that solves the problem in a more elegant or performant way, it is difficult to start using it. Rewriting an entire application is almost never an affordable option. The monolithic architecture pattern does not lend itself well to scalability.

Scalability

Scalability refers to an application's ability to grow (and shrink) as demand for its services changes without noticeably affecting the user experience. A badly performing e-commerce website loses customers quickly, making scalability very important. The first go-to solution is to scale horizontally and duplicate the application over many servers and load balance the traffic in a High Availability (HA) manner, with a passive peer that becomes active if the active peer goes down. X-axis scaling improves the capacity and availability of the application. This option does not have development cost implications but does result in higher hosting and maintenance expense.[3]

You can scale an application along the Z-axis. The application code is duplicated onto several servers, similar to an X-axis split, but in this case each server is responsible for only a fraction of the data. A mechanism is put in place to route data to the appropriate server, perhaps based on a user type or primary key. Z-axis scaling benefits from much the same performance improvements as X-axis scaling; however, it implies new development expense to rearchitect the application.

None of these solutions resolves the worsening application and development complexity. For this, you need vertical scaling.

The application can be scaled along the Y-axis. It is decomposed into functionality, service, or resource. The way you do this is entirely your choice and will depend on the situation, although division by use case is common. The idea is that each decomposed part should encapsulate a small set of related activities.

To visualize the X-, Y-, and Z-axis scaling, you draw an AKF scale cube,[4] as in Figure 15-4.

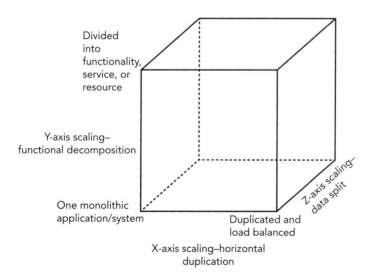

FIGURE 15-4: The AKF cube should have X-, Y-, and Z-axis scaling.

Decomposing into Services

The microservice approach decomposes a monolithic application along the Y-axis into services that satisfy a single use case or a set of related functionality. These services are then duplicated on several servers and placed behind a load balancer, X-axis split. The data persistence may be scaled along the Z-axis by sharding the data based on a primary key.

If you decompose the applications in Figure 15-3 along the Y-axis, you end up with the architecture in Figure 15-5.

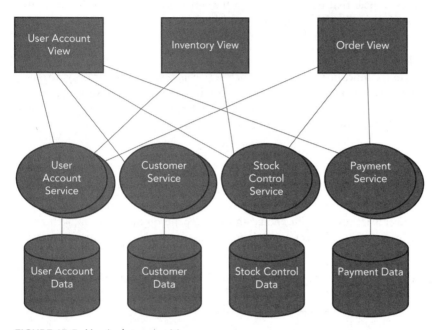

FIGURE 15-5: Y-axis decomposition

The front-end views have been split into separate applications that access the functionality of several back-end services. The services have been split from the monolithic application into standalone applications that manage their own data. You can achieve splits along the Z-axis by sharding the data and scaling along the X-axis by clustering and load balancing.

You have seen how to decompose a monolithic application into microservices and learned the importance of scalability for the continuance of an application.

Now you'll look more closely at the specific benefits and cost of the microservice architecture.

Microservice Benefits

From the development perspective, the benefits of a microservice architecture result from the size and agility of the small applications of which it consists. They are easy for developers to understand and for the IDE to manage. A large application that consists of many hundreds of modules can take considerable time to load, which negatively affects the developers' productivity. Each microservice application can be deployed quicker and often without the cooperation of other teams. Because each service stands alone, local changes to code do not affect other microservices; therefore, continuous development is possible. Each microservice can be developed by a dedicated team of developers who manage the deployment and resource requirements of their service independently of other teams.

The user interface (UI) is normally divorced from back-end development; your development team may never see a line of UI code. If you are programming to a REpresentational State Transfer

(REST) API (see Chapter 13, "RESTful Web Services"), you are only required to honor the resource representation contract, not to think about the way the front end will be implemented. This allows true separation of concerns.

From the perspective of application performance, the main benefit comes from being able to deploy each microservice onto its own tailored environment. The resource requirements of your microservice may differ from another, thereby allowing resource allocation to be fine grained. A monolithic application is deployed on one environment with shared resources.

Fault tolerance and isolation are increased. A fault in one microservice does not affect the operations of the others, allowing the application to continue to perform. In a system that uses MOM to communicate between services, messages destined for a failed microservice wait in the queue until the fault is resolved and the microservice (consumer) begins to consume the messages. If the application is scaled horizontally, there's no break in service because one of the duplicate microservices consumes the messages. In a monolithic application, such a fault could bring down the entire application.

Among all the benefits attributed to the microservice architecture, the most talked about is the ease with which you can change the technology stack. Because each microservice is small, rewriting it is not expensive. In fact, new microservices can be written in any language, allowing you to choose the most suitable language for solving the problem. Technology decisions made at the beginning of the project do not dictate the technology that you must use throughout the application's life.

Nothing in Life Is Free

The benefits of the microservice architecture do not come free. There are costs involved.

The ease with which you can develop a microservice makes it easy for the number of microservices to grow, and to grow very quickly. Fifteen microservices can easily become thirty or more, especially when different versions of the same microservice are counted. This poses several difficulties.

The responsibility for operations may move to the development team. With only a handful of services to maintain, it's not a difficult task, but as the number of microservices grows, the task of maintaining them increases. A significant investment needs to be made to ensure that the microservices are deployed and maintained. Processes need to be automated to reduce the burden of deploying and maintaining a large number of services. There may be a knowledge gap you need to fill, adding to the overall running costs.

Cross-cutting changes to semantics means that all microservices must update their code to keep in sync. This can be time consuming to perform and has significant retesting costs. Alterations to interface contracts and message formats can be the cause of such changes and require that all teams work in a coordinated way. Equally, failing to change an interface or message format early on in the project results in significantly greater costs as the number of microservices grows.

Duplicated code is something that you have been taught is bad, and it is. In a microservice environment, the risk of code duplication is high. To avoid coupling and dependencies, code must sometimes be duplicated, meaning every instance of that code must be tested and maintained. You may be able to abstract code to a share library, but this does not work in a polyglot environment.

The inherent unreliability and complexity of distributed systems are duplicated in a microservice environment. Every service may be hosted in a distributed way, communicating via networks that suffer from latency issues, incompatible versions, unreliable providers, hardware problems, and more. Constant monitoring of network performance is vital.

Conclusions

The monolithic architecture has been used for many years to develop applications and serves small applications and development teams well. It's easy to develop and test because IDEs are designed to manage these types of application structures. But as you have seen, it does not scale well and hinders development. It is difficult to introduce new technology, and refactoring is expensive.

Microservices decompose into logical services of related functionality. Their small size makes them easy for developers to understand. Development and deployment are continuous. Scalability is built into the architecture, and you are not stuck with initial technology decisions.

FINALLY, SOME ANTI-PATTERNS

The purpose of this book is to fill the gap between "classical" patterns and Java EE. You will find many books discussing anti-patterns, but there is no harm in discussing a few here.

Anti-patterns usually occur because of misuse of one or several patterns. A Java EE developer who has enough experience can easily list more anti-patterns than patterns. Here are a few that are common or that you may already have come across.

Uber Class

There is probably no single project without a huge class that serves many purposes and responsibilities. Not only does this violate Java EE principles, but such classes override basic object-oriented programming (OOP) principles and must be avoided.

Services that are overloaded with many responsibilities fall into the same category. If you are not a big fan of OOP, that's fine, but if you do want to continue to write code in an OOP language, it is best to keep your classes small and highly cohesive.

Although many others had expressed this anti-pattern, Reza Rahman may have first introduced the name.

Lasagna Architecture

Java EE promoted layers starting from the early days, which may have resulted in many unnecessary interfaces and packages. Although this pattern may look like an answer to uber class and monolithic applications, usually it complicates things unnecessarily.

Lasagna architecture in the OOP world is not much different from spaghetti programming in structural programming. Too much abstraction is unnecessary and provides no help. Interfaces and loose coupling are great tools only when you use them in the right amount, in the right context, and only when they are needed.

This anti-pattern has been expressed by many developers with many different names, such as Baklava Code. However, the name *lasagna* may have been first given by Adam Bien,[5] who is heavily against unnecessary use of interfaces.

Mr. Colombus

Almost all experienced Java EE developers want to invent or implement their own perfect solution. Most of the time these are only attempts to abstract and provide a better interface to a common library, such as logging or testing, where it may even go to extremes and rewrite an important functionality that has been supported by the open source community for years, such as an Object Relational Mapping (ORM) layer.

Although inventing something new may look appealing, reinventing something is just a waste of time. If you are going to write a new logging or an ORM framework, you should really have a good reason to do it. If you don't, you are rewriting a well-supported mature product, and most likely you'll end up maintaining it and providing all the support, tests, and future development alone.

Always make sure you have done enough literature searches on open source projects before starting to write a framework from scratch.

Friends with Benefits

One huge problem of J2EE was vendor locking. By the time J2EE 1.4 was released, most vendor servers only worked with the same vendor's tools and IDEs. This looked like a mutually beneficial relationship at first because the vendor provided professional support for its own tools, and open source tools and servers were left to the community to support. However, in the long term, many J2EE developers observed how open source tools and servers provided standard behavior and compatibility to Java specifications when vendors failed to do so.

There is nothing wrong with buying professional support and services and using tools, servers, and IDEs from vendors as long as the project is not locked to that vendor. Vendor locking may introduce problems that are impossible to solve without new releases and patches from the vendor, whereas building applications always make it possible to change to other vendors.

Bleeding Edge

Passionate developers love to use bleeding-edge technologies. For example, WebSockets were introduced many years ago, but they still suffer compatibility issues with old versions of browsers. No one can argue against the joy of learning something new and implementing a bleeding-edge technology in a project. However, it may become cumbersome to support such projects if you are targeting the mainstream.

A good approach to deciding which framework or technology to use is to see how it fits with your target user base. If you are building a banking application for clients who may still be using Internet Explorer 6, using WebSockets is the best choice (although most WebSockets frameworks provide fallback scenarios).

You always need to make sure an outsource library or framework is well supported, mature, and fits your project before moving on.

Utilityman

Utility classes and packages are common in projects. No one can argue that you need a class to perform some math operations, such as rounding or converting different number types. If you do have such utility or helper classes, you probably need to organize them with a package name of `util` or `helper`, right? No, in reality, they just help you collect junk. Because `util` and `helper` sound too generic, many classes are moved into these packages. Any class that may not be categorized easily will end up in your package. The generic name does not provide real information, so even though those classes are not used anymore, no one would dare to remove them.

If you have a great utility that everybody needs to use, just place it where it belongs with the current usage and provide proper documentation. You can move it to some more generic package in the future if needed.

Just like lasagna, Adam Bien first described and named this pattern.

NOTES

1. The complete list of HTTP methods is: GET, POST, DELETE, PUT, PATCH, OPTION, HEAD, TRACE and CONNECT.
2. Oracle's WebSocket API tutorial: http://docs.oracle.com/javaee/7/tutorial/doc/websocket.htm.
3. This could introduce a development cost if the system makes use of HTTP session data and there is not a clustered solution in place for HTTP session replication.
4. *The Art of Scalability: Scalable Web Architecture, Processes, and Organizations for the Modern Enterprise*, Martin L. Abbott, Michael T. Fisher. January 1, 2009.
5. Adam Bien. Author and Java Champion. www.adam-bien.com

PART III
Summary

16

Design Patterns: The Good, the Bad, and the Ugly

WHAT'S IN THIS CHAPTER?

➤ The good—how design patterns can lead to success

➤ The bad—how overuse and misuse of design patterns can lead to trouble

➤ And the ugly—how some "de-facto" standards can lead to failure

So far, this book has covered many of the classical design patterns from the GoF[1] book as well as some additional patterns that may find their way to becoming classics in the future. This book was written with the aim of being something that the authors would have bought themselves if they had not written it.

As is true with everything in life, design patterns do not always do good. They can do harm as well by leading you into implementing an anti-pattern. This chapter focuses on the good, the bad, and the ugly aspects of design patterns and hopefully provides a better approach for your heavy arsenal of patterns.

THE GOOD: PATTERNS FOR SUCCESS

As has been mentioned many times before, design patterns are the collective wisdom and experience of many smart developers. They unleash a great depth of experience that you can utilize to solve many common problems that occur in software development. Even in the early days of programming when using `goto` was considered legal (and acceptable), many projects failed. One of the early important resources on software engineering and project management was *The Mythical Man-Month* written by Frederick Brooks while he was managing development of OS360 for IBM.[2] Although the book was published in 1975, it still addresses many concerns and problems in modern software projects. At that time, one of the first design patterns in software was becoming popular: object-oriented programming (OOP). OOP was a set of design rules and patterns that enabled real-life situations to be modeled in code more effectively and easily. It simply offered a magic wand for designing, coding, and maintaining software. Smalltalk, C++, and Objective-C pioneered the early golden years of OOP. Although Edsger Dijkstra[3] commented that "Object-oriented programming is an exceptionally bad idea which could only have originated in California," it was the first major shift that changed how programs were written.

However, OOP was not a silver bullet either. First, using an object-oriented language did not really mean using an object-oriented approach. Developers were, and still are, allowed to write procedural code in any object-oriented language. Second, complex and badly designed objects being used were at least as capable at complicating things as any non-OOP systems.

In the early 1990s, the famous Gang of Four, Erich Gamma, Richard Helm, Ralph Johnson, and John Vlissides, published *Design Patterns: Elements of Reusable Object-Oriented Software*, which was the first book to bring together a collection of solutions to common problems as design patterns. That book covered 23 design patterns that have been referred to as classical patterns throughout this book, and they included code examples in C++ and Smalltalk. Over the years, many new patterns have been introduced and added to pattern catalogs by many great programmers such as Jim Coplien.[4]

However, design patterns are not language and platform dependent and can be implemented in any software project. Design patterns solve common problems and offer a common dictionary between developers. Instead of describing how you implemented a callback mechanism, which is only triggered when there is a change on the resource, you can say, "Oh, we have observers on x."

When Java was developed in the mid-1990s, many design patterns were integrated into its run time. Java made good use of design patterns in its internal design and exposed many patterns in the language itself by providing a default implementation application programming interface (API).

With the release of Java EE, even more patterns were introduced, many of which were published in the book *Core J2EE Patterns: Best Practices and Design Stratgies*.[5]

Reading pattern catalogues and learning their use cases does increase your knowledge of many common problems and how to solve them, even before they have appeared. This book has listed many war stories about how a particular design pattern has affected the project. These stories are from real-life experiences. Reading and memorizing a pattern is no guarantee of a magic solution, but it may give you some clues and hints about how to solve a problem when you come across a similar difficulty or challenge. Very soon, and with experience, you will end up addressing problems even before they have occurred by using an appropriate pattern.

Initially, the J2EE programming model relied heavily on Extensible Markup Language (XML) configuration and a heavyweight Enterprise JavaBeans (EJB) container. Beans needed to extend specific classes and implement each method to work properly. Very soon, this approach proved not to be productive and almost became an anti-pattern. Although Spring[6] offered a lightweight container approach, the upcoming design of Java EE favored inline code annotations over configuration files. The lightweight container and EJB based on Plain Old Java Objects (POJOs) offered a productive and easy-to-test programming model. Subsequent releases of Java EE offered many desired features, most of which have been covered throughout the book. Finally, Context and

Dependency Injection (CDI) introduced a new container with great flexible features. With the help of CDI, you can implement many patterns, such as observer and decorator, with little hassle.

WAR STORY

When I was given the responsibility to work on the Eclipse Libra project, I had limited knowledge of Eclipse plug-ins. After reading the only available book, *Eclipse: Building Commercial-Quality Plug-Ins*, by Dan Rubel and Eric Clayberg (Addison-Wesley, 2008), I decided to jump into the existing codebase in the Eclipse repository.

Very soon, I was amazed with the overall architecture of Eclipse and how the plug-ins were built. Design patterns such as adapter, decorator, strategy, memento, and many others were everywhere, used in the right context, and they provided an efficient and clear implementation.

Eclipse code repository is one of the best live sources for good implementation of design patterns in a real-world project that millions of developers use.

THE BAD: OVER AND MISUSE OF PATTERNS

The first training I received on design patterns simply blew my mind. The following month I spent all my time reading *Head First Design Patterns*[7] and next, of course, the GoF book. I was armed with the knowledge of patterns and was ready to use them. As time passed by, I realized I didn't even need to use inheritance and could build all models and object hierarchies with decorators. I even created a set of utility classes consisting of several singletons, some message busses for observers, and some generic decorator and observers that I always included when I created a new project.

I was always proud to show my code and let others see how great and sophisticated a programmer I was. It did not take long to realize my way of using design patterns was just over-complicating my code and adding too many layers during run time. Even simplifying the existing code resulted in better performance. Complex and sophisticated code does not make you a better programmer, and it doesn't make the code optimized and maintainable. Engineering is the art of using the right tool at the right place and building a system efficiently.

WAR STORY

I was once asked to implement a data structure to handle transactional database operations for a job I was applying for. I was to complete the code at home and send it back to the company for review via e-mail. The system would be able to add new values and perform a save operation once a commit was done. Also, the system would be able to go back to a previous state when a rollback was executed. Little

continues

---

continued

voices in my head were screaming, "Memento!" Although I had never needed to apply memento until that day, I knew it was a perfect match. The memento pattern would let me commit to a save point that I could then roll back. So I set about revising my knowledge of the memento pattern's implementation. I created my `Caretaker`, `Memento` and `Originator` classes, placed them in an internal package, and implemented the database logic code that uses internal memento classes.

I was proud and confident about the code I delivered. Surprisingly (for me), the company didn't want to continue with the interview process. Maybe it was looking for someone who would use a simple stack to push and pull values, but the code I delivered gave me confidence in my knowledge of design patterns, even for the patterns I don't use often.

After going back over the original question years later, I realized there were performance constraints of using minimal objects and an O(log N) runtime performance. My code was readable, clean, and maintainable, but it failed to address the key points that the interviewer asked in the first place.

If knowing a pattern blinds you to making good decisions, design patterns do more harm than good.

...AND THE UGLY

Design patterns and Java EE are old pals. However, this friendship did not always work out well. As J2EE became more accepted in the corporate world and began addressing large projects, design patterns came to the rescue. Many of the classical patterns from GoF found their place in J2EE applications. Enterprise patterns followed soon after to address common problems in the J2EE platform.

J2EE gained popularity and drove many new concepts such as Service Orientated Architecture (SOA) and Web Services. However, the complex structure of J2EE doomed many projects to fail. J2EE beans relied on extending classes and needed a heavyweight container on which to run. Because the beans rely on the container, the development process needed full-blown heavyweight servers to slow down the development and needed costly hardware to run on. Still, those enterprise containers were slow, resulting in sluggish restarts and refreshes. Testing and unit testing was hard to perform properly.

Besides, J2EE configuration was heavy and relied on XML files. Although separating the configuration and code seemed like a good idea, soon it turned out to be an XML hell. Heavy configuration was needed to create a simple bean.

As J2EE became the platform of the enterprise, consultants, architects, and vendors released sophisticated guidelines that resulted in over-complex, over-architected, and overly layered applications that were impossible to test and hard to develop (due to long restarts), debug, and deploy.

Luckily, Enterprise Java had a happy ending. The POJO and lightweight container movement led by Rod Johnson[8] gained a huge following and soon became a competitor to J2EE. Spring offered a lightweight container and the ability to run on simple Java servers. The POJO approach was great for testing and did not need the container most of the time, but even if the container was needed, it was not hard to use.

The success of Spring caused a renaissance in the Java Community Process. Java EE 5 was designed from scratch to support POJO EJB and lighter containers. Java EE had evolved and matured.

However, old habits and development techniques did not change overnight. Still, many developers follow the patterns of J2EE, creating overly layered and complex applications while not using the lightweight containers and servers. Just like the English language has changed since Shakespeare's time, platforms and programming languages have changed. Don't get stuck in the past by resisting change.

WAR STORY

It was the early days of J2EE 1.4, and we were to implement the next generation of banking systems. We had implemented all the best practices, patterns, guidelines, and anything else we could find in books and online resources.

Our application was heavily dependent on a particular vendor and was not portable. We had to run the vendor integrated development environment (IDE) and the vendor server, and this was in the age of 32 bits when Windows refused to address more than 3GB of RAM. The server and IDE were so slow when started in debug mode that we did not need breakpoints to stop execution.

The vendor assured us that the production environment was going to be fast; nevertheless, the development life cycle was like a ball and chain. We could easily go for coffee breaks while the server restarted.

Things got even more fun when we wanted to go live. The production environment turned out to be as slow as the development boxes. Soon we all had the habit of watching prod and test environment's memory statuses.

Finally, we hired a famous consultant to show us what we were doing wrong. He was an old and wise guy whom we treated like Gandalf. After reviewing our code for a few days, he asked us to delete almost all façades (we had façades for almost every bean) and all unnecessary interfaces (again, we almost had interfaces for interfaces). He also asked us to minimize our lasagna-like layers by cutting down the call hierarchy (EJB calling EJB calling EJB...).

It was the J2EE 1.4 days with heavy vendor servers, so nothing magical happened. Still, we gained some performance and at least achieved much readable code.

Assuming that everything may change, developing with needs for flexibility in mind does not offer an easier future but most probably a more crippled today.

SUMMARY

Design patterns are one of the most important, challenging, and useful topics in software. No object-oriented programmer would be complete without proper knowledge of common design patterns.

Good knowledge provides a great toolset for common problems you are likely to face. Java EE takes this a step further and introduces a much easier and integrated way to use design patterns in enterprise projects. Most patterns in Java EE have been introduced after long debates and pain, which ensures they are well implemented and mature.

All patterns described in this book rely on Java EE standards, so they are almost guaranteed to work successfully.

Still, patterns are neither silver bullets nor magic wands. If they are used extensively without reason, they tend to overcomplicate the project. Knowing a pattern does not necessarily mean you have to use it unless you know it fits and solves a potential problem.

Read and learn design patterns, and try to keep your memory fresh on where they fit and what problems they solve. You will save many lines of code and earn respect.

NOTES

1. *Design Patterns: Elements of Reusable Object-Oriented Software* (Addison-Wesley, 1994): Erich Gamma, Richard Helm, Ralph Johnson, John Vlissides.
2. *The Mythical Man-Month: Essays on Software Engineering* (Addison-Wesley, 1975): Frederick P. Brooks Jr.
3. Edsger Wybe Dijkstra was a Dutch computer scientist who received the 1972 Turing Award for fundamental contributions to developing programming languages.
4. James O. Coplien is an author, lecturer, and researcher in computer science.
5. *Core J2EE Patterns: Best Practices and Design Strategies* (Prentice Hall, 2003): Deepak Alur, Dan Malks, John Crupi.
6. A Java-based framework that provides many features including dependency injection and aspect-orientated programming.
7. *Head First Design Patterns* (O'Reilly, 2004): Eric Freeman, Elisabeth Robson, Bert Bates, Kathy Sierra.
8. Rod Johnson is an Australian computer programmer who created the Spring framework.

INDEX